CATALOGING AND ORGANIZING DIGITAL RESOURCES: A HOW-TO-DO-IT MANUAL FOR LIBRARIANS

Anne M. Mitchell
and
Brian E. Surratt

facet publishing

Copyright © 2005 Neal-Schuman Publishers

Published by
Facet Publishing
7 Ridgmount Street
London WC1E 7AE

Facet Publishing is wholly owned by CILIP: the Chartered Institute of Library and Information Professionals.

First published in the USA by Neal-Schuman Publishers, Inc., 2005.
This simultaneous UK edition 2005.

British Library Cataloguing in Publication Data
A catalogue record for this book is available from the British Library.

ISBN-1-85604-556-0

Printed and bound in the United States of America.

CONTENTS

LIST OF FIGURES
AND TABLES

PREFACE

Cataloging and Organizing Digital Resources: A How-To-Do-It Manual for Librarians addresses the dramatically changing collection, management, mediation, and preservation of information resources. Even modest-sized libraries now access dozens of licensed electronic products representing thousands of individual titles; seek out freely available resources on the Web; and digitize unique materials from their own collections.

Users now expect libraries to provide the best digital resources and deliver them easily. Beyond the technical aspects of handling online resources—which are complex and constantly changing—lays a nebulous array of legal, financial, and managerial concerns. How do libraries adapt to these new challenges? Many re-evaluate their collections, service priorities, and work processes, and even reassign job duties, create new positions, and bring together new departments to manage online content.

The standards for managing electronic collections tend to evolve more slowly than the resources themselves. Libraries must often adjust existing standards and develop local tools to facilitate access to their increasingly complex electronic collections. Today, as a new generation of systems and standards comes of age, the tools created are more sophisticated and interoperable than their predecessors; they are also more numerous and complex.

Electronic-resource management often refers to the tools and processes used to organize administrative metadata, such as license terms, vendor contacts, and usage statistics. *Cataloging and Organizing Digital Resources* covers the full spectrum of library operations involved in building and maintaining access to electronic collections; affecting every area of the library, from the initial selection process to the point of use. It focuses on the methods for organizing and providing access to information collections (known collectively as bibliographic control).

Confronted with burgeoning online collections and a changing technology landscape, each library must determine which bibliographic tool or combination of tools best suits its needs. Some libraries favor catalog access while others highlight alternative bibliographic tools; some libraries offer parallel access through both traditional and alternative tools, and a great many libraries mix a little of both. We wrote

Cataloging and Organizing Digital Resources to provide readers with an overview of the scope of online management concerns, the issues that influence bibliographic control in the online environment, and the variety of tools available for managing bibliographic data.

The online catalog serves as the library's best-established tool to organize and provide access to conventional information materials. We believe it will continue to operate in this capacity for the foreseeable future. The catalog is just one tool among many. The movement toward alternative bibliographic approaches, as well as the recent overhaul of traditional cataloging practices for electronic resources, has been propelled primarily by developments in the online environment. Although physical electronic media such as CD-ROM and DVD-ROM have special physical-management needs, from a bibliographic perspective these media are more akin to other physical resources with unique descriptive conventions, such as video recordings or maps, than to their online counterparts. *Care and Handling of CDs and DVDs: A Guide for Librarians and Archivists* (Byers, 2003) provides detailed guidelines for storing and handling direct-access electronic media, and the "Electronic Resources" chapter in *Cataloging Nonprint and Internet Resources* (Weber, 2002) offers step-by-step instructions for cataloging these resources. *Cataloging and Organizing Digital Resources* concentrates instead on online resources and the issues they raise for bibliographic control.

Chapter 1, "Thinking about the Organization of Digital Resources," examines the management of online materials, including collection development, acquisitions, and administration; and the special considerations for local digital libraries, including planning, processes, and resources.

Chapter 2, "Establishing the Cataloging Work Flow," looks at how libraries can perform original or copy cataloging for individual records and record sets and includes strategies for reviewing and updating entries.

Chapter 3, "Exploring Alternatives to Cataloging," lays out the strengths, weaknesses, and implementation of three alternatives to cataloging—Web lists, context-sensitive linking, and federated searching.

Chapter 4, "Determining Bibliographic Control in the Online Environment," outlines strategies for tailoring a library's bibliographic tools and practices to meet its own unique access needs.

Chapter 5, "Understanding Cataloging Rules and Guidelines," provides an easy-to-understand introduction to the record content and cataloging rules involved in organizing digital resources.

Chapter 6, "Analyzing the Bibliographic Structure of Online Resources," looks at the bibliographic characteristics of online information. This chapter will serve as a guide for the succeeding chapters that explore and explain various types of online sources.

Chapter 7, "Online Monographs: E-books and Manuscripts"; Chapter 8, "Online Serials: E-journals and Periodicals in Aggregator Databases"; and Chapter 9, "Online Integrating Resources: Databases and Web Sites," provide step-by-step instructions for cataloging the three different classes of online resources—monographs, serials, and integrating resources—according to the most current rules and standards. Coverage includes multiple examples for organizing and cataloging born-digital monographs; online reproductions; unpublished resources; born-digital, online-only serials; journals copublished in online and print formats; aggregator neutral records; continuously updating Web sites; and more. These chapters take into consideration the challenges of title changes and the discontinuance of print editions (as often happens when a record migrates from print to online). Each example features bibliographic characteristics, instructions for coding the *MARC 21* record, and the full *MARC 21* record.

Chapter 10, "Online Trends to Watch," forecasts the future importance and impact of new technologies on the cataloging and organization of digital resources.

Cataloging and Organizing Digital Resources addresses the fundamental dilemmas that all libraries face as they confront bibliographic control for online resources. Any library that selects online information for its collection must ultimately decide whether to catalog that information, how to maintain bibliographic control if the resources are not cataloged, and how to manage the proliferation of information resources and bibliographic tools in an effective and sustainable manner. This book provides a broad survey of the e-resource–management landscape and specific techniques for managing, accessing, and cataloging online information with ease.

We joined the library profession as electronic-resource catalogers at a time when online resources were proliferating exponentially and libraries had begun to look to cataloging and technical services to take the lead in managing these growing collections. Change has been the only constant in our daily work, and we are frequently exhilarated, overwhelmed, and frustrated all at the same time. Ultimately, the promise and potential of the online environment inspires our imaginations and sustains our inquiry and service. We hope that *Cataloging and Organizing Digital Resources: A How-To-Do-It Manual for Librarians* reflects our excitement about the future of managing and providing access to online resources, and that it will be not only practical but thought provoking as well.

REFERENCES

Byers, Fred R. 2003. *Care and Handling of CDs and DVDs: A Guide for Librarians and Archivists.* Washington, DC: Council on Library and Information Resources.

Weber, Mary Beth. 2002. *Cataloging Nonprint and Internet Resources: A How-To-Do-It Manual for Librarians.* New York: Neal-Schuman.

ACKNOWLEDGMENTS

We gratefully acknowledge the assistance and support of our colleagues at the University of Houston Libraries and the Texas A&M University Libraries. We would like to extend special thanks to Lisa Furubotten for her generous cataloging instruction and professional support, and to Jill Emery, Nathaniel Feis, and Richard Guajardo for their guidance and constructive feedback at every stage of this project. Thanks also to our editor at Neal-Schuman, Michael Kelley, who has been unfailingly patient and encouraging throughout the writing process.

1 THINKING ABOUT THE ORGANIZATION OF DIGITAL RESOURCES

INTRODUCTION

Online information resources are defined by their mode of delivery rather than the nature of their content. Journals, maps, data sets, software, slide presentations, books, and Web sites may have very little in common in terms of their information content, their audience, or the manner in which they are published and distributed, but they share a common set of attributes when they are made available on the Internet. It is difficult to overstate the degree to which online publication has affected library practices for organizing and providing access to information resources.

The universe of online information includes both resources created by external content providers, such as commercial publishers, educational institutions, and government entities, and digital objects created and hosted by the library itself. External online resources and local digital collections have very different management needs. The challenge in managing external resources lies in licensing, access control, and bibliographic control. Local digital resources pose issues including digitization and the development of tools to host and provide access to the content. In this chapter, the management aspects of the full spectrum of online information are discussed.

MANAGING ONLINE RESOURCES FROM EXTERNAL INFORMATION PROVIDERS

Perhaps the most monumental change that has accompanied the rise of online resources is the shift from ownership to access. The Internet is, by its very essence, a distributed system, and most Web-based content that a library might select and promote to its users is not owned by the library or hosted on library servers. Instead, libraries provide access to information hosted by external content providers, including individuals, businesses, nonprofit groups, educational institutions, government entities, and commercial information services. As any library that maintains a Web presence can attest, developing and hosting Web content is not a trivial exercise. Under the access model, the responsibility for file storage, resource development, data migration, and technical support resides with the content provider. In exchange for this convenience, libraries relinquish control over bibliographic stability and assurance of long-term access.

Libraries struggle with the dynamic behavior of online resources primarily because they cannot control it. Resources change in unpredictable ways and at unpredictable times, and every content provider has a slightly different approach to communicating these changes when they occur. In addition to the day-to-day complexity of managing remote resources, the access model has further ramifications for long-term preservation because a library cannot physically control any online resource it does not host itself. Valuable information resources can simply disappear from the library's collection if the host takes down the content or the library's subscription lapses. As online resources have grown in popularity and prevalence, libraries have become increasingly concerned about the impact that distributed ownership has on their ability to collect, organize, and preserve online information objects for sustained access (Keller, Reich, and Herkovic, 2003).

Work Flow Comparison

Management of online resources is not a discrete activity but an amalgam of interrelated management functions spanning all areas of the library. On a broad scale, the management functions that apply to online resources are identical to those for any other type of resource that a library might select and acquire: collection development, acquisition, bibliographic control, and access. Looking closer, however, it becomes clear that the work flow for online resources is markedly more complex, involving new elements as well as familiar elements in new combinations. New processes and technologies enter this work flow at every stage. As a result, it is common to overemphasize the learning curve for specific technical skills, such as negotiating a license, cataloging an online resource, or building a database. In fact, a much more daunting challenge lies in adapting organizational structures designed to manage physical materials to accommodate a vastly different work flow (Grahame and McAdam, 2004).

The following figures compare the work flow for materials in conventional formats with the work flow for online resources. Even when these processes are greatly simplified for schematic presentation, it is clear that adapting to online resources is not simply a matter of accommodating a greater volume of work, but also of changing the way functional units interact with library resources and with one another (Brown and Cox, 2001).

Monographs

> **Monograph**: A resource that is complete in one part of a finite number of parts, such as an electronic book.

Figure 1-1 illustrates the path that monographs in a physical format would take through the library. Although this diagram ignores the many procedural intricacies that occur in real-life library operations, it nonetheless clearly demonstrates the linear nature of this work flow. Note that the various stages bear a conspicuous resemblance to the administrative divisions and physical layout that are common in library technical services.

Serials

> **Serial**: A resource issued in a succession of discrete parts with no predetermined conclusion, such as a newspaper or journal. Serials are distinct from integrating resources, which absorb successive updates into a contiguous whole. Collectively, serials and integrating resources form a class of materials known as continuing resources.

Figure 1-2 illustrates the work flow for a serial in a physical format. It incorporates many of the same elements as the work flow for monographs, such as selection, acquisition, bibliographic control, and physical access. However, an added level of complexity is introduced by the fact that subscription management and cataloging take place at the title level, whereas receiving, processing, and physical access take place at the issue or item level. Physically and fiscally, serials are sufficiently different from monographs so that, over time, libraries with the resources to support separate functional units for monographs and serials have generally done so.

At the title level, the serials work flow is circular. Subscriptions come up for periodic renewal, at which

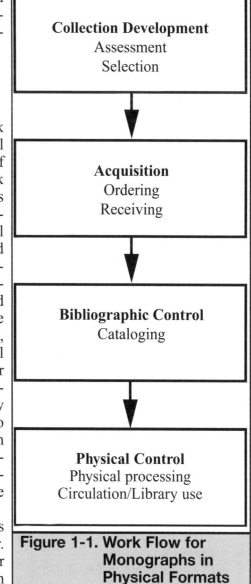

Figure 1-1. Work Flow for Monographs in Physical Formats

point the library makes either an active selection decision through a formal review or an implied selection decision through noncancellation. Over time, changes to the title, subject coverage, frequency, and other attributes require sustained bibliographic attention and potentially further review. At the item level, however, the work flow remains

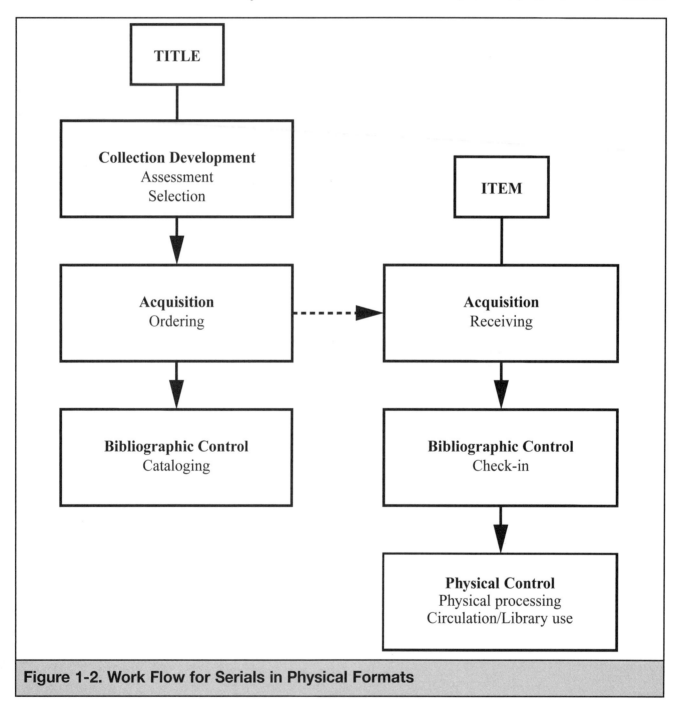

Figure 1-2. Work Flow for Serials in Physical Formats

fundamentally linear: new issues are checked in, placed on the shelf, and perhaps bound or discarded at a later time. Events that occur at the title level, such as title changes, publisher changes, or cancellations, have no effect on previous issues.

Online Resources

In some respects, online resources resemble serials: many online resources are of a continuing nature, and most fee-based online content is sold on a subscription basis even when the content itself is monographic. Indeed, many libraries have integrated electronic-resource management into their serials units for these reasons. However, online resources diverge fairly significantly even from the serials work flow, as illustrated in Figure 1-3.

The most unusual aspect of the work flow depicted here is the dynamic resource at the center. Physical resources are pushed through successive stages of their work flow, but a virtual resource in effect remains stationary while the library engages in various processes around the periphery that collectively result in access to the content. Effective communication is an essential component of this work flow because nothing about the resource itself necessarily indicates where it is in the process or who has responsibility for it at a given moment.

The expectation that online resources can be managed more easily and efficiently than their print predecessors is clearly not borne out by this diagram. Indeed, Figure 1-3 suggests that the management process for online resources is more resource intensive at every stage than the work flow for physical resources. The elements that are unique to this work flow, such as trial periods, license negotiation, administrative setup, and alternative bibliographic-control methods, require technical expertise and vendor relations. These requirements tend to push management processes to a higher level of the organization than the corresponding processes for physical materials. The sustained bibliographic maintenance of online collections as a result of dynamic characteristics also adds to the density of this work flow.

Open access: A publishing model that shifts the cost of scholarly publication from the consumer side to the producer side. Open access has the potential to dramatically alter the work flow for online-resource management in libraries that collect such materials. See Chapter 10 for a more in-depth discussion of trends in open-access publishing.

COLLECTION DEVELOPMENT

Collection development encompasses a cluster of selection and assessment activities that shape library collections over time. Because individual resources and the information marketplace as a whole are highly dynamic, collection development for online resources is a particularly intensive process.

Selection

Online information resources should be evaluated according to the same content standards that apply to information resources in any format. In addition, selectors should evaluate functional performance and technical requirements, which are as much a part of online resources as their intellectual content. Further evaluation criteria exist that are not based on characteristics of a resource per se but on the conditions under which it is made available. It is advisable to articulate explicit policies about critical criteria that a resource must meet before it will be considered for purchase. It is also beneficial to provide selectors

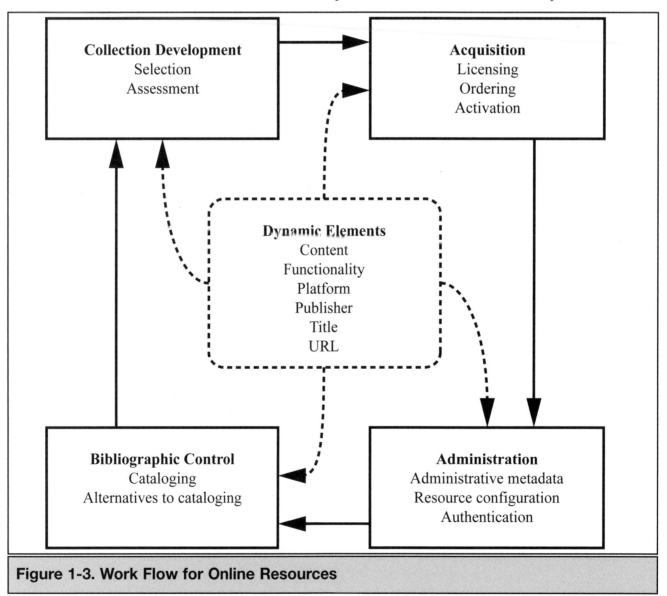

Figure 1-3. Work Flow for Online Resources

with evaluation guidelines specific to online resources highlighting the important evaluation criteria that are unique to this format. Table 1-1 breaks down these criteria in further detail.

Content

Most of the major content-related criteria for selecting online resources are markedly similar to the selection criteria for traditional

Selection Criteria: The Information Resource	
Content	• Subject matter • Audience • Authority • Accuracy • Thoroughness • Currency • Extent of coverage
Usability	• Ease of navigation • Accessibility • Search capabilities • Results display • Document quality • Output options • Server performance
Technical requirements	• Fonts • Plug-ins • Browser versions or settings • Proxy interaction
Selection Criteria: The Information Provider	
Pricing	• Free/fee-based • Basis of pricing • One-time/ongoing cost • Current content • Archival content • Bundled content • Combined formats
License restrictions	• Interlibrary loan • Course packs/Electronic reserves • Walk-in use • Remote access • Authentication method • Enforcement • Price cap
Reliability	• Longevity • Customer support • Adherence to standards

Table 1-1. Selection criteria for online resources

Extent of coverage: The duration and completeness of full-text coverage available with an online product. Consider the example of the *New York Times*, which has a variety of different levels of coverage available depending on the source. The newspaper's Web site makes the current day's news freely available, including images, interactive segments, and multimedia options. ProQuest offers current and historical coverage, including page images, as separate stand-alone subscriptions. In addition, anywhere from 4 to 24 years of text-only coverage is available in aggregator databases from Gale, LexisNexis, and other providers.

print resources. Any resource selected for the library, regardless of format, should be evaluated for the relevancy of its subject matter and appropriateness for the target audience, the authoritativeness of its source; and the accuracy, thoroughness, and currency of its content. In addition, it is important to assess the extent of the coverage provided by the online product in terms of both chronological coverage and completeness. Different online versions of the same title may offer vastly different spans of coverage, and some may reproduce sidebars, images, and other related material whereas others provide only the primary text. Therefore, it is important to verify that the version under consideration offers the necessary coverage and that this coverage justifies the cost of the resource.

Usability

Library resources in any format can and should be evaluated for usability, but online resources have a much wider array of functionality than other formats. Criteria affecting usability include how easily the user can navigate within the resource and locate the desired content or features. Closely related to navigation is how well the resource accommodates the needs of disabled users by including textual labels and descriptions for images, limiting the use of tables, providing ample target areas for links and buttons, and enabling users to resize text. These features indicate basic attention to good design in addition to addressing the needs of a specific user population. Any search functionality in the resource should be evaluated for ease, precision, and intelligibility of search results. Selectors should evaluate how resources are sorted and displayed as well as how easily they can be saved, printed, e-mailed, or output to citation software. Full text and media should be of good quality. Finally, selectors should examine resources multiple times at different times of day to assess server performance and look for the availability of mirror sites that could offset congestion at peak times or during scheduled downtime.

Technical Requirements

It is always wise to examine the technical requirements of new resources, and this is particularly important when the library provides on-site computing and needs to be sure it can support the online resources in its own collection. The selector should explore whether the resource requires any unusual fonts or software to be fully operational and note any performance problems encountered with particular browsers or browser versions. In addition, if the library is providing off-site access to its licensed resources and uses a proxy server to authenticate remote users, it is important that the resource can function in cooperation with the proxy server.

Pricing

Pricing models: Common pricing models for online content include direct purchase or subscription to individual titles, package subscription, free access with print, fee-based access with print, and one-time cost plus a nominal ongoing-access fee.

There are many factors to consider when evaluating the pricing for an online resource. First, it is important to ascertain whether an online resource is free or fee based. If there is a cost for a resource, it is important to determine whether the price is a flat fee for the site or is based on tiered pricing by type of library, number of sites or branches, or size of the user base. Archival online content may be priced according to a different model from that used for current content, so it is important to determine the pricing structure for the specific content the library needs.

Two factors in the pricing equation are particularly significant in the management of online resources: bundling and combined formats. Bundling is the practice of making online resources available as part of a suite, or collection, of separate titles. One important element of the selection process is assessing whether a desired resource is made available as an individual title, as part of a package, or both. Either option has both benefits and drawbacks for resource management.

Handling resources title by title allows libraries to have close control over the selection and processing of individual resources, but this approach also slows down every stage of the management process. Even if the library prefers to select resources title by title, the individual requests should be batched if possible for centralized review and processing. Not only is this practice more efficient than piecemeal handling of resources, but it also enables the library to uncover commonalities among requests; make vendors, subject areas, and types of content requested most frequently a priority; and move those resources through the remainder of the cycle together. This practice is particularly useful when selection responsibilities are distributed widely across an organization and individual selectors lack a cohesive picture of what their colleagues are requesting.

One alternative to title-by-title selection is to acquire collections, or packages, of online resources, such as a collection of e-books from a provider like netLibrary or a subscription package such as ScienceDirect. Subscription packages have long been a volatile political issue in libraries because of the high cost of commercial journals, but the debate continues because there are both benefits and drawbacks to the package approach. The library acquires access to a suite of titles at a substantially reduced unit cost, and this savings is further propagated by the increased efficiency of managing a single license, payment, and interface for multiple titles. In addition, some libraries find that titles they would not have subscribed to individually actually get significant usage through the subscription package. Despite the relatively lower unit cost of journals in subscription packages, the packages themselves can be extremely costly, and many libraries object to having to pay for a large number of resources they don't want in order to acquire the premium content they do want. In addition to tying up a large amount of money in a single agreement, subscription package may also limit budgetary flexibility by requiring that print subscriptions remain at a certain level in order to maintain online access at the agreed-upon price. In response to library demands for greater flexibility, publishers who pioneered the package subscription have begun to unbundle their subscription packages into smaller increments (Van Orsdel and Born, 2004).

Aggregator databases are similar to publisher packages in that the library acquires access to multiple titles through a single interface; the difference is that aggregations combine content from multiple publishers. Some aggregations behave like publisher collections by providing stable content and complete full text, while others function more like indexes that also happen to contain full text. The titles in an aggregator database are licensed from the publisher by the aggregator, which in turn does business with the library. Consequently, libraries have no direct control over the specific titles in the database. Although full-text aggregators can be highly useful for providing a critical mass of content in a particular subject area, it is not advisable to make selection decisions about specific resources based on whether or not they appear in a particular database.

> **Aggregator database**: A searchable database containing full-text articles from multiple sources and publishers, such as EBSCO's MasterFile Premier or InfoTrac's OneFile. Aggregator databases may be general purpose or subject oriented.

Online resources may be made available by one-time purchase, ongoing subscription or access fee, or in conjunction with a fee or subscription for the print version. In some cases, the online version may be considered the primary subscription and the print version an added format, a convention known as flip pricing. Whether the library acquires a work exclusively online or in conjunction with a print counterpart can have major implications not only for pricing but also for licensing and treatment in the library work flow. It is important that the selector be aware of the library's policy on online-only versus combined-format purchasing and know whether the desired resource actually gives the library a choice.

Some libraries have aggressively migrated their database and journal subscriptions to online-only format, and many more are following more circumspectly. Electronic books have not made as dramatic an impact as a replacement for print, but libraries continue to add electronic books to their collections as well. In addition, many libraries actively select Web sites and other Web-native content that has no direct equivalent in any other format. Online-only collections are not necessarily more cost effective than the corresponding collections in print, but they are certainly more cost effective than maintaining parallel content in multiple formats in terms of both direct cost and workflow efficiency.

Despite these advantages, there are several valid reasons why a library might prefer a combined print/electronic format over online-only. First and foremost, many online resources are simply not available as stand-alone products at this time, but are available only as an adjunct to the print version. In other cases, the library might want the convenience of online access but doesn't consider the online version to be a viable substitute for the print version because it lacks important coverage, functionality, or reliability. In addition, the library may perceive a need to maintain a tangible copy of a resource alongside the electronic version in order to meet current demand or long-term archival objectives.

The challenge of maintaining resources in multiple formats lies in tracking which resources are paid for as a combined subscription, which are freely available in conjunction with a print version, and which are simply acquired simultaneously. As a general rule, freely available resources can be managed more efficiently than fee-based resources because they require no licensing, payment, or authentication. Online content available for free in conjunction with print resources is an exception to this rule. Content providers have conceived countless variations on the free-with-print concept, including making all online content available with a current subscription, making available only that portion that corresponds to the library's print coverage, or offering a rolling window of coverage that may be revoked if the subscription is discontinued. These complexities should be a major consideration at the point of selection because they have significant consequences for the rest of the management process.

License Restrictions

Interpretation of the legal terminology in the licenses for online resources is best left to trained individuals who regularly review licenses. However, for selection purposes it is important to be able to recognize whether a license permits or prohibits activities that libraries consider to be part of their normal operations, such as interlibrary loan and document delivery, inclusion in course packs and electronic reserves, use by walk-in users not affiliated with the library, and authentication of authorized off-site users through a proxy server. In addition, selectors should be aware of language that leaves the library open to unchecked price increases.

Reliability

The reliability of online resources is largely contingent on the reliability of the content provider. With this in mind, the selector should consider the longevity and reputation of both the content provider and the specific product. It can take some time to work out the kinks in a product or business plan, and early adopters often bear the brunt of these hiccups in service. It is helpful to investigate the customer support available for the product in terms of both live assistance and online information. Communicating with the content provider can be highly instructive, because this can give the selector a good sense of how the company relates to its business partners. Finally, online products will be more reliable and interoperable over the long term if the content provider makes the effort to incorporate standards that are emerging in the information industry. Consequently, it is important to know whether products and content providers comply with existing standards or, better yet, if they are actively partnering with libraries and other stakeholders in the information industry in the development of standards.

Assessment

Ideally, assessment of online resources should take place both before and after the resources are selected. One of the advantages of online resources is that it is relatively commonplace to obtain access on a trial basis prior to making a selection decision. Unlike a canned product demonstration, the trial period gives the library an opportunity to explore a resource in detail and evaluate its performance in a live setting. Trials are useful for comparing similar resources, evaluating new platforms, and simply ensuring that big-ticket resources are thoroughly vetted prior to a final selection decision.

The library may not have the opportunity to customize a resource for trial access, so it is important to make evaluators aware of whether the trial resource is fully functional or not. Conversely, the trial may provide access to a full-featured version that includes content or functionality that the library does not plan to subscribe to. To ensure that trials run smoothly and generate responses that will be beneficial to the selection process, it is helpful to develop policies that articulate what kinds of resources the library will obtain on a trial basis, who is permitted to set up a trial, who may take part in the trial, and guidelines for evaluating trial products and submitting comments.

Assessment and selection are mutually sustaining processes, and nowhere is the relationship between these two more critical than in the development of online collections. The library incurs ongoing costs for many of its core online resources, such as electronic journals and research databases. In an era of escalating subscription costs and lean budgets, libraries must ensure that their collections provide both the intellectual content and the type of access that their users prefer. The nature and extent of online information varies widely across disciplines, so a wholesale flight to online access may not be feasible or desirable for all collections. However, the online-information marketplace is highly dynamic. As existing resources evolve and new products and publishing models enter the marketplace, libraries must continually assess their collection performance and user needs.

Libraries accustomed to gathering usage data for their physical collections may be amazed by the embarrassment of riches in the electronic realm. Usage statistics for physical resources are often based on circulation counts. Unfortunately, it is difficult to gather this type of information for many of the library's core resources, such as journals and reference materials, because these resources tend not to circulate. Shelving statistics can approximate, if not quite capture, the number of times a particular title leaves the shelves, but these data say nothing whatsoever about actual use. By comparison, online content providers are often able to gather usage data at a much higher level of detail. Libraries can supplement these data as well as gather data for resources that do not provide usage counts by reviewing proxy-server logs or employing click-through links that count usage, but these methods cannot provide information about how extensively a resource is used in a single session.

Initiatives to standardize reporting of electronic usage will further improve the quality of the usage data available to libraries. It is difficult to compare one resource or content provider to another when each provider has a different understanding of what constitutes a use and presents its statistics in a different format. The emerging standards and guidelines for usage statistics articulate a common language for usage terms and a common expectation for the depth and breadth of usage reports so that statistics can be compared without extensive manipulation on the library's part. A number of interested parties are working toward standardized usage reporting, including the National Information Standards Organization (NISO) and the International Coalition of Library Consortia (ICOLC), among others. The COUNTER (see sidebar) initiative has taken a notable leadership role in securing the cooperation of vendors to follow COUNTER guidelines, which are rapidly becoming a de facto standard among major information providers.

| **Counting Online Usage of Networked Electronic Resources (COUNTER)**: The COUNTER initiative works with vendors and publishers of online information to ensure consistent usage reporting. Standardized measures of online usage ensure that libraries can reliably compare usage data between one product or vendor and another. See the COUNTER Web site (www.projectcounter.org/index.html) for more information. |

Acquisition

The acquisition process for online resources is much more complicated than simply turning on access to the content. Because online resources are licensed from content providers rather than purchased outright, the library must negotiate the license before any order goes forward. Once the resource is paid for, the content provider must also enable the library to access the content.

Licensing: The license for an online resource is a contract containing specific legal terminology and is enforceable under the law. A basic overview of licensing issues and terms is available at the Liblicense Web site (www.library.yale.edu/~llicense/index.shtml).

Licensing

In order to acquire access to a fee-based online resource, the library must enter into a contractual agreement with the content provider. This agreement, known as a license, formally articulates the terms that govern how the library may use an online resource. These provisions define such concepts as authorized users and authorized use, restrictions on users or use, rights and responsibilities of both parties, and the legal protections available in the event of a dispute.

Initiatives across the digital information industry have attempted to establish standard licensing agreements that address the specific needs of libraries, but licenses still differ widely in their complexity and restrictions as well as the clarity of their definitions. Licenses are binding legal documents that content providers can and do enforce; libraries should be prepared to review licenses carefully or even refer them to legal counsel before entering into an agreement. Whether the library negotiates its own licenses or relies on a legal advisor, the library should be prepared to negotiate for advantageous license terms that address its particular needs and priorities.

Ordering

After the library signs a license for an online resource, it can proceed with the ordering process. Depending on the type of resource, the library might order directly from the content provider, manage online orders through a subscription vendor as it would for print subscriptions, or order through a consortium. Library consortia play an important role in the acquisition of online resources because of their ability to negotiate volume discounts on behalf of member libraries. In some cases, consortia even license online resources directly in order to provide access to all participating libraries.

Consortial discounts and subscriptions make it possible for individual libraries to gain access to resources they would otherwise have been unable to afford; small libraries in particular can see spectacular benefits from consortium membership. However, consortial subscriptions dilute local control of the collection, and resources that benefit some libraries in the consortium may not benefit all. At the same time, libraries run the risk of becoming reliant on resources funded from external budgets, which can have serious ramifications for individual libraries in the event that the consortium is forced to scale back its resources.

Activation

After the library has licensed and paid for an online resource, the vendor must provide a way for the library to access the content. As with most aspects of the online resource work flow, the activation process can be more complicated than one would expect. Vendors do not always notify the library when access becomes available, so the library may have to follow up repeatedly until access is available. In some cases, the vendor will notify only the individual whose contact information appears on the order, even though the ordering and resource-administration responsibilities may reside in entirely different areas of the organization. Some resources require the library to go through a complex, multistep process wherein the vendor gives the library a code that must be entered into an online form in order to activate the access. At the opposite extreme, vendors occasionally activate access to resources the library did not request at all. Patience and good communication both within the library and between the library and its vendors can help the activation step proceed considerably more smoothly.

Administration

Physical resources go through a variety of processing steps, such as labeling, bar coding, and security tagging. These processes ensure that an item can be stored, tracked, and kept secure while it is part of the library's collection. The administration stage for online resources fulfills a similar purpose, but rather than controlling the resources themselves, the library maintains an array of metadata about the resources that enables the library to maintain access.

Administrative Metadata

Catalogers tend to think of metadata in terms of bibliographic-resource description, but the publicly accessible metadata used in catalog records represents only a small fraction of the data that apply to online resources. Libraries must also manage information related to pricing schemes, license terms, vendor contacts, authentication, troubleshooting, and usage. Many libraries rely on a hodgepodge of spreadsheets, e-mail exchanges, and paper files to keep track of these data, but some libraries have built their own databases in order to streamline this process, and commercial systems are beginning to enter the market as well. The Digital Library Federation's Electronic Resource Management Initiative (ERMI) follows the development of

> **Electronic Resource Management Initiative (ERMI)**: ERMI is developing guidelines for the data that should be captured about online resources to facilitate their management in libraries. Examples of this kind of data include license terms, vendor contact information, records of the library's consideration process, and usage statistics. See the ERMI Web Hub (www.library .cornell.edu/cts/elicensestudy /home.html) for more information.

these tools and documents its evolving guidelines for the architecture of e-resource–management systems.

Resource Configuration

Many licensed resources provide an administrative console through which the library can activate a resource, retrieve usage reports, and in some cases, customize the interface. This customization might involve establishing links to the library's catalog, interlibrary loan service, full-text providers, or OpenURL resolver; adding preferred buttons or library-logo banners; or establishing search defaults and other functional preferences. Some content providers offer this level of customization but do not allow customers to manipulate their profiles directly, in which case the library must work through a customer-service representative to make these changes. Configuration preferences, customer-service contacts, and administrative passwords are among the configuration-related data elements that a library might include in its administrative database.

Authentication

A content provider must have a method for recognizing users who are authorized to access a library's licensed resources. User authentication can occur through the login/password method or by Internet protocol (IP) authentication. In conjunction with this method, the library may also provide a means of authentication—known as a proxy server—for its remote users outside the library network.

| **Internet protocol (IP) address**: The unique numeric address of each computer on the Internet. Robert E. Molyneux's (2003) *The Internet Under the Hood* is a useful guide to this and other networking terminology. |

Login/Password

Authentication by login and password is convenient in the sense that an individual user who knows the login and password can gain access to the resource from anywhere at any time. However, login/password presents some obvious management difficulties for the library, which must ensure that this information stays both current and secure. This mode of authentication is most feasible for libraries with fairly compact collections and a small, stable user population, such as a corporate or other specialized library. Libraries with a large number of resources and large, diffuse user populations, such as public and academic libraries, generally prefer authentication by IP address.

IP Authentication

IP authentication requires the library to register the unique IP addresses of its computers with the content provider. Users at registered computers are provided seamless access to the resource. The library must maintain a list of the IP addresses or address ranges it has supplied to the content provider, and redistribute this information to all content providers every time there is a change to the list. Libraries that are spread across multiple physical sites or reside on rapidly growing networks may have trouble staying abreast of changes to their IP ranges. It is critical that the library maintain regular contact with whoever is responsible for assigning its IP addresses so that updated addresses can be disseminated to content providers in a timely manner.

Proxy Servers

Generally speaking, libraries set up direct IP authentication only for their users in their own geographic domain, which may include only the computers in the library or computers in a wider area such as a business, school, or campus. This is an unfortunate limitation on access given that one of the most salient features of online information is that it is not location specific. The solution is a proxy server, which enables authorized users coming from outside the library's IP range to be authenticated as if they were physically in the library. The proxy server resides within the library's directly authenticated IP range. When a remote user tries to connect to a resource that is included in the proxy-server configuration, he or she is prompted for identification that can be verified against a database of valid users, such as a patron or personnel database. If the proxy server recognizes the identification as valid, the user is passed through to the resource just as if he or she were using one of the computers in the library building.

Proxy server: A server within the library that intercepts incoming traffic to restricted sites and prompts the user for identification. The identifying information is compared to a database of valid users, and correctly authenticated users are redirected to the desired online resource.

Proxy servers may rely on either browser configuration or a URL prefix to recognize library users. The browser configuration model requires users to enter the proxy-server address into the settings of their Web browsers. The browser essentially appends the proxy-server address to any link the browser points to, but the user is only prompted for identification if he or she links to a domain that is included in the server's configuration file. This method is efficient for the library because URLs are altered on the fly by the user's browser rather than in the hard-coded links. However, the browser-configuration model also tends to be unpopular with users who are intimidated by the browser preferences or do not have authorization to update the settings on their workstations.

The alternative to the browser-configuration model is the rewriting proxy, which does not require users to make any changes to their browser settings. Rewriting proxy servers require two things from the library. First, the library must maintain a configuration file containing the domain names of all the library's licensed resources. Online resources sometimes use multiple domains; all the alternative domain names must appear in the configuration file. In addition to every link for a licensed online resource, the library must add a prefix that redirects the URL through the proxy server. The principal drawback is that users are only prompted for authentication if they connect through the links that point to the proxy server for their library; users who discover the resource through a Web search engine, an external portal, or another library's catalog are simply turned away.

BIBLIOGRAPHIC CONTROL AND THE WORK FLOW

Bibliographic control is the first stage of the management process that makes content from external providers visible to library users, but bibliographic access cannot exist without the collection development, acquisition, and administrative steps that precede it. Trends such as open access notwithstanding, the complexity of the work flow for external online resources is unlikely to diminish; it is therefore critical that the activities culminating in online access are carried out as efficiently as possible. The tools and standards necessary to fully achieve this goal are still largely in their formative stages, but libraries can help to address this challenge by ensuring that the roles of those involved with electronic-resource management are widely understood within the library, and that policies and procedures exist to document and maintain consistency in management processes.

SPECIAL CONSIDERATIONS FOR LOCAL DIGITAL LIBRARIES

Libraries that create and manage their own digital collections provide a valuable service both to their local clientele and to other libraries seeking to link to online content. Local digital libraries improve access and visibility for rare, interesting, and intellectually significant content that would otherwise be inaccessible to most potential users because of geographical barriers or the condition of the resources. Libraries can set a positive example for other digital projects by employing high-quality digital formats, rich metadata, and open access.

It is possible to produce simple digital collections and ad hoc Web exhibits without a lot of specialized equipment or training, but this minimalist approach is not the best methodology for undertaking a major digitization project or attempting to manage substantive local digital collections. Digital projects require significant planning, expertise, technology resources, and institutional commitment both in the building stage and as the collections are managed and developed over time. This section presents a basic overview of the steps involved in building digital collections and highlights the important decisions that lead to successful digital projects. Building and managing a local digital library is a highly complex and multifaceted endeavor that will differ from site to site depending on the nature of the collections; the available personnel, budget, and infrastructure; and the library's service objectives with respect to its digital collections. The extensive bibliography of articles, reports, and technical specifications at the end of the chapter was compiled with this in mind. Consult it when planning a specific digital project.

What Is a Digital Library?

Born digital: Native to an electronic format. An information resource that is created in electronic form is considered to be born digital. An online resource that is digitized from another format, such as an e-book scanned from a print copy, is known as a retrospectively digitized resource.

The concept of the digital library encompasses a wide array of digital projects with very different scope, content, production models, and goals. For example, a public library might create a digital library to make its local history resources more widely available to the community, whereas an academic library might focus instead on gathering current teaching and research materials from its parent institution's faculty. One library may build its digital library with the aim of promoting access to materials, whereas another may be more concerned with preserving digital content. Some digital libraries are the result of retrospective digitization from older formats; others contain mainly "born-digital" content. For purposes of this book, a digital collection is any group of individual digital objects that share provenance, theme, or some other salient aspect in common. Digital library refers to any such collection or group of digital collections that a library creates or maintains locally.

Institutional Repositories

Institutional repository: A digital library intended to cumulate and preserve the output of a specific organization. Institutional repositories are chiefly used in educational institutions to archive and disseminate the scholarly output of faculty and students.

As libraries make progress in creating digital collections, more precise terminology is emerging to describe specific kinds of digital libraries. One example is the institutional repository, which is currently the focus of intense discussion and study among libraries supporting scholarly research and higher education. As the name suggests, an institutional repository is concerned with collecting, disseminating, and preserving the intellectual product of an organization. The mission of an institutional repository is to be "institutionally defined; scholarly; cumulative and perpetual; and open and interoperable" (Crow, 2002, 16). While in theory the institutional-repository model of coordinated self-archiving could apply to any constituency needing an online archive of its work product, the "scholarly" aspect and the language of "cumulative and perpetual" retention effectively restrict institutional repositories to the academic realm. At this early stage of development, most institutional repositories are being used to house traditional academic material such as scholarly articles and dissertations, but some are diversifying into other kinds of research and teaching tools that previously resided on personal and departmental Web sites and in professors' desks and filing cabinets.

In general, the planning, technology, and metadata issues associated with institutional repositories are much the same as for other kinds of digital libraries. However, some significant differences do exist as a result of how content is recruited for the repository. Whereas other kinds of digital libraries are based largely on the digitization of existing library and archival content that has already been evaluated, selected, and organized, institutional repositories look outward to their parent institutions to recruit content. As a result, institutional repositories often contain diverse, highly individualized collections. Libraries that have already implemented an institutional repository have spoken of the need to lower technology and policy barriers in order to ensure that a critical mass of content finds its way to the repository. In order to accomplish this, institutional repository planners should look for systems that make depositing digital objects into the repository as simple as possible, and be prepared either to assist depositors in following basic standards and creating metadata or impose these after the objects are deposited.

Planning for Digital Collections

The key to developing successful digital collections is planning. Careful and thorough planning allows the institution to develop goals, accumulate necessary resources, implement robust processes, and successfully anticipate outcomes.

Determining the Purpose of the Digital Collection

The first step in planning a digital library is determining what objectives a digital collection will help the library to meet. Creating and managing digital collections is highly resource intensive and should not be undertaken without a full understanding of the level of institutional support required for success. The most successful, useful, and sustainable digital libraries exist in harmony with the library's mission and priorities. Perhaps the most common reason for digitizing a collection is to increase access to high-demand resources. These typically include materials that represent the strength of a library's collections and highlight its relationship to its user community. For a public library, this might mean digitizing materials that are historically significant or that target a specific demographic segment of the library's clientele. An academic library is likely to focus on digitizing resources in the disciplines in which its parent institution is strongest.

Digital collections can also be used to provide access and visibility for underutilized or endangered collections. For example, an archive may have a collection of rare or fragile materials that are valuable to researchers, but cannot withstand frequent use. By digitizing the collection, the archive can provide a high level of access to the digital representations of the objects in the collection. The risk of this method is that the increased visibility of the collection may actually create a greater demand for access to the physical items.

Planning for Digital Library Processes

After determining the purpose of a digital project, the library must work through a series of processes that go into creating the digital collection:

- Selection
- Copyright research
- Digitization
- Ingest
- Metadata creation
- User-interface design
- Access control
- Preservation

These eight major processes are common to virtually all digital projects, but how these steps are implemented in a specific project will be highly dependent on local factors. For example, the size, type, and homogeneity of the collection; the condition of the materials; the desired quality of the digital files; the equipment and environment available for digitization; the skill of the technician; and many other factors have an impact on the process of digitization. An examination of each of these processes follows, including potential pitfalls and important decision points.

Digital Library Processes

Selection

When the library has finished planning a digital project and is ready to begin production, the first step is selecting the right collection to digitize. The collection should be chosen to support the purpose of the project, such as attracting the interest of a particular demographic or commemorating a landmark event. In many cases, the existence of an important collection is the impetus for attempting a digital project in the first place. The planners should take into consideration the space, personnel, equipment, and budgetary resources available to the project. The costs associated with digitization can vary based on the type, number, format, size, and condition of the collection and the level of digitization desired. These costs are discussed further in the discussion of the digitization phase.

Copyright Research

A critical step in selecting a collection for digitization is determining the copyright of the items in the collection. This can be a frustrating and time-consuming step because many of the objects that libraries digitize are not accompanied by a clear statement of ownership. The prevalence of historical resources in digital collections is not exclusively a result of topical interest. Resources in the public domain are the easiest to manage because they do not require the permission of the copyright holder, and many libraries that are new to digitization start with these. In addition, the use of public-domain resources means that the collection can be made freely available.

For collections that are not in the public domain, the copyright owner must be identified and permission to digitize and provide access to the collection secured. In such cases, the copyright owner has the right to determine what level of access is to be granted to the collection. The spectrum ranges from open access to highly restricted access. If the copyright owner restricts access, access control must be designed into the system, typically using a login/password or IP authentication model (see "Resource Configuration").

Digitization

Digitization is a complex process that is highly dependent on the physical characteristics of the objects in the collection. The technical specifications of digitization should be determined during the planning process to ensure that the library has the necessary resources at its disposal when the production phase begins. A digitization effort benefits greatly from the presence of a skilled technician with specialized knowledge of the digitization technology and, ideally, the type of resources being digitized.

Image Collections

Image collections are common among digitization initiatives because they have a high interest-to-difficulty ratio. That is, images are interesting to look at and also relatively easy to digitize because they are flat and often relatively uniform in size. A common example is a collection of photographs. The process of digitizing photographs depends on the physical characteristics of the collection. The digital images can be created by scanning or digital photography. A collection that is fairly homogenous, with photos of similar size and condition, can be scanned efficiently given the proper equipment and staff with adequate training. A collection of photographs of different sizes or in fragile condition requires a greater effort to digitize. For example, large photographs may require a higher-end scanner with a larger scanning surface to capture the image.

The library must also decide on its preferred technical standards for the digital images. Technical specifications for image quality are very specific, and special photographic training is useful if the library is going to be manipulating the digital images to any great extent. The Tagged Image File Format (TIFF) is considered to be the best standard for long-term image preservation, but archival-quality images are dense and their large file size can be burdensome for creation, storage, and delivery. To alleviate this problem, many digital libraries maintain an archival-quality image for preservation purposes but use a smaller image or a less-dense format, such as JPEG, for the public view.

Textual Collections

Collections of textual materials present a greater level of complexity than image collections. Textual collections can be digitized by creating image reproductions of documents, but this level of digitization is inadequate to encode the text of the document. Ideally, the text should be encoded as well in order to facilitate display and full-text searching. Therefore, digital reproductions of textual materials might consist of images only, images with hidden text, or images with text that can be displayed alongside the image.

The image content is digitized in the same manner as any other image, typically in the TIFF or JPEG format. The textual content may be reproduced using basic ASCII or Unicode characters, or it may be further marked up in a tagging language such as the eXtensible Markup Language (XML) to provide additional structure, search, and display capabilities. Digitization of the text may be accomplished using an automated optical-character-recognition (OCR) system or by technicians manually keying in the text. OCR does not automatically create XML tags, so these must be added in a later step if desired. The accuracy of OCR depends on the clarity of the text in the documents being scanned and is further affected by the quality of the scan itself. Statistical-sampling methods can be used to determine the accuracy of an OCR scan, and the output of an OCR scan can be manually corrected to increase accuracy. Manually keying the text is a highly resource-intensive process, but one that nonetheless may be required if the text does not provide sufficient clarity for successful OCR scanning. To ensure higher levels of accuracy, text can be double keyed, or typed in twice.

Audio, Video, and Multimedia Collections

Other types of media commonly found in digital collections include sound, video, and multimedia files. Each format requires special equipment, training, and software to manage adequately. Sound collections typically consist of either musical recordings or spoken-word recordings, such as recorded interviews and oral histories, but might also include other types of sound, such as birdcalls. In order to ensure that such a collection is digitized faithfully, it is helpful to have someone with expertise in the subject area as well as technical experts working with the project. Sound files may exist in various types of physical media, including legacy formats such as phonographic records and magnetic tape. Special equipment is required to convert the sound signals from the physical medium to a digital medium. Furthermore, there are multiple digital formats for sound files. As is the case for image files, different types of sound files provide different degrees of fidelity and system performance, and the planning process for a digital sound collection should include a discussion of appropriate formats for storage and delivery. Converting video to digital format is a similar, but still more complex process requiring special equipment and expertise. Like sound recordings, video can reside on a variety of source formats and can be converted to a variety of different digital formats. These should be evaluated during the planning process.

In-House Digitization versus Outsourcing

Based on the technical specifications of a digitization project and the library's available resources, the library must decide whether to perform the digitization in-house or outsource the project. Setting up a digitization program in-house requires specialized equipment and expertise. Even a relatively simple collection of small, homogenous photographs requires having a scanner, image-editing software, as well as an operator who knows how to use the scanner and has a basic understanding of digital-image formats. As more complex projects arise, the library should assess whether it wants to invest in the ongoing hardware and software upgrades and training updates that are needed if such projects are to be managed in-house, or farm out the project to a vendor who already has these things. The main consideration for outsourcing a digitization project is that the technical specifications should be determined by the project planners rather than prescribed by the outsourcing vendor. It is imperative to specify the formats and method of delivery of the final product so that the digital objects will function correctly within the scope of the overall project.

Born-Digital Collections

Libraries, archives, and museums are encountering an increasing number of resources that are born digital. This content can be virtually unlimited in terms of file formats and physical media. For example, there might be a document in an obscure file format (such as the WordStar word processor) stored on an obsolete physical medium (such as 5 $\frac{1}{4}$ inch floppy disks). Born-digital content is especially challenging because of the potential for obsolescence of the technology. With retrospective digitization of physical media, institutions can pre-plan the use of common standards that will have a greater probability of successful preservation over time. Born-digital content does not fit any preplanned standard of digitization. Therefore, born-digital objects may need to be migrated to more common formats and standardized before they can be used in a digital collection.

Ingest

The digitization process results in a quantity of disaggregated digital objects. Ingest is the process of moving individual digitized objects into a system that organizes the collection to achieve the digital library functions of description, access, retrieval, and preservation. There are typically two methods of ingesting digital objects: they can be ingested one at a time, or they can be batch loaded.

Ingesting Objects One at a Time

Most digital library systems have the facility to process digital objects one at a time. This method is common when the digitization process occurs just prior to ingest. This process is typically slower and less efficient than batch loading, but it can result in more thorough metadata and processing in general. The process begins by uploading the digital object. After uploading, the system will typically display a form for entering metadata. Other processes such as defining access controls and copyright may be included in the ingest process. In general, ingesting objects one at a time allows a high degree of description and control for each object.

Batch Loading

Batch loading is typically used when an entire collection has previously been digitized. In order to batch load a digital collection, it is important that it be somewhat organized at the outset. The collection may exist as a number of objects in a basic file system or may be partly organized with metadata or some other internal structure. The collection to be batch loaded must adhere to a format compatible with the digital library system, so preparation work may be required to format the collection for batch loading. Batch loading often requires the skills of a programmer or computer-systems specialist to preprocess the collection and execute the computer commands to ingest the collection into a digital library system. If the metadata is not already in the collection, it must be added after the fact.

Unique Identifiers and Persistent Locators

One of the purposes of digital library systems is to provide centralized control and stewardship of a collection to prevent loss of digital information. Digital information that is not centrally controlled or widely visible often suffers from format obsolescence or data corruption. Most information on the Web is not durable; links on Web sites are often broken and the content of pages changes over time. Good digital collections assign unique identifiers to content and provide persistent locators so that users can be confident that references to images, documents, and other digital objects will maintain their integrity in perpetuity. Two common systems for providing unique identifiers and persistent locators are the Handle system and the Digital Object Identifier (DOI) system. Compatibility with an identifier system should be built into the digital library.

Metadata Creation

Metadata is often defined as data about data. This definition is technically correct, but it fails to capture the many functions of metadata within the digital library. Catalogers are highly familiar with descriptive metadata, but because digital libraries have a content-management aspect as well as a bibliographic-control aspect, they involve other kinds of metadata. The three major categories of metadata are structural, descriptive, and administrative.

Structural Metadata

Structural metadata define logical or physical relationships among the parts of a digital object. For example, the Text Encoding Initiative (TEI) schema defines metadata tags that identify and relate separate parts of a textual document. The Metadata Encoding and Transmission Schema (METS) can define the complex relationships between dissimilar digital files. Encoded Archival Description (EAD) is a structural metadata schema for the creation of the complex, hierarchical finding aids used for archival collections. It is important to note that the EAD format applies only to the digital finding aids, not to the collections themselves.

Descriptive Metadata

Descriptive metadata define the bibliographic features of digital objects. The most commonly mentioned descriptive-metadata standard is the MARC format used by library catalogers for bibliographic description and access (see Chapter 5). Many libraries provide catalog access to digital collections at the collection level, but less frequently at the individual-object level. This is a consequence of cataloging tradition as well as the fact that this format is not optimal for individual digital objects. Complex catalog software is required to interpret MARC records, but digital objects cannot be stored in the library catalog; this means that the digital object has to be separated from its metadata. Instead of doing this, many libraries are using more straightforward schema that are more compatible with digital library systems. One such schema is the Dublin Core, which is discussed in greater detail later in this chapter. Although it is simple to use, Dublin Core has been criticized for lacking the level of detail needed for library applications. Another descriptive-metadata standard that is being developed as an extension schema for METS is the Metadata Object Description Schema (MODS). MODS promises to be semantically richer than Dublin Core and syntactically better adapted to modern computer networks than MARC.

Metadata: Data about data. Metadata can apply to any type of information object, but it is used most commonly in the context of digital-information objects. There are three broad categories of metadata: structural, descriptive, and administrative. Structural metadata defines the relationships among parts of a digital object. Descriptive metadata encapsulates the object's bibliographic characteristics. Administrative metadata relates to the creation, management, and preservation of the object, such as rights management or technical specifications. See NISO's "Understanding Metadata" (www.niso.org/standards/resources/UnderstandingMetadata.pdf) for more information.

Metadata Object Description Schema (MODS): MODS is still under development, but the Library of Congress is promoting this schema as a promising successor to both Dublin Core and MARC. MODS is designed to provide a rich and highly structured data environment for library applications and is XML-based for functionality in the Web environment. See the MODS Web site (www.loc.gov/standards/mods/) for more information.

Administrative Metadata

Administrative metadata provide information relevant to the creation, management, and preservation of digital objects. Administrative metadata include the technical metadata that are often embedded in digital objects, rights-management metadata regarding copyright and access control, and metadata used for preserving resources. An example of technical metadata is the header information embedded in a TIFF image. This information includes the dimensions of the image and information regarding the quality of the image. Rights-management metadata can be used to implement access policies on a network. Preservation metadata is less well defined, but it is an area of active and ongoing research. In general, any of the types of metadata discussed here can be helpful for preserving content over time.

User-Interface Design

Digital-library users interact with the collection through a Web-based user interface. The two most common functions of a user interface are object retrieval and display. Retrieval systems facilitate access to materials based on the criteria defined by digital library users. Display systems present the actual content of digital objects to users once the desired objects are found. Digital-library systems provide a broad range of capabilities for both functions.

Retrieval Systems

Retrieval is typically accomplished using a combination of a searching function and a browsing function. Search functions in digital libraries are closely tied to the metadata schema used in a collection. A rich metadata schema with highly structured content enables a high level of search capability, whereas simple metadata will only support simple searching functions. An example of a simple search function is single-box form that searches the unstructured full-text content of digital objects. A more sophisticated search function provides a multifield form that allows searches on specific metadata fields using controlled languages and Boolean-search capabilities.

Browsing Functions

Browsing functions are also closely associated with the metadata. Browsing functions utilize the structure and indexes imposed by metadata to present navigation options to users. An example of a simple browsing function is a display of digital objects ordered by accession number. A more sophisticated browsing function allows navigation by metadata fields more meaningful to users, such as title, author, or subject. Alternatively, a browsing function may allow navigation using logical structures in a document, such as an e-book reader that allows the user to access specific chapters or pages.

Displaying Digital Objects

Modes of display vary by type of object and digital-library system. Images may be displayed within the application that was used to access the item (such as a Web-browser window) or may open a new window of the same application, or even a new application, for viewing. Certain file formats are associated with specific viewers, such as Adobe's portable document file (PDF) format. Text can be presented in multiple modes, including hypertext presented in a Web browser, as documents of various formats, including Microsoft's Word format or PDF. Some objects packaged as e-books require special applications for viewing. Audio and video files are similarly diverse. The configuration of the digital-library system can greatly influence display. Some systems show relationships between and among objects; others do not. Some servers can be configured so that audio and video files can be played, or streamed, directly from the server. Otherwise, the file must be downloaded and played directly from the user's computer. Because audio and video files are typically large, failing to adequately design the system for access can create barriers to access that ultimately hamper the goals of the digital library.

Access Control

Access control refers to limiting access to the digital library through restrictions on computer networks. Access control is typically implemented to enforce copyright decisions. Collections that are in the public domain may be available under an open-access policy that does not require any access controls, but collections that are not in the public domain must be evaluated for copyright restrictions. Another justification for implementing access control is the desire to generate revenue from an online collection. An authentication system can be implemented with an online storefront service that requires payment to access collections. This technology is somewhat sophisticated and requires personnel with specialized skills.

Determining who may have access to a collection must be part of the planning process. Furthermore, while it may be easy to identify a class of individuals who will be granted access to a collection, implementing a system that unambiguously identifies these individuals can be challenging. Common methods include creating accounts that allow permitted individuals onto the network via login/password, or using IP authentication to allow access. Access control often requires troubleshooting and, therefore, adds an extra layer to the management of the system.

Preservation

Digitization is not a proven method for long-term preservation, and the development of digital libraries should be justified by the desire to enhance access to collections rather than preserve them. Nonetheless, digitization may be may be the only viable option for preserving content that is disintegrating or facing obsolescence. In general, the original objects should be preserved independently from their digitization.

Preservation of the digital objects themselves is also an important issue. Technology is progressing too fast to make reliable predictions about the future of digital media. The trend in digital-library policy is to make a good-faith effort to address digital preservation. Three different approaches exist for preserving digital objects: preserving bit streams as is, emulating systems and software, and migrating data to new formats.

Preserving Bitstreams

This level of preservation requires a commitment to preserve an exact copy of the bits of the file. Essentially, this is a promise to maintain the integrity of the file in its original state, using periodic checks to ensure fidelity. This approach does not address format obsolescence, nor does it make any effort to migrate the data to formats developed in the future or to maintain the applications necessary to access the digital objects.

Software/System Emulation

The second approach is emulation. For this level of preservation, the bits are maintained in the original format, as in the bitstream preservation approach. In addition to the preservation of bits, an effort is made to create applications that emulate the functions of the legacy applications that were originally used to access the objects. This method is highly risky and presumes that emulation is even possible with future technologies. Some research has been done in this area, but this method will only be validated if it is successfully implemented in the future.

Data Migration

The third approach is data migration. In order to implement this level of preservation, the institution assumes a commitment to move data to new formats as needed to prevent data corruption, obsolescence, or loss and to ensure continued access to the data. This approach is typically applied to high-profile collections for which continued access is considered to be a core purpose of the collection. Data migration is also risky. By assuming this responsibility, the institution is making a commitment to cover any costs associated with migrating the data. For some forms of digital information, there is no guarantee that it will even be possible to migrate the data.

The Importance of Standards

The best way for libraries to ensure the successful preservation of their own digital collections is to take a preemptive approach. Collections should be digitized using common file formats that have broad support and well-defined standards. The greater the number of institutions invested in any given format, the higher the probability that it will be maintained over time. Preservation is currently a hot topic for digital library research and one that deserves to be closely monitored by administrators on a continuing basis.

Resources Required to Develop a Digital Library

Hardware, Software, and Equipment for Digitizing

A great deal of equipment is required for conducting digitizing activities in-house. Simple image digitization can be achieved with a relatively inexpensive flatbed scanner. However, inexpensive scanners are limited in terms of physical dimensions, image quality, and throughput. There are a multitude of scanners on the market to meet a multitude of needs; the key is determining the minimum requirements for the digital initiative and finding the scanner that meets those requirements in the most cost-efficient manner. Beyond simple desktop-flatbed scanners, vendors offer scanners that can be sheet fed, scanners with large-format scanning surfaces, scanners that can automatically turn pages, and scanners bundled with image-manipulation software, just to name a few.

Large-format, rare, and delicate materials may require the use of a digital camera that does not physically touch the surface of the material. These are typically used with stands or cradles that can be minutely adjusted to hold the object. Camera setups tend to require a greater level of imaging expertise because there are so many variables, and the control of environmental factors such as lighting becomes more important.

Whether the material is digitized with a scanner or camera, image-editing software is a necessary component of image digitization. Just as scanners come in a broad spectrum of capabilities and prices, so does imaging software. Inexpensive desktop scanners typically come with simple software that allows for minimal image manipulation. Institutions that specify a higher quality for digital images will require more sophisticated software. Advanced imaging software allows for detailed editing, including color management, automatic correction of page curvature, and multiple options for output-file formats. OCR software may or may not be bundled with imaging software.

Textual materials are complex in multiple dimensions. Even pristine, mechanically produced documents, such as a memo printed from a computer, can introduce errors when subjected to OCR. Less-pristine documents, such as stained materials or pages that have been photocopied many times, tend to produce error-riddled output. OCR software is a developing technology, and software of the highest quality is technically sophisticated and quite expensive. Handwritten documents typically must be manually keyed, and even documents that have been processed using OCR require manual editing. If XML tagging is desired, this may have to be done manually as well. Professional-caliber text-editing software is another requirement for large-scale text digitization; standard word-processing software is inadequate for this purpose. Such software can provide powerful editing functions, such as color coding tags, collapsing and expanding hierarchies, managing tag libraries, managing schemas, and validating markup.

Digitizing audio and video is resource intensive. The equipment needed to digitize audio and video resources depends on the contents of the collection. At a minimum, the digitization facility must possess the equipment needed to play or produce an output from the physical objects. This could be anything from a wax cylinder player to 8mm videotape. The analog output device must be integrated with a device that can produce a digital version of the output. After the initial digitization, the sound or video files may require further editing that requires specialized equipment, software, and knowledge about both the format and content.

Hardware and Software for Managing a Digital Library

Following digitization, collections must be ingested into a digital library system. Digital library systems are typically installed on a pre-existing computer network. Therefore, network infrastructure must be included in the design. This includes raw magnetic storage for digital collections, networking infrastructure (domain-name servers, routers, and network cables), Web servers to provide internal and external access to the collection, and peripheral systems such as authentication systems that identify users on the network. Many libraries are already on such a network, but the development of a digital library may require enhancing some capabilities of the network, such as purchasing additional storage or additional servers.

Once the infrastructure is in place, a digital-library system, typically a complex set of software, must be implemented and integrated separately. Implementing and maintaining a digital-library system requires specialized computer knowledge. After implementation, staff must be trained to use the system, including how to ingest and provide access to digital collections, as well as general maintenance and upgrades for the system itself. A list of digital-library system vendors is included in the bibliography at the end of this chapter.

Like digitization, digital-library management can be outsourced to a vendor that provides digital-library service. This requires that the collections are hosted and maintained on Web servers owned by the vendor. It is important to remember that the content remains the intellectual property of the originating institution, and the vendor only provides the technical expertise to manage the content and make it available to authorized communities.

Personnel

Developing and maintaining a digital library requires a great deal of knowledge and oversight. Digitizing collections requires knowledge of relevant media formats as well as training on specific equipment and digital formats. Implementing and managing a digital library system requires a certain amount of computer-systems expertise. Successful digital-library project managers must possess a number of skills including a broad understanding of digital library design, project management skills, supervisory skills, budgeting skills, and accountability.

Developing a digital library is not a task that should be assigned as an added duty to employees with other responsibilities. Even a mature, robust digital library requires ongoing planning, development, and maintenance. Of course, the number of employees needed to sustain a library's digital projects depends on the size of the library and the scope of the collections. On the smallest scale, one person may be all that is needed to plan and develop a simple online image collection. At the opposite end of the spectrum, a cutting-edge digital library will employ specialists in each of the functional areas: imaging specialists for scanning, specialists for textual digitization, systems administrators and programmers to maintain computer systems, catalogers to create and maintain metadata, several project managers, and public-service librarians to assist patrons with collection access and use. The level of staffing should be appropriate to the specific needs and resources of the library, but a digital project can only thrive if it is staffed sufficiently to carry out all aspects of planning and production.

Dublin Core

Simple Dublin Core

The Dublin Core is a set of elements that can be used to describe a wide variety of digital resources. The standard consists of two levels: "Simple" and "Qualified." Simple Dublin Core consists of 15 elements:

- Title
- Subject
- Description
- Type
- Source
- Relation
- Coverage
- Creator
- Publisher
- Contributor
- Rights
- Date
- Format
- Identifier
- Language

Each element is optional and can be repeated. Dublin Core reveals its digital origins in the elements that do not correspond directly to anything in the MARC format, such as the **Rights** tag and a specific **Format** tag. Although Dublin Core does have conceptual crossover with other bibliographic-description formats such as MARC, Simple Dublin Core is far less complex than bibliographic-description in the AACR/MARC tradition. For example, compare the simple record below for a sound file rendered in Simple Dublin Core with the MARC records for monographic resources shown in Chapter 7:

```
<title>The Bends</title>
<creator>Radiohead</creator>
<publisher>EMI Records</publisher>
<date>1995</date>
<type>sound</type>
```

```
<format>mpeg</format>
<identifier>CDP 7243 8 29626 2 5<identifier>
<language>eng</eng>
```

Qualified Dublin Core

> **Dublin Core**: The Dublin Core metadata element set was developed to provide creators of online content with a flexible, easy-to-understand format for imbedding metadata in digital objects at the point of publication. The full set of Dublin Core elements and their refinements is described in-depth at the Dublin Core Web site (www.dublincore.org).

Simple Dublin Core may simply be too vague for certain applications, and Qualified Dublin Core exists to remedy this problem. Qualified Dublin Core adds one further element, **Audience**, and includes qualifiers for greater specificity that can assist in resource discovery. Qualifiers serve to narrow the definition of the basic 15 elements, not extend them into new domains

The Dublin Core qualifiers fall into two broad classes. The first class is element refinements, which make the meaning of an element narrower or more specific. The content of the element is still valid should the qualifier be removed. The second class of qualifiers consists of encoding schemes. These qualifiers indicate predefined schemes that aid in the interpretation of an element value. Examples of this type of qualifier are controlled vocabularies, formal notations, and parsing rules. The Dublin Core element **Date** has qualifiers of both types (see Table 1-2).

Syntaxes

The Dublin Core elements define metadata semantics, or the meaning of terms. The Dublin Core elements themselves are neutral in terms of syntax. That is, a separate syntax, or encoding scheme, must be employed to enter Dublin Core elements in a computer system. Fortunately, syntaxes have been defined for Dublin Core in the Resource Description Framework (RDF), an XML syntax for describing Web objects.

Dublin Core Element	Element Refinement	Element- Encoding Scheme
Date	Created Valid Available Issued Modified Date copyrighted Date submitted	DCMI Period W3C-DTF
Table 1-2. Dublin Core Qualifiers for the Date Element		

Application Profiles

Application profile: An interpretation of Dublin Core customized for a specific type of digital object, institution, application, or user community. An application profile contains specific information about how to apply the metadata elements and element refinements as well as the terms and syntax to use within the fields.

An application profile is an implementation of Dublin Core for a specific type of digital object, institution, application, or user community. Application profiles not only specify terms, but also explicate how the terms are to be used and provide policies and guidelines for implementing Dublin Core in the applicable context. An example of a Dublin Core application profile is the Electronic Theses and Dissertations Metadata Standard (ETD-MS). This application profile specifies how Dublin Core is applied to ETD collections produced by participants in the Networked Digital Library of Theses and Dissertations (NDLTD). It addresses both the semantics of the Dublin Core fields and the syntax of markup, using both XML and MARC. The NDLTD community benefits from this profile because it addresses concerns unique to ETD collections. For example, graduate students write dissertations under the guidance of a thesis advisor, typically a university professor. This role is unique to dissertations as a type of publication. The ETD-MS profile specifies how to record the thesis-advisor information using Dublin Core.

SUMMARY

The management of online information, whether local or external, is complex and multifaceted. Libraries must juggle information in multiple formats, work with a wide array of content providers, learn how to become content providers themselves, and employ a growing array of management tools. Libraries can rise to meet this challenge by clearly defining roles and lines of communications among the library's online resource managers, articulating policies and procedures for management tasks, and seeking out robust tools for managing metadata needed to prepare resources for the next stage, bibliographic control.

REFERENCES

Brown, Ladd, and Molly Brennan Cox. 2001. "Managing Electronic Resources in Technical Services." *Virginia Libraries* 47, no. 4 (October–December): 21–24.

COUNTER. "COUNTER: Counting Online Usage of Networked Electronic Resources." Oxford, UK: COUNTER (2004) Available: www.project-counter.org/index.html. Accessed January 27, 2005.

Crow, Raym. 2002. *The Case for Institutional Repositories: A SPARC Position Paper*. Washington, DC: Scholarly Publishing and Academic Resources Coalition.

Digital Library Federation Electronic Resource Management Initiative Steering Group. "A Web Hub for Developing Administrative Metadata for Electronic Resource Management." Washington, DC: Digital Library Federation (2004). Available: www.library.cornell.edu/cts/elicensestudy/home.html. Accessed January 27, 2005.

Grahame, Vicki, and Tim McAdam. 2004. *Managing Electronic Resources*. SPEC Kit 282. Washington, DC: Association of Research Libraries, Office of Leadership Services.

Keller, Michael A., Victoria A. Reich, and Andrew C. Herkovic. 2003. "What Is a Library Anymore, Anyway?" *First Monday* 8, no. 5 (May). Available: www.firstmonday.org/issues/issue8_5/keller/index.html. Accessed January 27, 2005.

Molyneux, Robert E. 2003. *The Internet Under the Hood.* Englewood, CO: Libraries Unlimited. SPARC. 2002. p.16.

Van Orsdel, Lee, and Kathleen Born. 2004. "Periodicals Price Survey 2004: Closing in on Open Access." *Library Journal* 129, no. 7 (April 15): 45–50.

Yale University Library. 2003. "Liblicense." New Haven, CT: Yale University Library Available: www.library.yale.edu/~llicense/index.shtml. Accessed January 27, 2005.

BIBLIOGRAPHY OF DIGITAL LIBRARY RESOURCES

Building Digital Libraries

National Information Standards Organization. 2004. "A Framework for Building Good Digital Collections." Bethesda, MD.: National Information Standards Organization. Available: www.niso.org/framework/forumframework.html. Accessed January 27, 2005.

National Initiative for a Networked Cultural Heritage. 2002. "The NINCH Guide to Good Practice in the Digital Representation and Management of Cultural Heritage Materials." Washington, DC: National Initiative for a Networked Cultural Heritage. Available: www.nyu.edu/its/humanities/ninchguide. Accessed January 27, 2005.

Building Institutional Repositories

Crow, Raym. 2004. "A Guide to Institutional Repository Software, v. 3.0." New York: Open Society Institute. Available: www.soros.org/openaccess/software/. Accessed January 27, 2005.

————. 2002. "SPARC Institutional Repository Checklist and Resource Guide." New York: Scholarly Publishing and Academic Resources Coalition. Available: www.arl.org/sparc/IR/IR_Guide.html. Accessed January 27, 2005.

Copyright

Budapest Open Access Initiative. 2004. "Budapest Open Access Initiative." New York: Budapest Open Access Initiative. Available: www.soros.org/openaccess/. Accessed January 27, 2005.

Harper, Georgia. 2001. "The UT System Crash Course in Copyright." Austin, TX: University of Texas System. Available: www.utsystem.edu/ogc/intellectualproperty/cprtindx.htm. Accessed January 27, 2005.

Digitization

Adobe Developers Association. 1992. "TIFF: Revision 6.0." Mountain View, CA: Adobe Systems. Available: http://partners.adobe.com/public/developer/en/TIFF6.pdf. Accessed January 27, 2005.

Chapman, Stephen. 2004. "Techniques for Creating Sustainable Digital Collections." *Library Technology Reports* 40, no. 5 (September/October): 1–64.

ITC-irst. 2004. "OCR and Text Recognition: Commercial Research and Products." Trento, Italy: ITC-irst. Available: http://tev.itc.it/OCR/Products.html. Accessed January 27, 2005.

Joint Photographic Experts Group. 2004. "JPEG 2000: Our New Standard." Joint Photographic Experts Group. Available: www.jpeg.org/jpeg2000/index.html. Accessed January 27, 2005.

Preservation and Imaging Department, Harvard College Library and Weissman Preservation Center, Harvard University Library. 2004. "Book Scanners and Tables: Links to Products and Reviews." Cambridge, MA: Harvard University Library. Available: http://preserve.harvard.edu/resources/bookscanners_table.html. Accessed January 27, 2005.

Text Encoding Initiative Consortium. 2004. "Text Encoding Initiative." Bergen, Norway: Text Encoding Initiative Consortium. Available: www.tei-c.org/

Western States Digital Standards Group, Digital Imaging Working Group. 2003, Jan. "Western States Digital Imaging Best Practices, Version 1.0." Denver, CO: Colorado Digitization Program. Available www.cdpheritage.org/resource/scanning/documents/WSDIBP_v1.pdf. Accessed January 27, 2005.

Handle and DOI Systems

Corporation for National Research Initiatives. 2004. "The Handle System." Reston, VA.: Corporation for National Research Initiatives. Available: www.handle.net. Accessed January 27, 2005.

International DOI Federation. 2004. "The Digital Object Identifier System." Oxford, UK: International DOI Federation. Available: www.doi.org. Accessed January 27, 2005.

Metadata

Caplan, Priscilla. 2003. "Metadata Fundamentals for All Librarians." Chicago: American Library Association.

Dublin Core Metadata Initiative. 2004. "Dublin Core Metadata Initiative: Making It Easier to Find Information." Dublin, OH: Dublin Core Metadata Initiative. Available: www.dublincore.org. Accessed January 27, 2005.

Eden, Brad. 2004. "Metadata and Its Applications." *Library Technology Reports* 38, no. 5 (September/October): 1–87.

Library of Congress. 2004. "MADS: Metadata Authority Description Schema." Washington, DC: Library of Congress. Available: www.loc.gov/standards/mads/. Accessed January 27, 2005.

———. 2004. "METS: Metadata Encoding and Transmission Standard." Washington, DC: Library of Congress. Available: www.loc.gov/standards/mets/. Accessed January 27, 2005.

———. 2004. "MIX: NISO Metadata for Images in XML Schema." Washington, DC: Library of Congress. Available: www.loc.gov/standards/mix/. Accessed January 27, 2005.

———. 2004. "MODS: Metadata Object Description Schema." Washington, DC: Library of Congress. Available: www.loc.gov/standards/mods/. Accessed January 27, 2005.

National Information Standards Organization. 2004. "Understanding Metadata." Bethesda, MD: National Information Standards Organization. Available: www.niso.org/standards/resources/UnderstandingMetadata.pdf. Accessed January 27, 2005.

National Information Standards Organization and AIIM International. 2003. "Data Dictionary: Technical Metadata for Digital Still Images." Bethesda, MD: National Information Standards Organization. Available: www.niso.org/standards/resources/Z39_87_trial_use.pdf. Accessed January 27, 2005.

W3C. 2004. "Extensible Markup Language (XML)." Cambridge, MA: Massachusetts Institute of Technology. Available: http://www.w3.org/XML/. Accessed January 27, 2005.

Western States Digital Standards Group, Metadata Working Group. 2003, Jan. "Western States Dublin Core Metadata Best Practices, Version 2.0."

Denver, CO.: Colorado Digitization Program. Available: www.cdpheritage.org/resource/metadata/wsdcmbp/index.html. Accessed January 27, 2005.

Digital Library Software and Services

DiMeMa. 2004. "CONTENTdm: Digital Collection Management Software by DiMeMa, Inc." Seattle, WA: DiMeMa. Available: www.contentdm.com. Accessed January 27, 2005.

Endeavor Information Systems. 2004. "ENCompass Solutions." Des Plaines, IL: Endeavor Information Systems. Available: http://encompass.endinfosys.com/. Accessed January 27, 2005.

ExLibris Group. 2004. "DigiTool: Digital Asset Management." Chicago: ExLibris Group. Available: www.exlibrisgroup.com/digitool.htm. Accessed January 27, 2005.

OCLC. 2004. "Digitization Services." Dublin, OH. Available: www.oclc.org/preservation/digitizing/default.htm. Accessed January 27, 2005.

VTLS. 2004. "VITAL." Blacksburg, VA: VTLS. Available: www.vtls.com/Products/vital.shtml. Accessed January 27, 2005.

Institutional Repository Software

DSpace Federation. 2004. "DSpace." Boston: DSpace Federation. Available: www.dspace.org. Accessed January 27, 2005.

University of Virginia and Cornell University. 2004. "The Fedora Project." Charlottesville, VA: University of Virginia. Available: www.fedora.info. Accessed January 27, 2005.

University of Southampton. 2004. "EPrints.org." Southampton, UK: University of Southampton. Available: www.eprints.org. Accessed January 27, 2005.

2

ESTABLISHING THE CATALOGING WORK FLOW

INTRODUCTION

Most cataloging instruction assumes that the cataloger possesses both the time to examine individual resources and the tools necessary to build complex bibliographic records. In practice, few libraries have the luxury of providing this level of bibliographic treatment for all online resources. The demand for online resources of all kinds is taxing libraries' ability to provide bibliographic control, and many libraries acquire a significant proportion of their online content in the form of collections developed by the content provider rather than individually selected titles. These collections vary in size and composition; common examples include e-book packages, aggregations of journals, and other databases containing full text or media. Libraries often want catalog access not only at the collection level but also for the constituent titles, of which there may be hundreds or even thousands. The cataloger must employ judicious timesaving measures to provide timely access to such a large volume of titles.

In broad terms, access to online resources through the catalog requires effort in two basic areas that are the same for library resources in any format:

- New cataloging

- Catalog maintenance

What makes online resources unusual are their rapidly growing numbers, their tendency to become available in large clusters as databases and collections are activated rather than as a continuous stream of incoming material, and the fact that they require frequent and sustained bibliographic maintenance. Within the broad categories of new cataloging and catalog maintenance, libraries have considerable latitude to apply different levels of bibliographic treatment. This chapter will address approaches to record creation that balance efficiency and access, and record-management strategies to simplify ongoing bibliographic maintenance for dynamic resources.

NEW CATALOGING

Two basic approaches exist for adding records for online resources to the library catalog. The resources can be cataloged one by one, or records for a set of resources can be loaded with a batch process. The approach that should be used depends on the nature of the resources to be cataloged and the level of staffing the library can commit to managing online resources. To date, online resources have tended to outpace libraries' management capabilities at every stage of the management process. As a result, most libraries are not in a position to produce full bibliographic records in-house for all of their online resources.

Many libraries have compromised by using a combination of methods to catalog different kinds of resources. For example, a library might designate as a high priority any online resources that are produced or hosted locally or individual titles to which the library subscribes directly, and create full-level catalog records for these resources. Meanwhile, the same library might prefer to use batch records for resources over which it has less direct control, such as the journals in an aggregator database. Although these choices significantly affect the cataloging work flow, it is not strictly a cataloging responsibility to identify priorities for bibliographic treatment but rather the shared responsibility of all the library's stakeholders, including those responsible for acquisitions, cataloging, reference, and user instruction.

> **Cataloging priorities**: Many libraries assign their highest cataloging priority to resources that the library pays for, resources that the library or its parent organization produce, and resources of immediate interest to its local user community.

INDIVIDUAL RECORDS

Individual bibliographic records are the most labor-intensive approach to providing access to online resources, but they give the library the most reliable control over the quality and composition of the records. The primary dilemma the cataloger faces in this category of record production, which includes both original and copy cataloging, is finding a balance between rigor and efficiency.

Original Cataloging

Although new online resources continue to emerge at a rapid rate, the need for original cataloging for certain kinds of resources is actually diminishing. Commercial producers of online monographs often make MARC records available for their collections, either through the bibliographic utilities or directly to their customers. Original cataloging for online serials has been greatly impacted by the Cooperative Online Serials Program (CONSER)'s recent aggregator-neutral cataloging

Aggregator-neutral record: A MARC record that is used to represent all online versions of a serial. Aggregator-neutral records do not contain any version-specific information other than the URLs where each version is available. See Chapter 9 for an example of an aggregator-neutral serial record.

policy. Prior to the aggregator-neutral record, versions of an online serial issued by different vendors each required a separate record, whereas today these versions are grouped together on a single online record. New cataloging rules for integrating resources also reduce the need for original cataloging by incorporating multiple iterations of an updating database or Web site into a single ongoing record. As a result of these developments, original cataloging is focusing increasingly on new or highly specialized titles and locally produced resources.

Catalogers often appreciate the intellectual challenge of original cataloging and the satisfaction of creating new records for other libraries to share, but the creation of original bibliographic records is a time-consuming process. If the cataloger is contributing original records to a bibliographic utility or union catalog, it is imperative to follow the standards that are in place for that shared system, even if the cataloger's library does not adhere to those standards internally. The efficacy of a cooperative catalog as a data source and the host organization's ability to perform automated database maintenance both rely on the uniformity of contributed records. Because of the time and care required for original cataloging, it is important for the library to establish its cataloging priorities and the level of service it is willing to provide in this area. The library may have an obligation to provide cataloging leadership, either formally through participation in a national cooperative cataloging program or informally within a consortial environment. Even if the library is not bound by an explicit commitment, it can offer a valuable service to the cataloging community by providing high-quality original cataloging for online information within its area of specialization and for any online resources produced by the library itself.

Original cataloging is an inherently complex process, but catalogers can streamline this process somewhat by batching resources with the same type of issuance or that come from the same source wherever possible. This practice improves the likelihood that the cataloger will be able to use a partially populated template to create a series of related records, saving time and minimizing the incidence of errors. Another measure that can greatly economize the cataloger's time over the long term but requires more up-front planning and buy-in from other stakeholders is the distribution of responsibility for metadata creation, particularly in areas that require significant expertise and interpretation of content, such as subject cataloging. For example, subject selectors could provide descriptions and point out significant subject aspects of the online resources they select, much as they would for a pathfinder or resource guide. Likewise, if a significant proportion of the library's original cataloging workload involves locally produced resources, such as theses and dissertations, it may be well worth the library's effort to work with the institution's thesis office to request that authors provide their own description and keywords.

Copy Cataloging

The most widely disseminated documentation of cataloging practice emanates from bibliographic utilities or from the Library of Congress and its affiliated cataloging programs (see Chapter 5). While these entities have an important role to play in guiding cataloging policy and practice, they also have particular needs, goals, and clientele that may be very different from those of the average public, school, special, or academic library. Although we strongly advocate adhering as closely as possible to national standards in order to promote the highest level of uniformity within and across library catalogs, the standards and practices that benefit a national library or a bibliographic utility may not necessarily be optimal for other kinds of libraries.

An example of this in action is the aggregator-neutral serial record. For the bibliographic utilities, aggregator-neutral records are a good solution to an earlier problem of multiple records existing for different online versions of the same title, often with very different levels of descriptive depth and subject access. The aggregator-neutral record ensures that no matter which electronic version of a journal a particular library subscribes to, identical cataloging copy will be available. However, while aggregator-neutral records serve as excellent master records, many libraries may find them difficult to use in their native form. For example, aggregator-neutral records do not include access points for vendor names or collection titles, nor do they provide any version-specific information about system requirements. Libraries that consider this information significant must add it as they copy catalog and ensure that local policies exist to document this practice. In addition, in a shared catalog in which the participants use different URLs for the same resource, aggregator-neutral records are problematic because the proliferation of links for multiple versions and sites on the same record can become a serious obstacle to usability.

This example highlights the fact that even though the library catalog is a well-established and highly standardized bibliographic tool, individual libraries manage and use their catalog records very differently. Cataloging standards have an impact on both workflow and database integrity, and diverging from widely followed standards should be a careful, necessity-driven, and well-documented process. Before departing from a standard or a recommended practice, the library needs to ensure that the desired outcome is indeed worth the effort of developing, documenting, and ensuring adherence to a local variation, and that the same result truly cannot be achieved within the boundaries of the existing standard. Both the local practice and its rationale should be clearly documented and frequently reviewed. Official standards and practices evolve over time, particularly in developing areas such as online resources. As the online landscape changes, the library should assess whether its local variations continue to serve their intended functions.

Local cataloging practices for online resources tend to focus on two areas: record content and cataloging work practices. Descriptive information can typically be generated with fairly minimal effort, but with the online resource residing just one click away from the catalog record, a record rich in access points provides much better access for the user than a record that emphasizes description. Therefore, the library may find it useful to articulate policies for adding uniform access points for vendors and collection titles, alternate titles, and form/genre headings to online-resource records that are far more comprehensive than the basic requirements for full-level records. In addition, the library should document its local practices for describing technical requirements and applying local subject descriptors and classification. It is also helpful to document any procedural instructions that differ from what is prescribed in external cataloging guidelines. For example, the prescribed sources of descriptive information for online resources are so broad that the cataloger can end up searching far and wide to gather information about a resource. As a practical matter, the library might decide that for copy-cataloging purposes the cataloger look no further than one click away from the title screen to find or verify descriptive information rather than searching deep within the resource or opening related documentation about the resource. This enables the cataloger to handle a greater volume of resources or spend more time concentrating on access points.

RECORD SETS

MARC record sets are a convenient alternative to cataloging online resources on an individual basis. Batch cataloging enables the library to get a large number of records into the catalog in relatively short order, but it also requires a conceptual shift from individual resources to groups of resources, and a shift in skills from examining and describing individual resources to working with an outside vendor, setting priorities for record quality, and assessing whether the overall quality of a record set is within parameters the library considers acceptable.

The increasing use of record sets can place unforeseen stresses on the local system that require the development of new policies to govern batch processes. More so than individual cataloging transactions, batch processes tend to affect system performance. The library may find it

Batch records: Loading large numbers of records into the catalog at one time can impair system performance. Libraries should avoid loading batch records during peak hours, and libraries that participate in shared catalogs should coordinate batch loads with their partner sites to minimize the impact on other staff and public users of the catalog.

needs to time batch record loads carefully to minimize the impact on other staff and public-catalog users. In addition, it can take time to become familiar with the technical aspects of loading record sets from unfamiliar sources and to learn to spot problem areas in the formatting of a record set that could potentially interfere with the load. The library may find that once it begins to accept record sets for online resources and grows accustomed to manipulating records in batch, this methodology can spill over to other kinds of resources, creating a significant shift in the way the cataloging unit is accustomed to working.

Full MARC

A variety of options exist for obtaining full MARC records for online resources. These include fee-based services, such as MARCIVE, WorldCat Collection Sets, and the MARC record services provided by serials-management systems. In addition, an increasing number of content providers are making MARC record sets available for their library customers for free or for a nominal fee. If no record set is available from a vendor or if the cost of doing business with a for-fee service is prohibitive, the library should consider organizing a cooperative or reciprocal cataloging effort with other libraries in the local area or consortial partners who have resources in common. This approach benefits the participating libraries while minimizing the cataloging burden on any particular one. The drawback is that coordinated efforts require advance planning, and all participants in the cooperative endeavor must agree on the division of labor, time commitment, standards, and expected timeline that the project will follow.

From a bibliographic perspective, the important issues to consider about record sets primarily revolve around quality control and opportunities for customization. In general, record sets that are contracted by the library for a fee or produced in cooperation with a group of libraries will provide the highest standards of quality, and also afford individual libraries the greatest opportunity to customize the records. Freely available record sets, on the other hand, are typically made available on an as-is basis. This doesn't necessarily imply that the records are inferior, only that the library may need to invest considerable time to customize the set for its own needs and should consider carefully how much effort it is willing to apply to free records. Whether free or for-fee, it is unusual for records supplied by an outside party to conform precisely to the standards the library would use for its own cataloging. It is important for the library to identify those elements that are critical to maintaining the integrity and effectiveness of its catalog. Important elements to look for include adherence to current standards for record format and description, use of authority-controlled access points; richness

Quality control: The library should carefully evaluate potential record sets before introducing them into the library catalog, just as it would evaluate new information resources. The library should identify priority areas for search and retrieval (such as subject headings, standard numbers, and authority-controlled access points) and database integrity (such as adherence to national cataloging standards and common thesauri) in order to assess potential record sets and communicate clear expectations to cataloging vendors.

of subject access; classification; uniformity of records within the set, suggesting that the provider has applied internal quality control; and the presence of a unique identifier for each record to facilitate record overlay in the event of updates.

Brief MARC

If no record set exists for a collection of resources but the library is concerned with providing title access at least at a general level, it is possible to generate brief records for the collection if the content provider makes a title list available. Brief MARC records tend to lack any form of subject access and generally consist of an uncontrolled title, a standard number, publication or coverage dates, URL, and in some cases a publisher name. Although such records are no substitute for full bibliographic treatment, libraries using this technique have anecdotally reported that usage of their online resources increased after brief catalog records were loaded despite the lack of subject access, suggesting that a minimal record is still preferable to no record at all.

Brief MARC records require only a bit of expertise with productivity applications and a MARC conversion program. Content providers typically make their title lists available in delimited text or spreadsheet form. These lists can be speedily converted to MARC records by using a mail merge, the word-processing function used to create form letters. The cataloger simply creates a mail-merge template formatted according to the requirements of the MARC software and identifies the vendor's list as the data source. In this example, the vendor supplies the ISSN, journal title, publisher, URL, and coverage dates:

```
=006  m\\\\\\\d\\\\\\\
=007  cr\unu
=022  \\$a«issn»
=245  00$a«journaltitle»$h[electronic resource].
=260  \\$a[S.l.] :$b«publisher»
=440  \\$aHealth & Wellness Resource Center
      electronic journals
=506  \\$aAvailable to subscribers only.
=655  \7$aElectronic journals.$2local
=710  2\$aGale Group.
=856  40$u«url»$3Full text available: «coverage»
```

In a matter of moments the template and vendor data are merged into a MARC-ready text file that the MARC utility can process into records and load into its catalog. This process requires a minimal investment of effort and the resulting records are essentially disposable, making this an ideal bibliographic approach for noncore resources or collections that are expected to be available only for a limited time.

MARC utilities: Programs that convert data in delimited text files, XML, and other data formats into MARC. This example is formatted for the MarcEdit utility; see the Library of Congress' list of MARC tools (www.loc.gov/marc/marc-tools.html) for more information.

RECORD MAINTENANCE

Record maintenance is an unavoidable aspect of providing access to online resources. A large proportion of online-resource maintenance results from changes to URLs and holdings statements, but resources also undergo changes to descriptive elements, intellectual content, and technical specifications. With the exception of link checking, it is difficult to automate the review process, but careful planning can greatly improve the long-term efficiency of record maintenance.

REVIEWING RECORDS

URL checking is the most basic step a library can take to maintain its bibliographic records for online resources. Link checking doesn't reveal much beyond whether the links in the catalog are live, redirected, or returning error messages. However, this information can help the library to investigate obsolete links and update or remove the records before a frustrated patron discovers them. Regular link checking can also provide documentation about resources that have a correct URL in the catalog but suffer from recurring down time. More subtle alterations, such as title, coverage, technical, and editorial changes, will not be evident from a URL report but require physical review by a human. Most of these changes can be readily remedied by the cataloger if found, but substantive technical and editorial changes that affect the quality or usability of a resource should be referred to the selector for the relevant subject area if possible. This distributes the burden of intellectual review outside the cataloging department, and also enables those with the appropriate subject expertise to assess the resource and make an alternative selection if necessary.

URL checking: If different areas of the record, such as the URL, coverage dates, descriptive information, and subject coverage, are being reviewed by different people, the division of labor should be clearly articulated to all participants, and specific procedures should exist for communicating the desired changes back to the cataloger.

Regardless of who is responsible for reviewing catalog records, it is important to establish a timetable and a process for systematic review. One advantage of cataloging online resources is that the records have a date stamp and can be easily identified for scheduled review. The library should identify a schedule for periodic review that will be frequent enough to catch problems before they reach a critical mass, but not so frequent that reviewing online resources completely monopolizes staff time. For example, an automated URL check can be run on a weekly basis, whereas editorial content might undergo human review anywhere from quarterly to once a year, depending on the number and type of resources involved.

UPDATING RECORDS

Online resources can change in unpredictable ways, but the library can position itself to respond efficiently by staying alert to those changes that are announced and by building catalog records in a way that facilitates easy update and removal. Content providers often distribute information about upcoming changes as a service to their customers. Such announcements may be issued by a variety of means, including personal contacts, distribution lists, newsletters, and Web sites. Regardless of the medium, this type of communication enables the library to receive advance notice of changes and implement catalog maintenance in an orderly manner that minimizes the impact on library users. It is critical that those responsible for the maintenance of online resource records receive information about upcoming changes in a timely manner, either directly or through a designated contact person within the library. In many cases, the appropriate contact person will be someone involved with licensing or resource acquisition because those roles tend to involve a high level of interaction with vendors. Thus, it is critical that the lines of communication between that individual and the cataloging unit are open and flexible.

The library should strive for batch updates wherever feasible, because automated updates are considerably more efficient than updating records one by one. Batch updates are greatly simplified when records contain access points or locally defined coding that enable the library to isolate groups of resources by a variety of criteria, such as type of issuance, vendor, collection title and, for records originally loaded as a set, the date and source of the record set. Uniformity among individual records and within record sets also improves the success of batch changes. Rigorous adherence to standards is an important element of this process; from a record management perspective, it matters less whether those standards are local or external than the degree to which they are understood and followed.

SUMMARY

Online resources are numerous and potentially volatile, and getting them under control can be a daunting task. Libraries that prefer catalog access for online resources should take care not to let the perfect become the enemy of the good, spending so much time building excellent bibliographic records that scores of resources go uncataloged. Cataloging options exist at every level, from good-enough brief records for ephemeral content to precise and carefully researched records for original and high-priority cataloging. Online resources are pushing libraries to think about cataloging and catalog maintenance in a systemic way, identifying priorities and seeking efficiencies throughout the cataloging work flow.

REFERENCE

Library of Congress Network Development and MARC Standards Office. 2004. "MARC Specialized Tools." Washington, DC: Library of Congress. Available: www.loc.gov/marc/marctools.html.

3 EXPLORING ALTERNATIVES TO CATALOGING

INTRODUCTION

Libraries that prefer to organize and provide access to online resources using tools other than the library catalog have a variety of options. In this chapter, we will discuss the alternatives that are most widely used at this time, including Web-based resource lists, context-sensitive linking, and federated searching. Whereas online catalogs evolved from an established tradition of bibliographic theory and practice, these new tools have emerged in response to specific problems of organization and access in the online environment. At present, alternative bibliographic tools are considerably less standardized and less transparent than library catalogs based on *Anglo-American Cataloging Rules, 2nd Edition* (Joint Steering Committee, 2002) and MARC. Integrated library systems typically do not reveal their underlying programming to competitors, but libraries are able to use that software to build their own local databases of catalog records using highly standardized and widely disseminated schemas, such as the MARC format. By contrast, many vendors of alternative bibliographic tools populate and manage the tools themselves, closely guarding the inner workings of their proprietary systems. Implementation of alternative bibliographic tools will, therefore, vary widely from library to library, depending on what system is used and how extensively it is customized. For this reason, we do not focus on the specific techniques of implementing these tools, but instead address their general functionality in relation to planning and policy decisions.

WEB LISTS

Many libraries maintain their own Web pages, which provide links to Web sites, e-books, databases, and other online resources. Some libraries refer to these pages with straightforward titles like "Databases," "Internet Links," and "Online Journals," whereas others use more abstract terminology, such as "Article Searching," "Reference

Tools," and "Research Guides." Some of these pages offer a simple title arrangement, others are subject oriented and heavily annotated, and still others present complex and highly structured metadata. The common denominator among these tools, simple or complex, is that they provide a locus of bibliographic description separate from the library catalog. In the absence of a common nomenclature, we refer to all such tools as Web lists, regardless of how they structure bibliographic data or what type of resources they include.

BACKGROUND

> **Web lists**: Web pages that provide links to online resources. Web lists may be simple or complex; common formats include alphabetical title lists and subject-related groupings. The Auburn University Libraries (www.lib.auburn.edu/ejournals/ Atitles.html) provide a straightforward alphabetical list of e-journals. The Pike's Peak Library District arranges selected Web sites into subject categories (http://library.ppld.org/ WebPicks/Admin/WebPicksByCateg ory.asp?keyword=Consumer). The MIT Libraries' VERA database uses a complex interface and displays rich metadata for its electronic resources. (http://libraries.mit.edu/ vera)

> **Using Web lists**: Web lists provide users with the most direct path to online access because they are simple and highly visible. Resources that the library promotes as starting points for the user (such as online databases) and cohesive high-use collections (such as e-journals) are good candidates for Web lists.

Web lists for online resources have two primary advantages over catalog access: visibility and flexibility. Web lists isolate collections of resources and enable the library to position these collections within easy reach of users browsing the library's Web site. The library can highlight a particular collection by giving it a more prominent position on the site, providing visibility for high-demand resources. Locally developed Web lists also give the library full control over every aspect of the bibliographic tool, from the underlying structure to the record format to the design of the user interface. This affords libraries the freedom to organize resources according to their own preferred criteria, relax bibliographic standards without compromising an existing database, and customize the appearance of the display.

Web lists were an early alternative to catalog access for resources that were perceived as too transient to manage through the catalog. In addition, Web lists addressed the perception that users would find searching the traditional catalog for online resources to be counterintuitive. Indeed, many libraries that do catalog their online resources have hedged their bets and provided access through Web lists as well (Boydston and Leysen, 2002). Web lists are not necessarily the ideal form of access for all online resources, but there are certainly cases in which using the catalog as the primary access point simply doesn't make sense. Online databases provide one such example. Relative to other kinds of online resources, online databases normally comprise a fairly compact collection and, although their contents may be wildly diverse, serve a common purpose as starting points for information seekers. That is, online databases are bibliographic tools in their own right, and the links to them should be as visible as possible rather than buried within another database.

Many early Web lists were produced in static HTML, which is relatively easy to manipulate with minimal technical expertise. However, hard-coded pages are difficult to scale as collections grow because their arrangement is static and, therefore, not conducive to frequent or large-scale changes. Many libraries now use software such as Access,

FileMaker Pro, and SQL to build Web-accessible databases of online resources. Although building a database requires somewhat more technical expertise than creating a static Web page, the database model nonetheless represents a major step forward for bibliographic control by enabling the library to manipulate the metadata elements in the records independently of the user interface. This structure makes it possible to break down bibliographic description into more detailed and specific data elements, which greatly simplifies input, maintenance, and standardization and allows the library to reconfigure the presentation of resource descriptions without affecting the underlying data.

LIMITATIONS

The challenge of using Web lists to manage bibliographic data lies in finding the appropriate balance between efficiency and complexity. Although they are quickest to produce and easiest to maintain, the simplest Web lists are a data-poor form of bibliographic control. A basic title list is effective only if the user is seeking a known title, and extensive lists may require detailed descriptions in order to disambiguate similar resources. It is possible to offset these problems by enriching descriptions and providing access points based on subject matter or other criteria to organize the collection into coherent subsets. However, as the collection grows, the description must become more complex and the subsets more specific in order to maintain the usability of the list, at which point the library is maintaining a secondary data structure that is potentially a close imitation of the library catalog.

As Web lists become more sophisticated, they also become more complicated to manage. Web tools with advanced features, such as search functions or Web interfaces for public and administrative use, require progressively higher skill levels in Web programming and designing for usability. In addition, the use of relational databases capable of reflecting complex relationships among data elements requires expertise in programming and database design. Furthermore, policy and work flow issues are subject to the same trial-and-error process as the technical details. Libraries have long since established what standards will be followed and who is responsible for new input, database maintenance, technical upkeep, and development decisions with respect to their online catalogs, but they are starting from scratch with their Web lists. It is important that the library's ability to manage resources using a Web list does not become overwhelmed by the challenge of managing the tool itself, particularly if the reason for using a Web list in the first place is efficient management of ephemeral resources with low direct cost, such as aggregator journals and freely available Web sites.

IMPLEMENTING WEB LISTS

As a first step toward building a Web list, the library should consider how the tool will manage bibliographic data. With the use of Web lists, the library has considerable freedom to create a bibliographic apparatus uniquely suited to its collection and its users, but that apparatus must essentially be invented out of thin air. Metadata formats less rigid than MARC, such as Dublin Core (see Chapter 1) can be used to structure bibliographic data. If no established schema exists that meets the library's needs, the library can start with a schema that comes close and then tailor it for local needs, or invent a format wholesale. The library isn't bound by *AACR2* or MARC standards for its Web lists, but it is useful to follow some standard if the library anticipates any need to migrate data into or out of the tool to share with other libraries or applications. The library should also consider whether it will use existing rules and vocabularies to describe the resources or create its own guidelines. This is particularly important if the responsibility for data input is distributed among multiple individuals or departments. Again, it is useful to keep in mind whether the library will be creating its data locally or importing it from some other source that may have its own content standards in place.

The library should also consider how the list is populated and maintained. Database software greatly facilitates batch-data loads, and most software is capable of exporting data sets to other file formats, such as spreadsheets or delimited text files, so that the data in the Web list can be used in other applications. For input at the individual element or record level, Web-based input interfaces allow people who lack the technical expertise or authorization to interact directly with the software to contribute to the database. This enables the library to distribute responsibility for record content to the appropriate personnel regardless of their technical ability. However, developing an effective and user-friendly input interface requires some Web programming expertise and close cooperation between those responsible for designing the input tool and those who use it to contribute data.

Not all Web lists are designed or maintained by the library. In recent years, many libraries have turned to outside vendors such as TDNet and SerialsSolutions to manage their largest and most volatile collections, the journals in their aggregator databases. These journal-management services, termed "publication access–management systems" (PAMS) in a recent NISO white paper (Jones, 2002, p. 4), enable libraries to provide access to full-text titles in aggregator databases that are too numerous and too volatile for libraries to catalog individually. Some libraries simply use the service's data set to populate their own Web tools, while others have turned their journal-management services into full-fledged

Publication–access management systems (PAMS): Also known as journal-management services, PAMS exist primarily to help libraries provide title-level access to the serials in their aggregator databases, which are too nebulous for individual libraries to track on their own. PAMS can also maintain links to freely available online serials and to titles and collections to which the library subscribes directly.

serials-access tools that incorporate not only aggregator journals but also direct subscriptions, open-access titles, and even print serials.

The major limitations of publication access–management systems stem from loss of control at both the data level and the interface level. Title lists compiled by database vendors are notorious in cataloging circles for their casual treatment of important features such as title changes and ISSNs. Publication access–management services aggregate title lists from multiple vendors into a single data set, resolving conflicts from one vendor to another as best they can. The resulting service provides access to titles that would otherwise have been buried in separate databases, but the bibliographic data are not always congruent with most libraries' local practices. In addition, libraries relying on publication access–management systems to maintain a public Web interface to the data may have concerns about retaining a sufficient level of control over the appearance or functionality of the site, an important consideration if local branding is a high priority.

With the development of context-sensitive linking services, the need for title-level access tools for the journals in aggregator databases is likely to diminish. However, the core function of these services, tracking serial holdings, makes them useful in the management of context-sensitive linking tools because their data can be used to populate link resolvers. In addition, the most advanced of these services provide value-added features, such as tables of contents and alerting features, that other systems do not currently provide.

CONTEXT-SENSITIVE LINKING

Context-sensitive linking: The ability to link from a bibliographic citation to the specific library's available options for full-text delivery and related services. Context-sensitive linking, also known as reference linking and OpenURL linking, is based on the OpenURL Framework detailed at http://library.caltech .edu/openurl/Standard.htm. OpenURL makes this type of linking possible by converting metadata from a source citation into a context-specific URL and resolving that URL against a library-specific database of target resources known as a knowledge base.

Users want to be able to connect from citations in online databases directly to full-text documents without having to search in multiple databases and collections to find a copy that is available to them. In the past, searching in online databases could bring users to a frustrating dead end. If a user found a citation that did not link directly to a full-text document, it was necessary to note the publication title and look again in the library's catalog or Web lists to determine whether the resource was available from the library. If no copy was immediately available, the user had to know about the existence of interlibrary loan in order to have any access at all to the desired document. Context-sensitive linking solves this problem by seamlessly integrating citations from online databases, catalogs, and bibliographies with full-text content and related services across disparate interfaces and content providers. Context-sensitive linking is also library-specific, so users are offered only the links and services they are authorized to access.

BACKGROUND

Most libraries are already familiar with context-sensitive linking on a small scale because many online databases have made it possible for libraries to set up links from citations back to the library catalog or to other databases from the same provider. One example is EBSCOhost's "SmartLinks" feature, which can link records in a citation-only database, such as *PsycInfo,* to articles in full-text EBSCOhost databases to which the library also subscribes. Alternatively, some providers will automatically link to full-text content from a limited number of selected partners. ABC-CLIO provides this type of linking directly to articles available from JSTOR, Project Muse, History Cooperative, and a short list of other services and publishers. The drawback to this approach is that users' retrieval options are contingent on their starting point: the same citation in two different databases might yield very different retrieval options, depending on what each database is able to link to. By maintaining its own link resolver, the library can reduce these disparities and move closer to a universal linking environment.

Context-sensitive linking consists of three parts: sources, targets, and the link resolver that connects them. (See Figure 3-1). A source is a database where the user's search originates, such as an online database or the library catalog. When a source database is OpenURL enabled, it means that the vendor allows the library to add a link or button for its OpenURL tool to the user interface. When the user clicks that link or button from a search result, the source database pushes metadata from the citation to the link resolver. The resolver compares these metadata with its internal knowledge base of titles and holdings to determine whether the library has access to the document in any of its targets, the full-text resources that the user wants to retrieve. The link resolver then links to the full document, or other related services, based on a database of linking syntaxes for the various targets.

Using an example from Chapter 8, suppose that a user has found a citation to an article in the *American Journal of Bioethics* in an online database. The article begins on page 13 of volume 3, number 2. The OpenURL link might build the metadata from that citation into a query that looks something like this:

```
http://linkresolver.library.org/main?issn=1526-
5161&date=2003&volume=3&issue=2&page=13
```

The link resolver compares these metadata with its own internal knowledge base, generally using the ISSN as the primary match point because it is the most uniform metadata element for a journal. If the library has access to the appropriate holdings of *American Journal of Bioethics* to fulfill this particular query, the server then builds a link to the appropriate targets based on the established syntax for those targets.

> **Using context-sensitive linking**: Context-sensitive linking relies on the exchange of metadata among the source database, the target database, and the link resolver. As a result, context-sensitive linking is most applicable to resources that are associated with standardized identifying metadata, such as an ISSN, ISBN or DOI, and that are cited in source databases that can be OpenURL enabled, such as online indexes and institutional repositories.

The user is then presented with a list of retrieval options that may include links to the full-text article and/or other related services such as those appearing in Figure 3-2. These additional options often include links to the library catalog, links to interlibrary-loan forms pre-populated with citation information, or links that launch related searches in Web search engines and open-access databases.

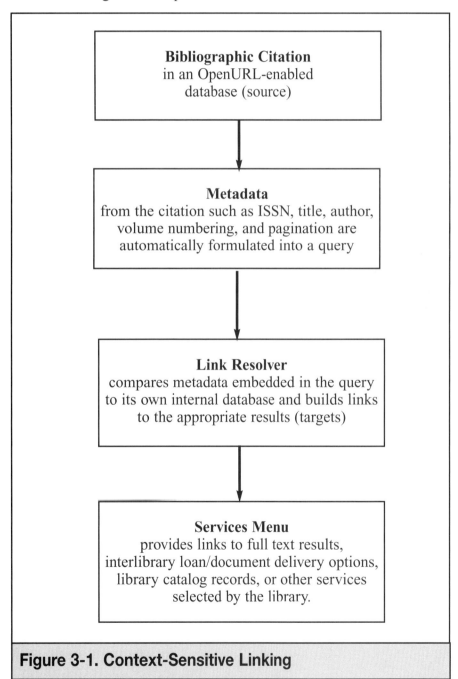

Figure 3-1. Context-Sensitive Linking

LIMITATIONS

There are two major limitations to context-sensitive linking tools at this time. The first is a lack of standardization among sources and targets in terms of their technical ability to interact with context-sensitive linking software. Sources must be OpenURL enabled in order to work with a link resolver. Although many major database vendors are OpenURL compliant, this functionality is far from universal. Among sources that are enabled, individual vendors do not always make it possible for the library to fully customize the link from the source to the local resolver. This creates a serious user-education issue for libraries because users must learn to recognize different links to the same service depending on which database they use. This lack of standardization also applies to target content. In order for context-sensitive linking to function optimally, the resolver should be able to link to the target at the document level. However, this is not always possible because of the way the target database is structured or the level of linking that the content provider will allow. As a result, some targets can only be resolved at the title or search level, meaning that the user potentially has to redo the search in the target database.

Context-sensitive linking can also break down at the data level. The smooth operation of an OpenURL tool depends on the accuracy of the source citation and the kinds of data the source pushes to the resolver. For example, if the source database has an incorrect ISSN associated with a citation, the link resolver may not find any matches in its knowledge base even if the relevant content really is available. This problem can be alleviated if the source is able to push additional metadata, such as a journal title in addition to an ISSN, providing another avenue for link resolution. The utility of a context-sensitive linking tool also depends on the integrity of the resolver's knowledge base. The problems associated with managing OpenURL knowledge bases are no different from those of managing journal holdings in a library catalog or Web list. Journal holdings are volatile and titles and standard numbers are often haphazard, and it is difficult to maintain information about missing content and embargoes that will affect the user's access.

IMPLEMENTING CONTEXT-SENSITIVE LINKING

As with any other bibliographic tool, the library should consider both how the OpenURL tool works and how the library plans to manage it. OpenURL products employ different technologies and, therefore, interact differently with sources and targets. The library should look for a tool that works best with its own sources and targets, and also

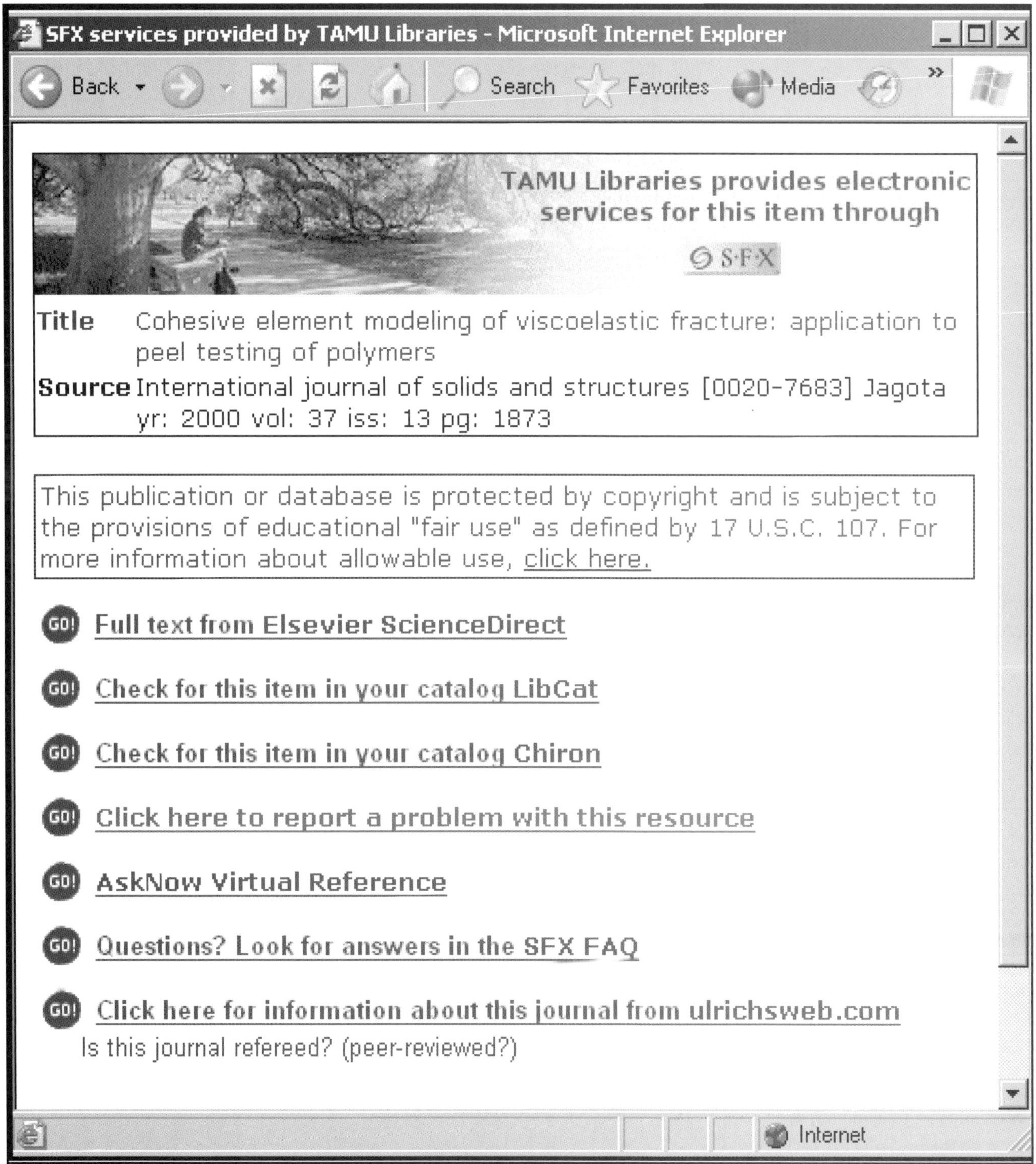

Figure 3-2. OpenURL-Services Menu

enables the library to have control over its public-menu options, including preferences for the order and wording of displays and the addition of extended services, such as linking to the library catalog, linking to interlibrary loan services, or searching additional databases.

While open-source tools exist for context-sensitive linking, most libraries are likely to purchase a system from a vendor. Most of the major players in the information-services industry, such as integrated library–system vendors, serial-management vendors, and major content providers are represented in the OpenURL market (see Table 3-1). The library should assess the advantages and limitations of a context-sensitive linking tool that is integrated with other services versus a stand-alone tool. An integrated system is likely to interact more smoothly with other components in the product suite than a separate stand-alone service, and the library already has a business relationship with that vendor. Although an integrated product may be easier to manage, it may not be the optimal service for meeting users' needs; this is a tradeoff that every library must consider for itself.

Context-sensitive linking tools vary considerably in terms of the amount of control the library has over the system and the interface. A locally managed system gives the library maximum control over the knowledge base, linking syntaxes, and public-display options, but also requires that the library have the resources and technical expertise to manage the service. Many libraries rely on the OpenURL vendor to populate and update the knowledge base, create the linking syntax, and provide technical support for the system. Most vendor-managed systems do provide some degree of customization, but the nature and extent of that customization depends on the specific product, and the library may have to work through the vendor in order to make changes to the service.

Context-sensitive linking tools provide an invaluable service to users by streamlining their information retrieval process. These tools are relatively new, and their environment is still chaotic. As more libraries and vendors discover what makes a good OpenURL service and as bibliographic services and content providers become more compliant with developing standards, these services can truly develop to their full potential.

Federated searching: Also known as metasearching, federated searching allows the user to search across multiple online databases simultaneously through a single interface. Most federated search systems can sort results by title, author, date, and other metadata; some are capable of ranking results by relevancy and deduplicating identical results from multiple sources.

FEDERATED SEARCHING

Federated-searching software allows users to search multiple networked information resources from one user interface. For example, a federated-searching service may enable a user to search the local online

Vendor	Product Name	For More Information
EBSCO Publishing	LinkSource	www.linkresolver.com/Libraries.html
Endeavor Information Systems	LinkFinder*Plus*	www.endinfosys.com/prods/linkfinderplus.htm
Ex Libris	SFX®	www.exlibris-usa.com/sfx.htm
Fretwell-Downing Informatics (FDI)	OL^2™	www.fdgroup.com/fdi/pdf/OL2overview.pdf
Innovative Interfaces, Inc.	WebBridge	www.iii.com/mill/digital.shtml#map
Openly Informatics, Inc.	1Cate	www.openly.com/1cate/
Serials Solutions, Inc.	Article Linker™	http://serialssolutions.com/articlelinker.asp
SIRSI Corp.	Sirsi Resolver™	www.sirsi.com/Sirsiproducts/openurl.html
TDNet	TOUR — TDNet OpenURL Resolver	www.tdnet.com/News_In_20.html
UKOLN	OpenResolver	www.ariadne.ac.uk/issue28/resolver/

Table 3-1. Context-Sensitive Linking Services

Using federated searching: Federated searching brings together multiple bibliographic tools into a single search and display interface. This type of one-stop interface is a good starting point for new library users as well as for users who want to cast a wide net with their searches.

catalog, catalogs of other libraries, licensed full-text databases, online journals, and content-rich Web sites from one search screen. The results are typically presented in a uniform format, and may be ranked by relevancy or sorted on various criteria. The main benefit of federated searching is that it provides patrons with access to a broad spectrum of information resources through a single tool.

While the concept behind federated searching is simple, the technology is complex and the implementation and management of federated-search systems require knowledge, skill, and planning. Furthermore, federated search systems have inherent limitations that must be understood in order to optimize the service for a particular library. Training is required for library staff and instruction should be provided to patrons. Because this is a relatively young technology, future advances will no doubt require ongoing maintenance by library policy makers and systems staff. This section will review the background of federated searching, discuss the technology of these systems, discuss their capabilities and limitations, and review trends in the development of federated search systems.

BACKGROUND

Web search engines began gaining prominence in the mid-1990s. Major sites such as Yahoo!, AltaVista, and Google emerged as starting points for finding information on the Web. Eventually, metasearch

Z39.50: Z39.50 is a protocol that facilitates communication between computer systems. It is particularly popular among libraries because it allows a uniform method of accessing diverse information resources, such as online databases produced by different vendors and that run on different systems. As long as a database is Z39.50 compliant, the Z39.50 commands can be used to access it, thus the user does not have to learn any proprietary system commands. Z39.50 is session specific; that is, it is best for conducting one federated-search at a time and retrieving results for a specific query (Finnegan and Ward, 1997).

Open Archive Initiative Protocol for Metadata Harvesting (OAI-PMH): OAI-PMH (Open Archives Initiative, 2004) is a protocol for metadata harvesting detailed at www.openarchives.org/OAI/2.0/openarchivesprotocol.htm. Libraries can use this standard to collect metadata from other systems. OAI-PMH is typically used to build large repositories of metadata from diverse resources. This repository can then be used as a basis for building other services, such as a Web-based catalog.

Application programming interface (API): An API is a set of software functions that an application uses to access the functions of an operating system or other low-level software. In the context of federated searching, the federated search tool might use an API to interact with the search functions of the target databases.

engines that cumulated the results from multiple search engines became popular tools.

Users quickly came to rely on search engines as a way to retrieve information from the Web, but Web search engines have major limitations. First, they only search publicly available Web sites. Web search engines are blind to online content that requires subscription and authentication, such as the full-text databases to which libraries license access (Fryer, 2004). Furthermore, authentication techniques vary from resource to resource, increasing the difficulty of interoperability with search software. For example, some resources authenticate via a manually entered user identification and password while others use IP authentication via proxy. Second, Web search engines use fairly simple search techniques that are not sufficient for library purposes. Most search engines index the full text of Web sites without considering the context of the information and fail to utilize catalog records and metadata that mark up content for resource description and bibliographic control. For example, a general Web search engine cannot distinguish between a work by Bill Cosby and one about him. In fact, this is partly by design. When search engines experimented with indexing metadata, unscrupulous site developers abused this feature by packing their metadata with common search terms in order to increase traffic to their sites. In response, search engines deliberately stopped indexing metadata and developed other methods for indexing and ranking sites. Another technological limitation is that much online content resides in databases that can only be retrieved by an interactive Web site. Because search engines must have actual HTML to index, a great deal of free content is thus overlooked. Some search engines have developed methods to access content in these databases, but the techniques are still somewhat limited.

Clearly, Web searching is a valuable tool, but there is so much online content available that more reliable tools are needed to access the highest-quality information. The challenge for libraries was to create a tool that possesses the good qualities of Web search tools (simple interface, the ability to search many resources, ranking and sorting of results) but provides greater access to the rich content available by subscription and in heterogeneous formats. Recognizing this need, researchers, vendors, and institutions have developed federated search engines. These new systems possess sophisticated features to support library functions. Most important, they have the ability to search across heterogeneous data repositories, including MARC-based library catalogs, abstracting and indexing databases, full-text databases, electronic-journal collections, citation databases, and Web sites. They do this by using a host of search protocols, including Z39.50, OAI-PMH, HTTP, XML, and proprietary APIs. Although a variety of protocols are used for searching, federated-search tools can aggregate the results into a common format for presentation purposes. These tools can also sort results based on criteria such as relevancy, date, or author, and are capable of managing the complex problem of authentication.

LIMITATIONS

Despite the significant benefits of federated searching, there are limitations to the technology (WebFeat, 2003). First among these is the lack of uniform authentication standards. For this reason, some databases are inaccessible to federated-search systems. There are efforts underway to standardize these protocols, and if the popularity of federated- search systems grows, market forces may encourage vendors to standardize methods for authentication.

Although some federated search engines claim to have a feature that eliminates duplicates from search results, perfect deduplication is not possible for a variety of reasons (Tennant, 2003; WebFeat 2003; Fryer 2004). Most federated-search systems download results in sets, and deduplication is only performed within these finite sets rather than across all search results. Deduplicating the full results would take too much time and computing power for the average user. Furthermore, comparing resources for deduplication is hampered by differences in search, retrieval, and metadata standards. Some duplicate resources may indeed be truly identical, but some may represent versions or editions that may share some characteristics, such as the same title and author, but have other important differences. Current systems do not support this level of refinement.

The popularity of the Google search engine demonstrates that users want the most relevant resources to be at the top of the results, but this is difficult to implement in federated-search engines (Tennant, 2003; WebFeat 2003; Fryer 2004). This is hampered by the quality of the source metadata, which often does not include abstracts or full text. The availability of this information is improving for new born-digital resources but will continue to be a problem, particularly for older resources. Relevancy ranking is just one method of sorting resources. Other sort criteria, such as date, title, or author, can be applied to the results, but these and other sorting methods remain problematic because of the lack of standardized metadata in the records retrieved by the federated-search tool. Because federated-search engines retrieve results from a variety of sites and databases, they encounter records expressed in MARC, Dublin Core, and various proprietary schemas. Inconsistencies among record formats limit the ability of a federated - search engine to sort reliably.

A common misconception is that federated-search systems are as good as, or can improve on, native search interfaces. This is simply not true (WebFeat, 2003). In fact, because of the need to standardize the search across heterogeneous resources, federated-search systems essentially use a lowest-common-denominator search. They are not well suited to precise information retrieval and are best used to complement, rather than replace, the search interfaces of native databases (Gerrity, Lyman, and Tallent, 2002; Luther, 2003; Tansey, 2003; Webster 2004). Despite their sophistication, federated-search systems do not meet all users' needs in the same manner (Tennant, 2003). A patron of a public library or an undergraduate student may be satisfied with a few results from a broad search. Users with sophisticated information needs, such as graduate students or faculty engaged in scholarly research, may be best served by using a federated search as an initial starting point to help identify potential resources and search strategies (Fryer 2004) for more focused searching in individual databases. It is important that this information is communicated to library staff and users throughout the system's life cycle.

The most common method for implementing a federated-search system is to purchase it from a vendor (see Table 3-2). Some institutions have created their own systems, such as the California Digital Library's "Searchlight" system (Tennant, 2003), but this is relatively rare. Installation of a federated-search system requires technical skill informed by policy decisions. These systems consist of a software package that is installed on a computer network. Once installed, the system consists of a Web-based public-user interface and a Web-based administration console. Additional system maintenance may require access to the server on which the system resides. After installation, the system must be configured for local use. This includes configuring the search system to communicate with specific databases, customizing the public interface to provide the desired user experience, and adding local library branding to the user interface.

Customizing the public interface is a very important step (Luther, 2003). Federated-search systems are infinitely configurable, and a library that chooses to install a federated-search system must base the design of the service on the library's resources, mission, and users (Tennant, 2003). Because these are powerful, enterprise-level systems that can accommodate a great deal of customization, each library must decide how much of its staff's time can be used to implement the system (Fryer, 2004).

The simplest possible installation is a single keyword-search box that searches all of a library's databases without presenting any search options to the user, similar to the simple search box of the Google search engine. Contrast this with a service designed to meet the needs of a large research library. Such a system provides advanced searching on specific fields (such as author or title), allows the user to select individual databases or subject groupings, and provides multiple options

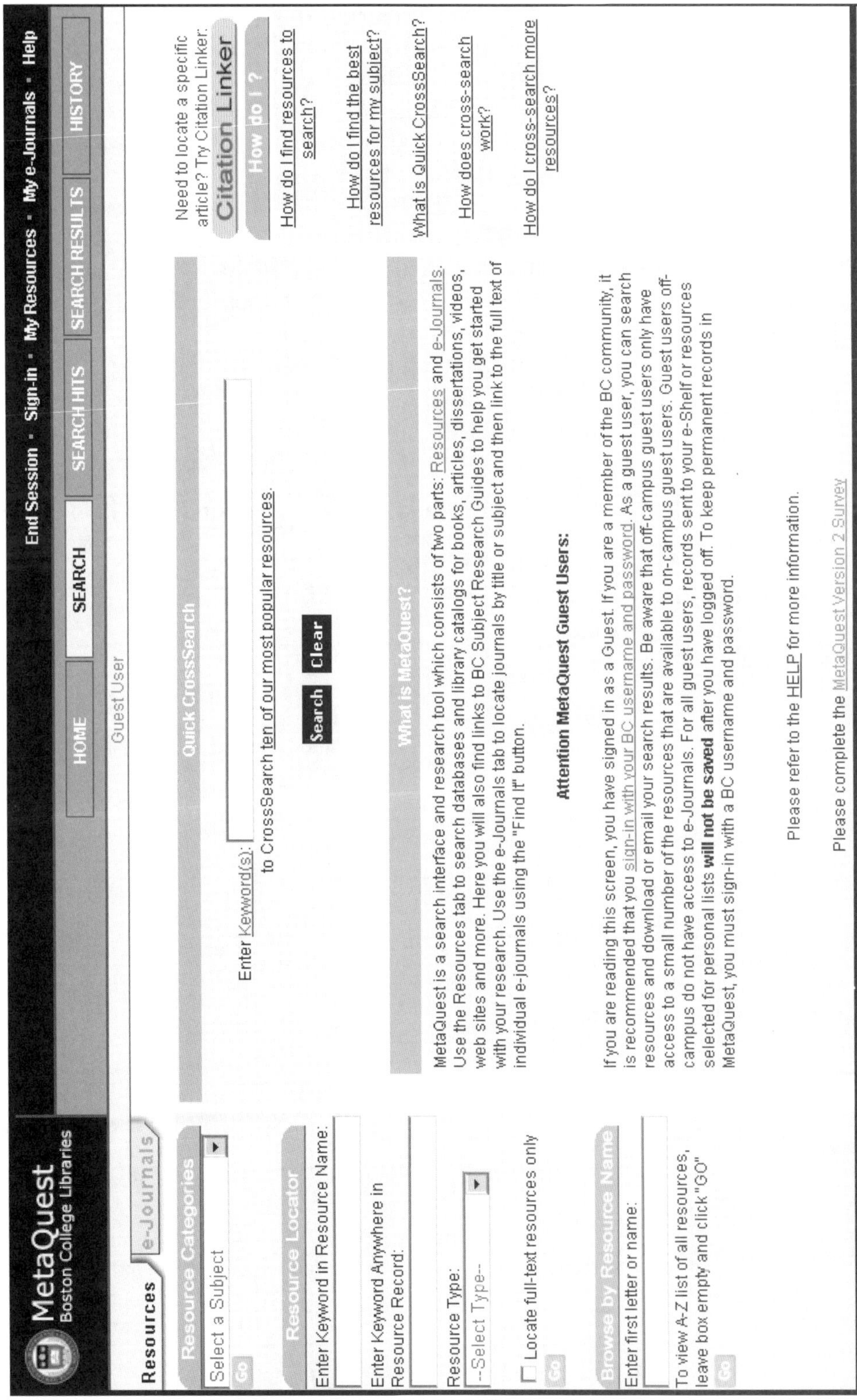

Figure 3-3. Federated-Search Menu

for organizing and downloading the results. These examples are two extremes, with literally infinite possibilities for customization in between. Ideally, the library should approach federated searching as a service that affects all aspects of library operation in order to select the variation that is best suited to the library's needs.

During a typical installation, the search protocols must be set up for each library resource (Lewis, 2002). This includes setting up Z39.50 profiles, establishing OAI harvesting systems, configuring customized HTML, XML, and unique API connections. When doing this, the library has to keep in mind the final form of the user interface. Setting up search protocols involves deciding what metadata to search, how to search it, and how to present the search results. Because of the myriad standards involved, each database has to be evaluated and set up individually. Once the database connections are set up, the user interface has to be configured with the appropriate search boxes and options. The

Vendor	Product Name	For More Information:
Auto-Graphics, Inc.	AGent™	www4.auto-graphics.com/product_agent.html
BiblioMondo	ZONE-Pro™	www.bibliomondo.com/site/solutions/search.php
Blue Angel Technologies, Inc.	MetaSearch Solution	www.blueangeltech.com/Solutions /MetaSearch%20Solution.pdf
BrightPlanet Corp.	Deep Query Manager	www.brightplanet.com/products/dqm.asp
DYNIX	Horizon Information Portal	www.dynix.com/products/hip/
Endeavor Information Systems	ENCompass Solutions	http://encompass.endinfosys.com/
Ex Libris	MetaLib®	www.exlibris-usa.com/metalib.htm
Fretwell-Downing Informatics (FDI)	FDI Zportal	www.fdgroup.com/fdi/marketing/zportal_choice .html
GIS Information Systems, Inc.	Polaris® PowerPAC™ Portal	www.gisinfosystems.com/Polaris/SubSys /PowerPAC_small.pdf
Index Data ApS	Keystone	www.indexdata.dk/keystone/
Innovative Interfaces, Inc.	MetaFind	www.iii.com/mill/digital.shtml#map
MuseGlobal, Inc.	Muse Metasearch™	www.museglobal.com/solutions/discovery _tools.html
Open Text Corp.	Livelink® Federated Query Server	www.opentext.com/products/livelink /federated-query-server/
SIRSI Corp.	Sirsi SingleSearch	www.sirsi.com/Sirsiproducts/broadcastsearch.html
The Library Corporation	YouSeeMore™	www.tlcdelivers.com/tlc/youseemore.asp
VTLS Inc.	Chameleon iPortal	www.vtls.com/Products/gateway/
WebClarity Software Inc.	WebClarity Resource Gateway	www.webclarity.info/products/gateway.html
WebFeat, Inc.	WebFeat™ Prism	http://www.webfeat.org/products/prism.html

Table 3-2. Federated-Searching Services

search interface can be relatively simple or quite complex. The library has to decide which fields to make available for searching and may offer multiple choices, including a simple search, complex queries, or customized queries based on subject areas or other criteria. The user interface may be set up to search all resources at once, to search clusters of resources in related subjects, or to allow the user to select which databases to search.

The library also needs to consider how results will be formatted (Luther, 2003). The results may be given one standard format, or the interface may be set up to allow the user to customize the presentation of results. This includes the presentation of individual records and the options for sorting results. Results can be presented as brief views of metadata, comprehensive or long views of metadata, and perhaps the full text of the resources. Sorting may be controlled by a relevancy algorithm or based on metadata, such as title, author, or date. Query results may be delivered by various means (Luther, 2003), including an on-screen view or formatted for printing, e-mail delivery, or output to citation software. Users can save queries to run at a later time, and intelligent information discovery services can be set up to run favorite queries automatically and deliver the results on a pre-set schedule.

Following installation, the library must provide staff training so that library personnel are knowledgeable about the use of the federated search tool (Gerrity et al., 2002). Staff who work with the public should, at minimum, be trained in the basic functions of the system in order to assist users and, ideally, should also be fluent in the advanced features in order to support the full functionality of the service.

IMPLEMENTING FEDERATED SEARCHING

The key to a successful implementation of a federated-search service is branding and promotion (Gerrity, et al., 2002). Rather than merely putting a search box on the Web site and hoping users find it, a better approach is to give the service a catchy name and logo as part of a marketing campaign to attract users. Some ideas for marketing include press releases, opening day ceremonies, outreach to library users, posters and other visual marketing materials, and word of mouth at library service points and as part of library outreach and formal instruction.

Federated-search systems are still relatively young (Tennant, 2003; Fryer, 2004) and likely to mature further in the near term as vendors develop software and services, so ongoing maintenance is an important part of the library's implementation plan (Lewis, 2002). In addition, the library's online content is constantly changing and growing, and it is important to keep the search and authentication protocols up-to-date as resources are added, dropped, or changed. Staff responsible for maintaining the system as well as staff directly serving the public should be aware of these issues as part of the planning process.

By providing a single interface for searching multiple, heterogeneous resources, federated-search systems provide a valuable service to library users. In order to make the most of these systems, libraries must implement federated searching carefully and market it vigorously. Staff training, user instruction, system maintenance, and assessment of the service must be ongoing. With the help of a comprehensive plan, a federated-search system can become a valuable component of a library's public services.

SUMMARY

Web lists, context-sensitive linking, and federated searching are three increasingly popular approaches to online access in libraries. These tools are designed to provide users with an efficient and transparent information discovery experience in the online environment. Libraries can employ Web lists to streamline and customize access to any kind of online resource, thereby creating metadata and user interfaces as simple or complex as necessary to meet specific needs. Context-sensitive linking applies chiefly to traditional publications such as journals, books, and book chapters, enabling users to link directly from OpenURL-enabled discovery tools to full-text content without needing to know where the full text resides. Federated searching further simplifies the search process by applying a common interface to a variety of searching tools.

Many libraries are using these alternative bibliographic tools to supplement or complement their library catalogs, but these tools have not yet matured. The online information environment is a jumble of proprietary, open-source, and home-grown tools and resources. As a result, systematic information sharing and retrieval are less efficient in the current environment than they could ultimately become, and information providers are moving toward greater interoperability in response to this problem. A more immediate issue for libraries is the cost of these new bibliographic tools, in terms of both the direct cost of commercial systems and the indirect costs of developing, maintaining, and promoting multiple bibliographic tools. Chapter 4 discusses how to balance these alternative bibliographic tools with traditional catalog access based on local needs and priorities.

REFERENCES

Boydston, Jeanne M. K., and Joan M. Leysen. 2002. "Internet Resources Cataloging in ARL Libraries: Staffing and Access Issues." *The Serials Librarian* 41, no. 3/4 (June): 127–145.

Finnigan, Sonya and Nigel Ward. 1997. "Z39.50 Made Simple." Queensland, Australia: Distributed Systems Technology Centre, University of Queensland. Available: http://archive.dstc.edu.au/DDU/projects/ZINC/zsimple.htm. Accessed February 1, 2005.

Fryer, Donna. 2004. "Federated Search Engines." *www.onlinemag.net* 28, no. 2 (March/April): 16–19. Accessed January 27, 2005.

Gerrity, Bob, Theresa Lyman, and Ed Tallent. 2002. "Blurring Services and Resources: Boston College's Implementation of MetaLib and SFX." *Reference Services Review* 30, no. 3: 229–241.

Joint Steering Committee for the Revision of AACR2. 2002. *Anglo-American Cataloging Rules,* 2nd ed., 2002 rev. Chicago: American Library Association.

Jones, Ed. 2002. *The Exchange of Serials Subscription Information.* Bethesda, MD: National Information Standards Organization.

Lewis, Nicholas. 2002. "Talking about a Revolution? First Impressions of Ex Libris' MetaLib." *Ariadne* no. 32 (July) Available: www.ariadne.ac.uk/issue32/metalib. Accessed January 28, 2005.

Luther, Judy. 2003. "Trumping Google? Metasearching's Promise." *Library Journal* 128, no. 16 (October 1): 36–39.

McDonald, John, and Eric F. Van de Velde. 2004. "The Lure of Linking." *Library Journal* 129, no. 6 (April 1): 32–34.

National Information Standards Organization (NISO). 2004. "The Proposed OpenURL Framework Standard." Bethesda, MD: NISO Available:

http://library.caltech.edu/openurl/Standard.htm. Accessed January 28, 2005.

Needleman, Mark H. 2002. "The OpenURL: An Emerging Standard for Linking." *Serials Review* 28, no. 1 (Spring): 74–76.

Open Archives Initiative. "The Open Archives Initiative Protocol for Metadata Harvesting." Open Archives Initiative (2004) Available: www.openarchives.org/OAI/2.0/openarchivesprotocol.htm

Tansey, Mike. 2003. "Intelligent Content and Technology Integration." *Special Supplement to EContent and Information Today* 20, no.6 (June): S6–S7.

Tennant, Roy. 2003. "The Right Solution: Federated Search Tools." *Library Journal* 128, no. 11 (June 15): 28–30.

Walker, Jenny. 2001. "Open Linking for Libraries: The OpenURL Framework." *New Library World* 102, no. 4/5: 127–133.

WebFeat, Inc. 2003. "The Truth about Federated Searching." *Information Today* 20, no. 9 (October). Available: www.infotoday.com/it/oct03/hane1.shtml. Accessed January 27, 2005.

Webster, Peter. 2004. "Metasearching in an Academic Environment." *www.onlinemag.net* 28, no. 2 (March/April): 20–23. Accessed January 27, 2005.

4 DETERMINING BIBLIOGRAPHIC CONTROL IN THE ONLINE ENVIRONMENT

INTRODUCTION

The online catalog is the library's most important tool for organizing and providing access to local collections. In the context of online resources, it is also the most hotly debated. Site-specific bibliographic tools enable libraries to guide their users to locally selected resources and provide access to licensed content that is inaccessible to Web search engines. For many years now, libraries have supplemented or even replaced catalog access to online resources with their own Web-based lists and finding aids. Today, libraries also have access to the federated searching and context-sensitive linking tools discussed in depth in Chapter 3. These tools represent an approach to managing bibliographic data that is fundamentally different from a catalog or Web list because they mediate among existing bibliographic databases and full-text resources rather than describing those resources directly. Regardless of the specific tools involved, the library's bibliographic strategy for online resources must be able to grow with the collection, keep pace with evolving standards, and capitalize on emerging technologies in order to remain effective over the long term. In this chapter, we will compare how library catalogs, Web lists, OpenURL services, and federated search tools facilitate search and retrieval, provide access to collections, and interact with existing infrastructure and procedures.

CHARACTERISTICS AFFECTING BIBLIOGRAPHIC CONTROL

Online resources have challenged established bibliographic-control practices as a result of three unique characteristics:

- scale and structure
- dynamic content
- dynamic functionality

The rapid proliferation of online resources over the past decade has given libraries ample opportunity to experience these characteristics firsthand. The dynamic nature of the online information landscape is unlikely to change as long as it remains technology driven, and so the library's ability to harness the positive aspects of online information and mitigate its potential pitfalls depends on the development of efficient tools—or combinations of tools—for bibliographic access.

SCALE AND STRUCTURE

In the nonelectronic environment, the traditional mode of publication is a cohesive intellectual work associated with a single physical object, such as a book, or a succession of closely related physical objects, such as the issues of a journal (Svenonius, 2000). Even if the user is ultimately seeking only a subset of a work, such as a single track on a music CD or an article in a journal, he or she must obtain the entire physical object in order to reach the specific content. Libraries have therefore created bibliographic tools that describe resources at the level most consistent with the physical objects that reside on their shelves, while specialized indexing and abstracting services provide bibliographic access at greater levels of specificity. By contrast, online-information resources vary enormously in scale from individual documents to massive aggregator databases. Apart from the internal policies of individual libraries, there is no objective basis for providing access to resources at any particular level of granularity; what one library considers a collection of individual documents, another might consider a single resource with many parts.

For the most part, traditional publication types such as books and journals have retained their distinctive structure in electronic form, and libraries typically provide access to these at the title level as they would for the corresponding print resources. However, online-content providers have already begun to diverge from these conventions to a significant degree. At one end of the electronic-publication spectrum, content is being issued in increasingly granular increments, including individual articles or chapters made available in advance of the larger publication. At the opposite extreme are full-text aggregators, which dissolve many separate publications into a single mass of searchable content. In either case, the journal persists as a kind of brand name even though the articles are dissociated from the issue/volume structure that most people would recognize as a journal.

Online resources also alter the relationship between information objects and the bibliographic-control superstructure. For information resources in physical formats, the catalog is essentially a finding aid. The user searches a detailed collection of bibliographic descriptions to

> **Granularity**: The level of detail at which a bibliographic entity is identified. For example, an aggregator database could be considered the primary information object, each of its constituent journals could also be considered an object of bibliographic interest, as could each individual article in the database. Article-level bibliographic access represents a higher level of granularity than database-level access.

> **Rapid online publication**: Online journals in the sciences are leading the way toward disengaging individual articles from the traditional issue/volume format. One example is the "Online Early" service available with some of the journals from Blackwell Publishing. A slightly different approach is used by the open–access BioMed Central journals; these online-only journals use traditional issue and volume designations, but a closer look reveals that each individual article is an issue of the journal and that the volume is simply comprised of all articles published in a given year.

determine whether the library owns any material that meets his or her information need, and if so, where it is found in the physical collection. The process of obtaining and using the material takes place beyond the confines of the catalog. In the online environment, the bibliographic tool is both a finding aid and a point of entry; from the user's perspective, organization is indistinguishable from access. New approaches to bibliographic control such as context-sensitive linking and federated searching attempt to optimize this access factor. These tools are not designed to store descriptions of information objects but to provide users with the most efficient gateway to their desired content, regardless of where that content is stored or the user's point of origin.

DYNAMIC CONTENT

The effort required to produce and distribute a physical publication places certain practical limitations on who is able to publish and how frequently a publication can be revised. In the online environment, publication and revision can be accomplished almost instantaneously by updating data elements in a database or by uploading files to a server. As a result, many online information resources are subject to change on a frequent, or even continuous, basis. In addition, content providers often take advantage of the ease of online publication and the multimedia capabilities of the Web by publishing bonus articles, media clips, and other extended content that supplement the primary content. This added material may appear online separately from the primary content, or be available for a limited duration.

Dynamic content affords online resources a level of currency unrivaled by any other format, but it also has an impact on both the integrity of individual resource descriptions and the viability of the collection as a whole. Online serials, which in libraries primarily take the form of magazines and journals, are revised through a succession of discrete updates. Updates may be predictable, such as current issues added at regular intervals; or unpredictable, such as a one-time addition of backfiles. Although serial updates can be difficult to track accurately, the new content remains distinct from the content that existed prior to the update. The overall nature of the work may shift over time, but existing content is typically not altered retrospectively. Integrating resources, on the other hand, absorb revisions into a seamless whole. With each new revision, the previous iteration of the resource ceases to exist, and it can be difficult to determine precisely what has changed. At no point can the library be certain that the bibliographic descriptions for its online resources accurately reflect those resources in real time, or that a particular resource is still appropriate for the collection after multiple iterations.

DYNAMIC FUNCTIONALITY

Plug-in: A small software module that extends the functionality of a larger program such as a Web browser. Libraries often encounter resources that require plug-ins for Flash, Adobe Acrobat, and various media players, to name a few common examples. In order for the information resource to be fully operational, users must have the necessary plug-ins installed on their computers.

Like information content, the visual design, navigation aids, and functional components of an online resource are important features affecting accessibility; these aspects of a resource can change considerably over time. Online information resources have become increasingly sophisticated and media-rich, and often require a variety of software plug-ins to access page images, media files, and animation. An increasing number of online resources also require the user to tinker with the Web browser in order to clear the cache, adjust privacy settings to accept cookies, or enable JavaScript. Many online resources incorporate search capabilities, provide multiple output options, interact with citation software, and link out to other content providers. Functional characteristics such as these can have a major impact on the usability of a resource, yet these elements are largely absent from the traditional bibliographic description.

Hypertext links facilitate a loose, multidirectional mode of information discovery that is unique to the Web, but each link is also an individual functional element that can obsolesce independently of intellectual content. These links exist not only among information objects, but also between information objects and bibliographic services, the online catalogs, databases, and Web lists that link to them. When an online resource migrates to a new URL, the bibliographic access must follow. Advance announcements of planned migration, provider-side redirects, and persistent uniform resource locator (PURL) resolvers can minimize the impact of link rot, but these courtesies are far from ubiquitous.

Persistent uniform resource locator (PURL): A URL that points to a centralized resolution service instead of to the resource itself. The PURL resolution server associates the PURL with one or more specific URLs and redirects the user to the resource. When the library links to a PURL instead of to a specific URL, any change to the URL will be invisible to the library user as long as the PURL service incorporates the new URL.

MANAGING MULTIPLE BIBLIOGRAPHIC TOOLS

Among the approaches we present in this book, traditional cataloging currently provides the best-developed system for bibliographic control. The modern cataloging apparatus has evolved over many decades to incorporate physical description, intellectual access, classification, and authority control. Libraries have an enormous investment in their own catalogs and in shared systems to support cooperative cataloging, and we predict that library catalogs will continue to play an important role in online access for some time to come. However, every bibliographic tool has strengths and weaknesses, and the library catalog is no exception.

The advantages of traditional cataloging are its widely accepted standards and relatively robust systems. Library catalogs throughout the English-speaking world share a common record format and input conventions. Although online catalogs differ somewhat from vendor to vendor, these systems were developed to automate pre-existing bibliographic-control practices that were already well standardized. By contrast, newer approaches, such as federated searching and context-sensitive linking, began as entrepreneurial responses to specific problems created by online information; these tools are becoming standardized only now that their application has become widespread. Online catalogs have been in existence for many years and have mature infrastructures that can accommodate even very large collections of online resources. In addition, many online catalogs are part of a larger integrated library system that combines bibliographic data with acquisitions records, holdings information, and even e-resource management data, greatly streamlining the overall management process.

There are two major drawbacks to providing access to online resources through the library catalog: (1) the complexity of the cataloging process and (2) the content of the resulting records. First, cataloging is a resource-intensive process, a fact that libraries have found problematic in light of the volume and volatility of online content. The cataloger is expected to examine individual resources and then record information about them in surrogate records using a complex network of interrelated standards and input conventions. Within the records themselves, access points must be justified by elements of the description, and many data elements are recorded in both free text and coded form. Cataloging an online resource according to prescribed rules is simply not an efficient process, and, even when the cataloging is technically flawless, the resulting record does not necessarily contain the optimal data for management and use of the resource. For example, cataloging rules give the cataloger detailed guidance for handling different kinds of title information, and the MARC record format provides a structure for the cataloger to articulate titles proper, uniform titles, variant titles, series titles, and related titles with great subtlety. By contrast, important characteristics such as technical requirements and access restrictions are relegated to note fields, which are typically not machine-actionable in the way that traditional access points are. These notes are typically not searchable, and the cataloger is given little specific instruction about what level of technical detail to bring out or how to express it. Reports of the demise of the catalog (Tennant, 2002) are greatly exaggerated, but the need for local flexibility and the emergence of nimble technology in the Web environment has drawn libraries away from a one-tool model of bibliographic control.

Machine-actionable: A machine-actionable data element uses coding and syntax that can be interpreted and displayed automatically. In library catalogs, highly structured access points like title and author are machine actionable—they can be searched and sorted according to the rules that govern the system. The system has more difficulty parsing free-text notes; typically data can be retrieved from these fields only by a broad keyword search, if at all.

BUILDING A BIBLIOGRAPHIC STRATEGY

A seminal cataloging text defines bibliographic control as "the process of creating, arranging, and maintaining systems for bibliographic information retrieval" (Taylor, 2004, 501). This is a compelling definition because it identifies bibliographic control as a process that is sustained and developed over time rather than a specific outcome. This perspective certainly resonates with the current trend toward multiple approaches to organization and access. At the same time, Taylor's definition implies that information retrieval is the sole objective of a bibliographic system. While this may be true in concept, since the advent of integrated library systems many libraries have come to rely on their catalogs to support a host of management functions, such as quantitative assessment, fiscal administration, and access control in addition to bibliographic control. If a library adopts a bibliographic tool that does not perform these auxiliary functions, separate tools must exist to do so.

As a library explores various approaches to organizing and providing access to its online resources, it is important to consider potential bibliographic tools from a variety of perspectives:

- information retrieval
- access to collections
- management needs

Regardless of a bibliographic tool's potential information-retrieval capabilities, that tool cannot provide effective access to information resources if its functionality is incompatible with the collection it is intended to support, or if the library cannot maintain it efficiently. This is particularly true for online resources, which exist as a collection only to the extent that the library provides access points to them.

INFORMATION RETRIEVAL

At its most fundamental level, bibliographic control serves two complementary purposes: identification and collocation. A unique bibliographic record represents each information object in a collection, while common data elements within the records provide the basis for collocating related resources across the collection. From the user's perspective, a bibliographic tool should offer a reliable means of finding information resources that correspond to various search criteria, and sufficient information about each individual resource to disambiguate similar results. These basic objectives have been articulated in a variety of different ways since the dawn of modern cataloging (Svenonius,

Functional Requirements for Bibliographic Records ([FRBR] IFLA Study Group. 1998): *FRBR* is an approach to bibliographic control that is gaining momentum in the online environment. The *FRBR* model articulates the complex relationship between intellectual content as an abstraction and the reality of information objects. *FRBR* also relates the specific needs of information-seeking users to each element of the bibliographic record and prioritizes the data elements according to those goals. *FRBR* is a conceptual model rather than a metadata format or a set of cataloging rules; it is unclear when or if existing library catalogs will incorporate the *FRBR* model, but its principles are likely to guide the development of post-MARC bibliographic tools. See Chapter 10 for a more in-depth discussion of *FRBR*.

2000), but the underlying concepts remain relevant today even though bibliographic tools have begun to diverge from the catalog model. Consequently, the library should first evaluate how a potential bibliographic tool addresses these objectives.

Identification

Metadata schema: Also known as metadata schemes, the schema is the framework that defines a set of metadata elements and the relationships among them. Metadata schema familiar to libraries include the highly structured MARC format, the more flexible Dublin Core, and the free-form descriptions and keywords found in Web-page headers. Libraries working with their own digitization projects will encounter many more metadata schema specific to text, image, and media files and archival resources. See NISO's "Understanding Metadata" (www.niso.org/standards/resources/ UnderstandingMetadata.pdf) for more information.

Bibliographic tools identify and describe information objects through the use of metadata schema. Metadata schema provide a framework for the application of metadata by defining the elements that comprise a record and establishing the relationships among them. Input rules and formal vocabularies further define how the specific attributes of an information object are expressed; this is the role of cataloging and classification rules. The richness and granularity necessary for the metadata schema to work effectively will vary according to the size, homogeneity, and purpose of the collection it supports. In general, metadata for resources in large, diverse, or highly specialized collections must be more exhaustive and detailed than the metadata for small, uniform, generalized collections. However, given the tendency of online collections to grow and subdivide over time, it is important to consider the scalability of the metadata schema when evaluating a bibliographic tool.

Traditional catalog records contain a variety of data elements transcribed from the resources they represent as well as additional elements formulated by the cataloger to ensure that each description is unique, even when the differences among resources are very subtle. Subject thesauri tend to focus on the specific subject matter of a resource, while classification systems situate a resource within the context of a broader discipline. For a small collection, this level of detail and specificity can seem like overkill. However, library catalogs are designed to provide bibliographic control for collections of thousands or even millions of volumes. At that scale, the utility of a rich and detailed metadata schema becomes clear. Libraries that assembled simple lists of links to various resources when the Web was in its infancy soon had the need to differentiate among multiple versions of the same content, distinguish among resources with similar titles, and subdivide broad subject categories as the resources proliferated, only to discover that enhancing metadata retrospectively is difficult and time-consuming.

Newer bibliographic tools such as federated search engines and context-sensitive linking operate much differently from the traditional catalog or a similar information surrogate model, such as a list of resources by title or subject. Federated search tools do not actually contain bibliographic data of their own, but instead provide a mechanism for simultaneous searching of other bibliographic tools, such as indexes, catalogs, and full-text collections. Depending on the specific system, a library may have considerable latitude to customize the metadata elements that appear in the search results, but the metadata itself comes from an external source and its richness and accuracy are a function of the source database. Similarly, the ability of a federated search mechanism to reliably collapse duplicate results is dependent upon the uniformity of metadata across the various source databases and the richness of the metadata that those sources return to the federated search.

Whereas federated search tools serve as a bridge between users and bibliographic data, context-sensitive linking tools mediate between bibliographic data and content. Federated search tools broadcast the user's search to multiple databases and return the cumulated results; context-sensitive linking tools start with an individual search result and use its metadata to determine the retrieval options available to the user. When the user finds a citation in an OpenURL-enabled database, that database pushes its own metadata to the linking tool, which compares that metadata to its internal knowledge base and offers library-specific links to available versions. The knowledge bases for OpenURL tools primarily contain holdings information rather than bibliographic description; they do not provide subject access, classification, or descriptive detail, but rather they require an external record in a catalog, index, or other bibliographic tool as a starting point. It is the responsibility of the library or the library's contracted vendor to ensure the accuracy of the tool's knowledge base, but the richness and accuracy of the source metadata is beyond the library's control.

Collocation

A bibliographic tool must also provide a means of collocating resources that share similar attributes. Alphabetical title lists of online resources are easy to organize and maintain, but a straight alphabetical arrangement is only effective for information retrieval if the user is seeking a known item. A collection of any significant size requires a more sophisticated data structure capable of parsing the collection into manageable subsets, either through a precoordinated arrangement or on the fly, as is the case with a searchable database.

The library catalog has a highly refined ability to collocate related resources through the use of controlled access points such as uniform titles, linking entries, and subject headings. The cataloger uses these elements to describe the intellectual characteristics of individual resources and establish the logical relationships among them, and external authority lists are used to define the standardized form of access points for consistent retrieval. Authority control is critical to the collocation function because it establishes the relationships between the entry form of the access point and other forms of the same information as well as the relationship between one uniform heading and another. To date, cataloging is the only form of bibliographic control that has a fully realized authority structure.

Federated searching poses interesting collocation challenges because it pulls results from many different sources and reassembles them in a secondary interface. Federated search tools generally provide a variety of options for sorting and filtering results, but the multiplicity of output options cannot conceal the fact that a cross-database search is a relatively blunt instrument compared to the search capabilities that most databases provide through their native interfaces. Federated search tools are designed to cast a wide net; therefore, they operate most effectively when they search the most universal metadata elements for widely applicable terms. As a result, these tools cannot collocate related resources as reliably as tools based on richly detailed metadata schemas and controlled vocabularies, even when the individual source databases provide these.

Context-sensitive linking services play a somewhat different role in collocating resources because they perform a retrieval function rather than a search function. In terms of the user's query, the collocation function is carried out by the source database that the user is searching. What context-sensitive linking accomplishes very efficiently is the collocation of access points. These tools are designed to present to the user a set of possible paths that originate from their search result. These paths may include services such as interlibrary loan forms or Web searches for related information, as well as full-text versions of the document itself. In terms of organizing the access points, the library can specify its own priorities about the order in which multiple providers are listed or the context in which certain options appear.

ACCESS TO COLLECTIONS

A bibliographic tool can follow one of two broad approaches to organization and access: it can integrate online resources with other materials in the library's collection, or it can isolate them on the basis of format. Although some tools tend to be more format-focused than others, this relationship is not strictly a function of a particular technology but can be greatly influenced by the library's choices at implementation. This in turn is influenced by whether the library prefers to approach its collection as an integral whole across multiple formats, consider the online collection independently of other formats, or treat different kinds of online resources as discrete collections of their own.

By integrating online resources with other formats, the library can streamline its work processes and present intellectually related resources in a cohesive collection, but its ability to accentuate and manipulate online resources is diminished. Separating online resources from other formats gives the library greater flexibility and control in the management and presentation of its online collections, but it also disconnects these collections from related material in other formats. Neither approach is more correct than the other; each is dependent on the individual library's preferred approach to access and the composition of its particular collection.

Integrating Online Collections

When to integrate: An integrative approach to access brings online resources together with other formats. This approach works best for online collections that are closely related to print resources, for online collections that are not sufficiently robust to stand on their own, and for libraries that prefer to approach their collections as a unified whole.

Bibliographic tools that integrate online resources with the rest of the library's collection are best suited to resources that are closely associated with other formats, resources for which online is not the preferred mode of access, and online collections that lack the depth or cohesion to stand alone. Many online publications, such as books, journals, and indexes, are reproductions or near analogs of materials that libraries have long collected in print. Given the close relationship between these resources and their print counterparts, libraries need a bibliographic system capable of collocating these resources across multiple formats. This approach is also useful in disciplines that are underrepresented in the online environment or that emphasize content that many users may still prefer to use in print, such as art reproductions or works of long fiction. In such cases, users may be less inclined to seek out online content because their needs are not reliably met by the available online collection. Isolating online resources with different bibliographic treatment further reduces their visibility by forcing users to use multiple tools for information retrieval.

The library catalog is the quintessential integrative tool because it is already the access point for the majority of the library's resources. The practice of cataloging is itself content— rather than format—oriented. For example, an online map is first and foremost a map, and its bibliographic record is organized to bring out all the characteristics that apply uniquely to maps, while the electronic aspect is ancillary. This approach emphasizes the fundamental similarity of resources that share a common bibliographic aspect regardless of publication format. The predominance of content over format in the cataloging model is also evident in the wide acceptance of combined-format serial records (see Chapter 8) and in the treatment of many electronic books as reproductions rather than new editions (see Chapter 7).

The catalog is also the database of record in many libraries, particularly research libraries that have consciously cultivated their collections to be scholarly repositories (Burke, Germain, and Van Ullen, 2003). Although the catalog is not necessarily the only means of access to electronic resources at such institutions, it is relied upon to represent the authoritative record of the library's collection in all disciplines and formats. Not surprisingly, online collections in these libraries tend to emphasize research resources with established reputations and strong connections to print counterparts that predate the Web, such as journals, indexes, and reference works. By cataloging these materials in their online form, the library ensures continuity between archival volumes and current content as print resources are migrated to online form, and it preserves a complete record of the collection.

The catalog certainly does not have a monopoly on format integration. Indeed, even a simple Web page with a list of library resources can perform cross-format integration to the extent that it points users to resources that are not online. Although context-sensitive linking tools were designed primarily to provide efficient access to online journals, they nonetheless perform a powerful integrative function that did not previously exist by linking article-level bibliographic tools, such as indexing and abstracting services, directly with online content. Depending on the library's particular implementation, OpenURL tools can also point users back to the catalog, which brings online resources back together with conventional formats. Federated-search technology is integrative by design because it pulls many separate tools together into a single search interface. Even if the library manages its online resources entirely through tools external to the catalog, through the use of a federated search engine the catalog can be re-integrated with other bibliographic tools.

Isolating Online Collections

When to isolate: Isolating online resources with their own bibliographic tools gives the library flexibility and control. This approach works best for online resources that do not have a strong relationship with other areas of the collection or require different kinds of metadata from those used for traditional materials, and for libraries that prefer to use different bibliographic approaches for different areas of their collections.

The principal drawback to merging online resources with other formats using a single tool is that the library loses flexibility and precision in providing access to its online resources. Any information-retrieval system will perform optimally when the records in its database share a common scale, richness, and vocabulary. However, the library may want lean, minimally structured metadata for highly volatile resources, such as freely available Web sites or journals in aggregator databases, but it may prefer rich, detailed metadata for more durable, locally significant resources, such as its own digitized archival materials. Attempting to combine these approaches with traditional materials in the library catalog will gradually diminish the integrity of the catalog and reduce the library's ability to address the specialized bibliographic needs of its online resources. Bibliographic tools that isolate online resources from other formats are best suited to resources that differ from the majority of existing library materials in scale, content, behavior, or function; freely available resources that do not require the full spectrum of management activities; and resources that comprise a cohesive collection in their own right. Instead of attempting to shoehorn different bibliographic approaches into a single information retrieval mechanism, the library might instead provide access to some or all of its online content using tools devoted solely to online resources.

An online list of resources, whether static or database driven, is a prime example of a tool that tends to be used to isolate online resources. Although such a list works much like the catalog in the sense that it contains its own bibliographic data, libraries often turn to this type of solution when they want to bypass the catalog search process, capture attributes of online resources that the catalog cannot easily accommodate, maintain a less-rigid standard of bibliographic control, or offer a different interface to online resources from what the catalog provides. To return to the example of an online map, a library choosing to emphasize format over content might make the map accessible through a Web page linking to online maps, relate it thematically to other online resources through a pathfinder, or include it in a broader e-resource tool that provides access to the library's online collection as a complete entity. Any of these approaches will isolate the map from its printed counterparts represented in the catalog, but connect it with other resources that share its online aspect.

If federated searching and context-sensitive linking tools are not configured to incorporate the library catalog, users can effectively bypass the catalog for many kinds of searches because these tools take them directly to article-level access. We anticipate that the variety of publications that can be effectively accessed in this manner will grow concurrently with developments in online publishing. In their present incarnation, federated searching and reference linking are chiefly used to provide access to journal articles. This is largely because commercial-article databases and the serial publications to which they provide access offer a highly structured data environment ideally suited to automated query formulation. However, as these linking technologies become more widespread, it is likely that an increasing share of bibliographic databases and full-content resources, both commercial and open access, will be developed with these tools in mind.

MANAGEMENT NEEDS

The library should consider two separate but related management concerns as it investigates various bibliographic tools. First, it is important to determine how extensively a particular tool provides resource management and decision support in addition to user access. If a bibliographic tool cannot provide these additional services to the extent the collection requires, the library will need to establish another layer of tools and practices to carry out these functions. This leads directly to the second critical issue, the library's ability to manage the tools themselves. Access that appears seamless to the user requires an increasingly complex coordination of technology, workflow, and information resources. If the library embarks on a bibliographic-control strategy too complex to sustain, it runs the risk of impeding rather than facilitating online access.

Managing Information Resources

Libraries have a strong impetus for systematic collection analysis motivated by changing modes of publication and ongoing budget pressures. Collection assessment informs institutional comparison, collection restructuring, and budgetary decisions, and the library's bibliographic tools play an important role in supporting passive measures, such as the size, cost, and subject composition of the collection. A library that has an institutional obligation to report collection statistics or plans to make selection decisions about print resources based on the availability of electronic access will benefit from a tool that clearly relates online resources to their print counterparts, distinguishes free resources from fee-based ones, and enables the library to analyze the collection according to a variety of criteria. At present, the library catalog is the tool with the richest environment for collection assessment because it provides not only plentiful bibliographic data, such as physical description, subject access, and classification, but also related administrative metadata, such as cataloging dates and financial records.

In the age of integrated library systems, bibliographic records in the library catalog serve as the hub for a complex network of administrative metadata, such as selector information, order status, and input dates, indirectly related to resource description. In this model, fiscal control of the collections budget is closely tied to the bibliographic system. Although high-quality open-access resources are beginning to gain a foothold in the information marketplace, fee-based resources remain the most stable, content-rich, and highly developed electronic materials that most libraries make available. Not surprisingly, the need for bibliographic tools that can efficiently integrate resource description with administrative metadata tends to follow monetary expenditure: the library cares more about managing the resources it pays for than those it does not. For example, freely available Web sites and journals in aggregator databases can be excellent information resources. However, most libraries approach these resources as found objects because the library has no direct monetary investment in them and no contractual guarantee of their long-term availability. For such resources, efficient provision of access is a more pressing concern than management support, and the ideal bibliographic approach for such resources will emphasize efficiency over depth.

Managing Tools

The development of alternative bibliographic databases for online resources has been an object lesson in understanding matters of scale. There was a time when a simple list in static HTML could provide adequate access to the library's online resources. As online information proliferated and diversified, the tools and processes associated with managing online content became more complex. Alphabetical title lists were replaced with more complex descriptions, and static Web pages were phased out in favor of more powerful and flexible Web-accessible databases. These transitions inevitably demanded more of everything from the library: more software, more server space, more systems and metadata expertise, more ongoing attention to maintenance and development. As bibliographic tools themselves proliferate, the library must be prepared for the challenge of managing multiple systems. Theoretically, special-purpose tools provide superior access to collections with unusual needs and characteristics. However, each new tool has its own unique manner of managing bibliographic data, and implementing new tools requires planning, policies, setup, training, and ongoing maintenance. These problems are exacerbated by the fact that all bibliographic tools, even the library catalog, are experiencing growing pains as a result of online resources.

SUMMARY

Now that libraries have a variety of bibliographic tools at their disposal, it is possible for each library to pursue a bibliographic-control strategy tailored to its unique institutional philosophy, collection, and management environment. The library should think carefully about the suitability of potential solutions before committing its resources to any particular tool, but given the relative ease of manipulating bibliographic data in electronic form, the library should not hesitate to pursue a promising tool out of concern for its potential longevity. No single bibliographic tool will be the magic bullet for managing online resources, but we believe that as online collections continue to grow and diversify many libraries will pursue a similar variety among their bibliographic tools.

REFERENCES

Burke, Gerald, Carol Anne Germain, and Mary K. Van Ullen. 2003. "URLs in the OPAC: Integrating or Disintegrating Research Libraries' Catalogs." *Journal of Academic Librarianship* 29, no. 5 (September): 290–297.

IFLA Study Group on the Functional Requirements for Bibliographic Records. 1998. *Functional Requirements for Bibliographic Records, Final Report.* Munich: K. G. Saur.

National Information Standards Organization (NISO). 2004. "Understanding Metadata." Bethesda, MD: NISO/ Available: www.niso.org/standards/resources/Understanding Metadata.pdf. Accessed January 28, 2004.

Svenonius, Elaine. 2000. *The Intellectual Foundation of Information Organization.* Cambridge, MA.: MIT Press.

Taylor, Arlene G. 2004. *Wynar's Introduction to Cataloging and Classification.* Englewood, CO: Libraries Unlimited.

Tennant, Roy. 2002. "MARC Must Die." *Library Journal* 127, no. 17 (October 15): 26–28.

5 UNDERSTANDING CATALOGING RULES AND GUIDELINES

INTRODUCTION

Modern cataloging is a cooperative endeavor that requires a high level of standardization in order to be widely applicable. Most libraries attempt to follow the cataloging rules, standards, and guidelines that originate at the national or international level because these are the most highly developed and widespread. National libraries, professional organizations, and policy groups have invested their time and considerable expertise in developing rules and standards so that catalogers do not have to reinvent the wheel. That said, individual libraries have unique systems and service needs that require them to diverge from established standards and practices. The result is that multiple layers of alternative practices exist for individual libraries, cooperative networks, and proprietary systems. The resulting maze of interrelated rules and standards can be divided into two broad categories:

¥ record content

¥ content designation

In addition, a great deal of secondary analysis exists at the national, system, and local levels to mediate between content rules and record formats. Although these guidelines do not carry the weight of an official standard, many of them are either so widespread or so essential to the smooth functioning of a local system that they are at least as critical to catalogers in the field as the standards themselves. This chapter will serve as an introduction to the major sources of rules and guidelines that will be referenced throughout the subsequent cataloging chapters.

> **Record content and content designation:** Content designation refers to the structure or tagging of the bibliographic record, while record content refers to the data that actually populate the record.

RECORD CONTENT

One important element that distinguishes traditional cataloging from newer bibliographic systems is its highly developed standards for record content. Standards for record content encompass both the descriptive aspect and the intellectual aspect of the bibliographic record. Descriptive cataloging rules and guidelines govern which physical aspects of an information resource are represented in the bibliographic record and how each data element should be recorded, while intellectual access is standardized through the use of established subject thesauri, subject-cataloging guidelines, and classification systems.

CATALOGING RULES

Anglo-American Cataloguing Rules, second edition, 2002 revision (AACR2): the principal source for cataloging rules in the English-speaking world. *AACR2* covers both bibliographic description and the formulation of uniform access points.

Continuing resources: Resources that are successively updated and have no predetermined conclusion. The category of continuing resources includes both serials, which have updates that remain discrete, and integrating resources, which absorb updates into the whole.

In the English-speaking world, the primary source for rules pertaining to descriptive record content is the Anglo-American Cataloguing Rules, second edition, 2002 revision, colloquially known as *AACR2* (Joint Steering Committee for the Revision of AACR2, 2002). *AACR2* is an independent set of cataloging rules that does not refer to any higher authority. AACR2 tells the cataloger both what elements to take from the information resource as the basis for the bibliographic description and how to record it in a systematic manner.

AACR2 is divided into two sections that separately address description and access. Chapter 1 provides general rules for describing information resources; additional chapters that address variations for specific material types, publication formats, and modes of publication supplement this basic chapter. The cataloger uses multiple chapters in tandem to describe resources that reflect more than one category. For online resources, the cataloger will rely on *AACR2, Chapter 9*, which sets down the rules for description of electronic resources. This chapter has recently been updated to address online resources more explicitly than previous versions. Many online resources will also require the use of the newly revised Chapter 12, which covers continuing resources. The access portion of *AACR2* provides detailed instructions for how to select and formulate access points such as uniform titles; place names; and the names of persons, corporate bodies, and conferences.

RULE INTERPRETATIONS

Library of Congress Rule Interpretations (LCRI): The Library of Congress internal guidelines for interpreting *AACR2*. Other libraries follow the *LCRI* in order to harmonize their own cataloging practices with the copy emanating from the Library of Congress.

The Library of Congress (LC) publishes copious documentation about its cataloging practices. The primary document relating to record content is the Library of Congress Rule Interpretations or LCRI (Hiatt, 1989). LCRI follows AACR2 chapter by chapter and is intended to elucidate vague or complicated rules, indicate areas where LC practice differs from the official rules, and, in instances in which AACR2 permits optional practices, indicate which option the Library of Congress follows.

LCRI is essentially a manual of local practice for catalogers at the Library of Congress rather than an autonomous set of rules, and individual libraries might find that the rule interpretations that best serve the Library of Congress are not ideal for their local catalogs. However, a great share of the cataloging copy in many libraries emanates from the Library of Congress, and by following *LCRI* those libraries are taking a major step toward standardizing local cataloging decisions.

COOPERATIVE CATALOGING

PCC, CONSER, and BIBCO: The Program for Cooperative Cataloging (PCC) is a network of libraries and other affiliated institutions such as vendors and research centers. PCC serves as a source of cooperative cataloging and policy development. PCC oversees the Cooperative Online Serials Program (CONSER) and its nonserial counterpart BIBCO (Bibliographic Record Cooperative Program, a name the group does not use). Both CONSER and BIBCO publish cataloging guidelines for their participating institutions that many other libraries follow as de facto national standards.

The Cooperative Online Serials Program (CONSER) is a component of the Program for Cooperative Cataloging (PCC), a network of libraries and affiliated institutions engaged in cooperative cataloging and policy development. CONSER publishes a set of guidelines for serials cataloging called the *CONSER Cataloging Manual* (Hirons, 2002). Module 31, the subset of the manual that deals with online serials, provides an in-depth analysis of the cataloging rules that apply to online serials and synthesizes these rules with CONSER policies for creating and maintaining records for remote-access serials in the MARC format.

BIBCO is the PCC component devoted to cooperative cataloging of nonserial resources, including both monographic resources and the newly established integrating resources. BIBCO is responsible for nonserial resources in any material type or format, but has issued two documents that particularly affect online resources. These are Appendix A of the *BIBCO Participants' Manual* (Hixon, Banush, & Crist n, 2002), which provides extensive cataloging guidelines for integrating resources such as Web sites and databases, and the *BIBCO Core Record Standard for Monographic Electronic Resources* (BIBCO, 2003), which would apply to online books, manuscripts, and nontextual resources issued monographically. Both of these documents mediate between the rules that govern record content and the deployment of those rules in the MARC format.

For the most part, the documents produced by CONSER and BIBCO are procedural manuals for member institutions rather than formal standards. However, the records that result from these programs are widely disseminated and relied upon to reflect the most current cataloging policy and a uniformly high level of quality control. As a result, CONSER and BIBCO documentation effectively articulate a national cataloging standard. As is the case with *LCRI*, the more closely a library adheres to these cooperative cataloging guidelines in its own catalog, the more uniform its catalog records and information retrieval will be.

RELATED DOCUMENTATION

In addition to the basic description and access points, bibliographic records for online resources may also include subject headings, genre headings, and classification numbers. This type of intellectual access is customary in bibliographic records for conventional materials, and these elements are recommended, though not essential, for online resources (Library of Congress Cataloging Directorate, 2003; Wilson, 2001). Subject, genre, and classification elements can follow a great variety of established vocabularies and classification systems, or they can reflect local practices. The subject headings and classification schedules that the Library of Congress issues are perhaps the best-known tools for providing intellectual access, but many other vocabularies and classification tools exist that are based on specific disciplines, publication types, and audiences. Like the rules for resource description, tools for intellectual access are accompanied by yet another set of interpretive guidelines that tell the cataloger how to apply them in the bibliographic record.

CONTENT DESIGNATION

Content designation refers to how the metadata in the bibliographic record are formally structured or tagged. Whereas cataloging rules and guidelines tell the cataloger how to gather and record the data elements that comprise the bibliographic record, standards for content designation establish common metadata schema that define data elements and the relationships among them. Since the inception of online cooperative cataloging, standards for content designation in bibliographic records also ensure that these records can be transmitted intact from one system to another.

MARC RECORDS

Machine Readable Cataloging (MARC): The most common schema for bibliographic metadata currently in use in libraries. The MARC record format was originally designed to automate production of printed catalog cards, and is closely based on the arrangement of *AACR2*.

Bibliographic records created for use in online catalogs are primarily tagged in the Machine Readable Cataloging (MARC) record format. The MARC format was originally developed to automate the production of printed catalog cards. Although MARC records do include unique elements that do not have an analog in the printed card, on the whole this format is closely aligned with the structure and content of bibliographic records as expressed in *AACR2*. As a practical matter, catalogers contributing to an online catalog will encounter *AACR2* almost entirely through the MARC lens.

The official standard for MARC records is the *MARC 21 Format for Bibliographic Data* (LC Network Development and MARC Standards Office, 1999). The full MARC standard addresses other data types in addition to bibliographic data, such as authority records, serial holdings records, and classification numbers. However, for purposes of this book we will use the generic abbreviation *MARC 21* to refer to the standard for bibliographic data. The Library of Congress, which promulgates the *MARC 21* standard, has also issued format-specific guidelines such as *Guidelines for Coding Electronic Resources in Leader/06* (LC Network Development and MARC Standards Office, 2003), which elaborates on the codified fixed-length fields in the MARC record.

COOPERATIVE CATALOGING

The *MARC 21* standard describes an ideal MARC record, but catalogers seldom interact with the MARC record in its purest form. Instead, they work with online cataloging systems such as bibliographic utilities and integrated library systems that apply the standard selectively according to their own system requirements and business models. Catalogers who work with a particular utility on a regular basis may come to think of that proprietary MARC implementation as the generic MARC record. In fact, these services add or ignore fields or subfields, refine tags, provide specialized cataloging templates, and display their records in a distinctive manner.

The OCLC Online Computer Library Center publishes its own internal standards in *Bibliographic Formats and Standards* (OCLC, 2002) and further elucidates the correct application of these standards in the OCLC system through a series of technical bulletins. The Research Libraries Group provides a similar variety of guidelines for users of its RLIN21" service. In addition, the bibliographic utilities publish supplemental guidelines that clarify how to create and update records for materials in unconventional formats; an example of this is Cataloging Electronic Resources: OCLC-MARC Coding Guidelines (Weitz, 2003). For serials cataloging, CONSER publishes the *CONSER Editing Guide* (LC Serial Record Division, 1994), which provides useful guidelines specifically for serial records. As mentioned above, the manuals for CONSER and BIBCO cataloging practice provide guidance for record coding as well as record content.

| **Bibliographic utilities**: |
| Clearinghouses for shared cataloging. The OCLC and RLIN databases are national bibliographic utilities with many member libraries and other participants contributing and updating records in a centralized database. Member libraries download records from the bibliographic utilities when they copy catalog. |

LOCAL GUIDELINES

As MARC records are migrated from system to system, they seldom make the transition completely intact. Local library catalogs are configured according to different parameters for accepting or rejecting fields when a record is created or downloaded from a bibliographic utility, for validating tags and indicators, displaying records, and applying local fields for control data. Depending on the system, individual libraries may be able to further customize these features to such a degree that the same basic software functions quite differently from customer to customer.

Not all local variations to MARC records occur at the system level. The MARC format also designates a number of fields for local use. These fields are not codified in any external standard but are unique to the individual library; libraries that use local fields will necessarily have local guidelines for coding and populating these fields. Over time, libraries also develop distinctive practices for adding, enhancing, or deleting certain fields and interpreting definitions of fields and field tags to accommodate their local needs.

Many libraries began cataloging online resources before highly specific cataloging guidelines were in place to address their unique needs. As a result, catalog records for online resources often vary dramatically from library to library. We strongly advocate that libraries conform to national cataloging standards and avoid system-specific work-arounds to the greatest extent possible. This practice will ensure the most systematic cataloging over time and the greatest flexibility in moving bibliographic data among online systems.

SUMMARY

Although most cataloging standards and codes of practice are densely laden with detail, they cannot anticipate every potential variation among resources and systems. As a result, catalogers frequently encounter situations that are not clearly addressed in any existing documentation, or find that different sources contradict one another. This is particularly true in the area of online resources, which are evolving so fast that the standards and practices for cataloging them are still somewhat unsettled. The daunting array of separate cataloging codes and guidelines can be a major obstacle to the cataloger s productivity. In the following chapters, we endeavor to synthesize the many rules, standards, and guidelines that apply to online resources into a set of recommended practices for cataloging the most prevalent types of online resources while also providing a rich context for our cataloging decisions.

REFERENCES

BIBCO. 2003. *BIBCO Core Standard for Monographic Electronic Resources.* Washington, DC: Program for Cooperative Cataloging. Available:

www.loc.gov/catdir/pcc/bibco/coreelectro.html. Accessed January 27, 2005.

Hiatt, Robert M. 1989. *Library of Congress Rule Interpretations*. Washington, DC: Library of Congress Cataloging Distribution Service.

Hirons, Jean L., ed. 2002. *CONSER Cataloging Manual*. Washington, DC: Library of Congress Cataloging Distribution Service.

Hixson, Carol, David Banush, and Ana Crist n, eds. 2002. *BIBCO Participants' Manual*. Washington, DC: Program for Cooperative Cataloging. Available: www.loc.gov/catdir/pcc/bibco/bpm.pdf. Accessed January 27, 2005.

Joint Steering Committee for the Revision of AACR2. 2002. *Anglo-American Cataloguing Rules*, 2nd ed. 2002 Rev. Chicago: American Library Association.

Library of Congress Cataloging Directorate. (2003, Jan. 15) Cataloging Directorate Strategic Plan Goal 4, Group 2 : Processing Rule Analysis Group Report. Washington, DC: Library of Congress. Available: www.loc.gov/catdir/stratplan/goal4wg2report.pdf. Accessed January 27, 2005.

Library of Congress Network Development and MARC Standards Office. 1999. *MARC 21 Format for Bibliographic Data*. Washington, DC: Library of Congress Cataloging Distribution Service.

Library of Congress Network Development and MARC Standards Office. 2003. Guidelines for Coding Electronic Resources in Leader/06. Washington, DC: Library of Congress. Available: www.loc.gov/marc/ldr06guide.html. Accessed January 27, 2005.

Library of Congress Serial Record Division. 1994. *CONSER Editing Guide*. Washington, DC: Library of Congress Cataloging Distribution Service.

OCLC. 2002. *Bibliographic Formats and Standards*, 3rd ed. Dublin, OH: OCLC Online Computer Library Center.

Weitz, Jay. 2003. Cataloging Electronic Resources: OCLC-MARC Coding Guidelines. Dublin, OH: OCLC Online Computer Library Center. Available: www.oclc.org/support/documentation/worldcat/cataloging/electronicresources/. Accessed January 27, 2005.

Wilson, Mary D. 2001. Flying First Class or Economy? Classification of Electronic Titles in ARL Libraries. *Portal* 1, no. 3 (July): 225—240.

6

ANALYZING THE BIBLIOGRAPHIC STRUCTURE OF ONLINE RESOURCES

INTRODUCTION

This chapter introduces a methodology for analyzing online resources prior to cataloging. It defines basic bibliographic questions that should be answered for each resource and explains how to apply them to the cataloging process. The answers to these questions, such as the type of issuance of a resource, strongly influence the process of cataloging. A thorough understanding of these principles is key to making the best use of the following chapters.

Each cataloging chapter is based on one of the major types of issuance: monograph, serial, and integrating resource. Each chapter begins with a definition of the type of issuance under discussion. This is followed by a bibliographic analysis of a classic example (called a "Long Example") leading to a description of how to catalog the resource. The focus is on creating *MARC 21* records. *MARC 21* tagging for each example is thoroughly described, generally in the order of control fields, fixed fields, and variable fields, with the variable fields discussed in numeric order. The names of *MARC 21* fields, numerical tags, and subfields are expressed in bold text: **Title proper (245).** The contents of MARC records are expressed in fixed-width courier text:

```
245  00    D-Lib magazine ‡h [electronic
           resource].
```

After an in-depth description of a classic example, significant variations are analyzed in "Short Examples." These passages focus on the aspects of bibliographic description that are influenced by the online nature of the resources. For example, rather than addressing the title and statement of responsibility in general, the discussion will focus on how this area is coded for online resources in particular. This approach assumes a degree of familiarity with basic cataloging practice and principles. Some common cataloging topics that are not specific to electronic resources, such as subject headings and classification, are not discussed in depth.

> **Type of issuance**: The type of issuance refers to whether a resource is published as a monograph, a serial, or an integrating resource.

DEFINITION OF ONLINE RESOURCE

> **Electronic resource**: Electronic resources include online resources as well as digital resources in a physical carrier such as a CD-ROM or DVD-ROM.

Electronic resources come in many varieties. In fact, the boundaries between electronic resources and other forms of media are sometimes difficult to distinguish. For the purposes of this book, we use the definition found in the glossary of *AACR2* (Joint Steering Committee for the Revision of AACR2, 2002, Appendix D-3.):

> Material (data and/or program(s)) encoded for manipulation by a computerized device. This material may require the use of a peripheral directly connected to a computerized device (e.g., CD-ROM drive) or a connection to a computer network (e.g., the Internet).

> **Mode of access**: The method by which one gains access to the intellectual content of the resource. Online resources are electronic resources with a remote mode of access, meaning that the resource is accessed over a network rather than run on the user's own hardware.

Online resources, the topic of this book, are a subset of electronic resources. Specifically, they are electronic resources with a remote mode of access. Mode of access, as defined in *AACR2* 9.0A, refers to the method by which access is gained to the intellectual content of the resource. Resources that are issued in a physical carrier, such as a magnetic or optical disk, must be inserted into a computer in order to gain access to the contents. These items are considered direct-access resources. Resources that are stored in a way that requires access via a computer network, such as the Internet, are known as remote-access resources. This includes resources that may be accessed via Gopher, file transfer protocol (FTP), or hypertext transfer protocol (HTTP). The mode of access of a resource is important because this information is coded in the fixed field of the *MARC 21* record and determines the type of issuance and physical description of the resource.

BIBLIOGRAPHIC CHARACTERISTICS

Library of Congress Rule Interpretations (LCRI) 1.0 has some sage advice when it comes to cataloging electronic resources: "Before creating a bibliographic record, determine what is being cataloged" (Hiatt, 1989, 1.0, p.1). Unfortunately, online resources present myriad ambiguities, creating an atmosphere where answering this seemingly simple question is often daunting. Perhaps the "what" portion of this question is most problematic as online resources can be defined in many ways, depending on which characteristic of a given resource one is attempting to define. For the purposes of cataloging, the body of literature is beginning to standardize the significant characteristics that must be defined to establish bibliographic control. For online resources, the following characteristics should be defined prior to cataloging:

- significant bibliographic aspect
- type of issuance
- sources of information
- born digital versus reproduction
- **type of record** code
- **bibliographic level** code
- *MARC 21* workform

SIGNIFICANT BIBLIOGRAPHIC ASPECT

Significant bibliographic aspect: Significant bibliographic aspect refers to the granularity of the resource to be cataloged. For example, a large Web site may contain digital objects or services that could each be cataloged separately. The cataloger must determine at what level the resource will be cataloged.

The first task in cataloging online resources is determining the significant bibliographic aspect of the resource to be cataloged. This concept is also known as the granularity of the resource. The key question is whether the work that is being cataloged is part of a larger work, and if so, at what level should the work (or collective work) be cataloged. In most cases, this question will be unambiguous, as the cataloger will be working with an item that is clearly an independent bibliographic work, such as a single e-book. However, for online resources, it is not uncommon to encounter works that are a part of a larger work. An example of this might be a complex Web site that consists of academic journals, searchable databases, and multimedia files, any one of which may be cataloged as an independent entity. Once the cataloger has specified the significant bibliographic aspect of the resource, care must be taken to apply the rules of cataloging consistent with this decision. The concept of significant bibliographic aspect is discussed at length in *LCRI* 1.0.

TYPE OF ISSUANCE

Type of issuance refers to the method of publication, distribution, or reproduction of a resource. If a resource is updated, the method of updating must also be considered. There are three types of issuance: monograph, serial, and integrating resource.

Monograph: A resource that is complete in one part or a finite number of parts, such as an electronic book.

Monographs are resources that are complete in one part or intended to be complete in a finite number of parts. The most common type of online monograph is the e-book. An example of an e-book is an electronic edition of William Shakespeare's *Hamlet, Prince of Denmark* from the Project Gutenberg Web site (www.gutenberg.org).

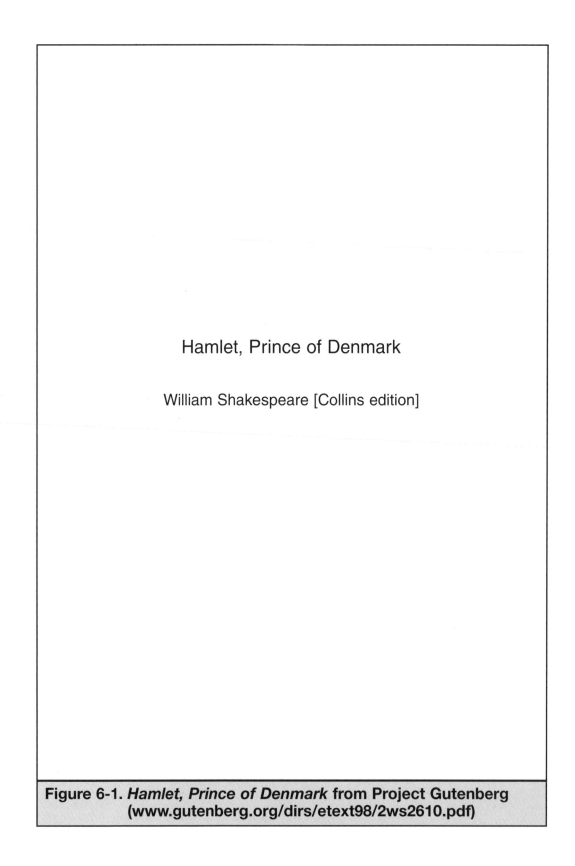

Figure 6-1. *Hamlet, Prince of Denmark* from Project Gutenberg (www.gutenberg.org/dirs/etext98/2ws2610.pdf)

Serial: a resource issued in a succession of discrete parts with no predetermined conclusion, such as a newspaper or journal. Serials are a type of continuing resource.

Integrating resource: a resource in which updates are combined into the whole and do not remain distinct, such as a Web site. Integrating resources are a type of continuing resource.

Serials are continuing resources that are issued in discrete parts, with no predetermined conclusion. The discrete parts are usually presented as new issues that are chronologically labeled. An example of a remote-access serial is the online journal *Public Library of Science: Biology* (www.plosbiology.org).

Integrating resources are continuing resources in which updates are combined into the existing resource. Currently, there are two kinds of online integrating resources, namely updating databases and updating Web sites. An example of an updating database is the Internet Movie Database (www.imdb.com).

An example of an updating Web site is Yahoo! News (http://news.yahoo.com).

The three types of issuance are defined in the *AACR2* glossary. Type of issuance as it relates to online resources is discussed in detail in *LCRI* 1.0.

SOURCES OF INFORMATION

Sources of information: The chief source of bibliographic information is the preferred part of the resource from which the cataloger should take bibliographic data; prescribed sources of information are secondary sources of bibliographic data if the preferred source does not provide the relevant data.

For online resources, the chief source of information is the resource itself. The rule of thumb is to use information that is "formally presented," including home pages and main menus. If the information is presented in varying degrees of fullness, prefer the source that provides the most complete information. If no information is available from the resource itself, then take this information from documentation or other accompanying material. The allowable sources of information for online resources are discussed in *AACR2* 9.0B.

BORN DIGITAL VERSUS REPRODUCTION

Born digital: An information resource that is originally manifested in an electronic format. The alternative is a retrospectively digitized resource, one that is scanned or copied from a pre-existing nonelectronic format.

Online resources may either be born digital (originally manifested in an electronic format) or reproductions of physical items. An example of a born-digital resource is a journal that publishes new issues online. To contrast this with a reproduction, consider the example of a rare book that has been digitized using photographic-image files to reproduce a facsimile of the printed book.

Cataloging for each of the two cases is different, so this distinction must be made before cataloging. Sometimes, it is not entirely clear if the resource itself is born digital or an electronic reproduction. For example, many online serials provide both past issues and newly published issues online. Sometimes, the past issues are presented as scanned images of the print editions, sometimes as text files that have been transcribed from the print. New issues are typically published online concurrently with the print version and thus can be considered born digital. A good rule of thumb is to assume the resource is born

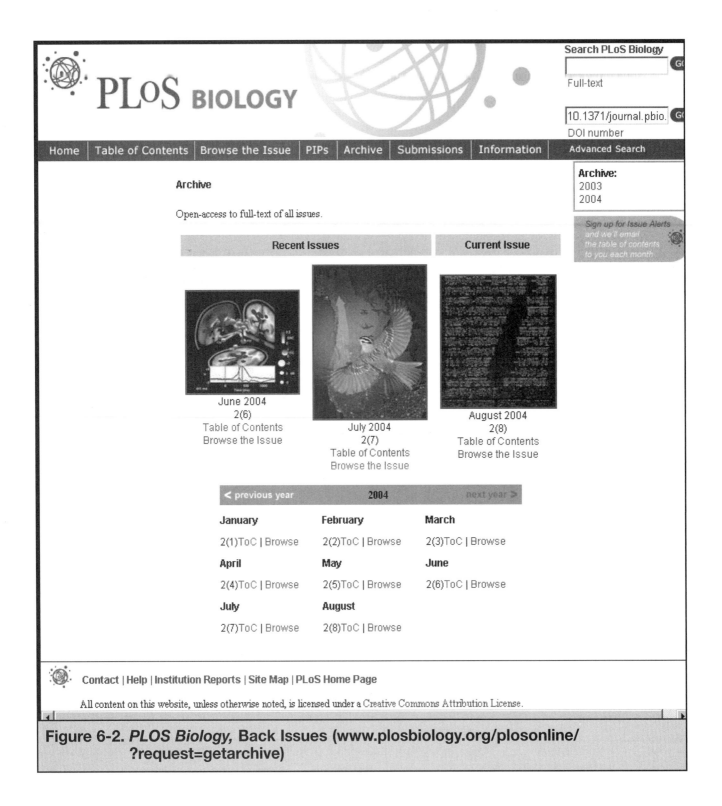

Figure 6-2. *PLOS Biology,* Back Issues (www.plosbiology.org/plosonline/ ?request=getarchive)

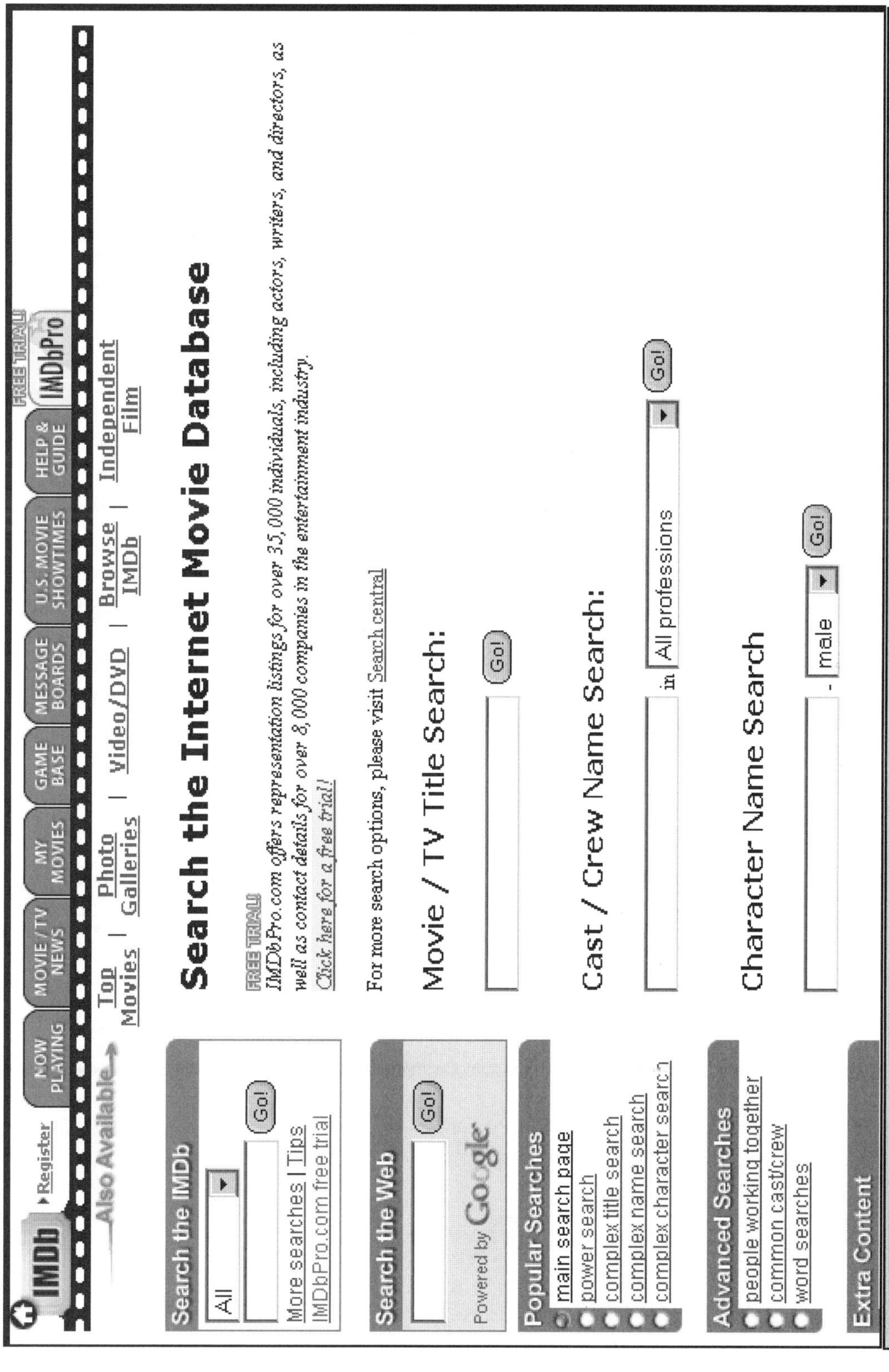

Figure 6-3. Internet Movie Database, Search Screen (www.imdb.com/search)

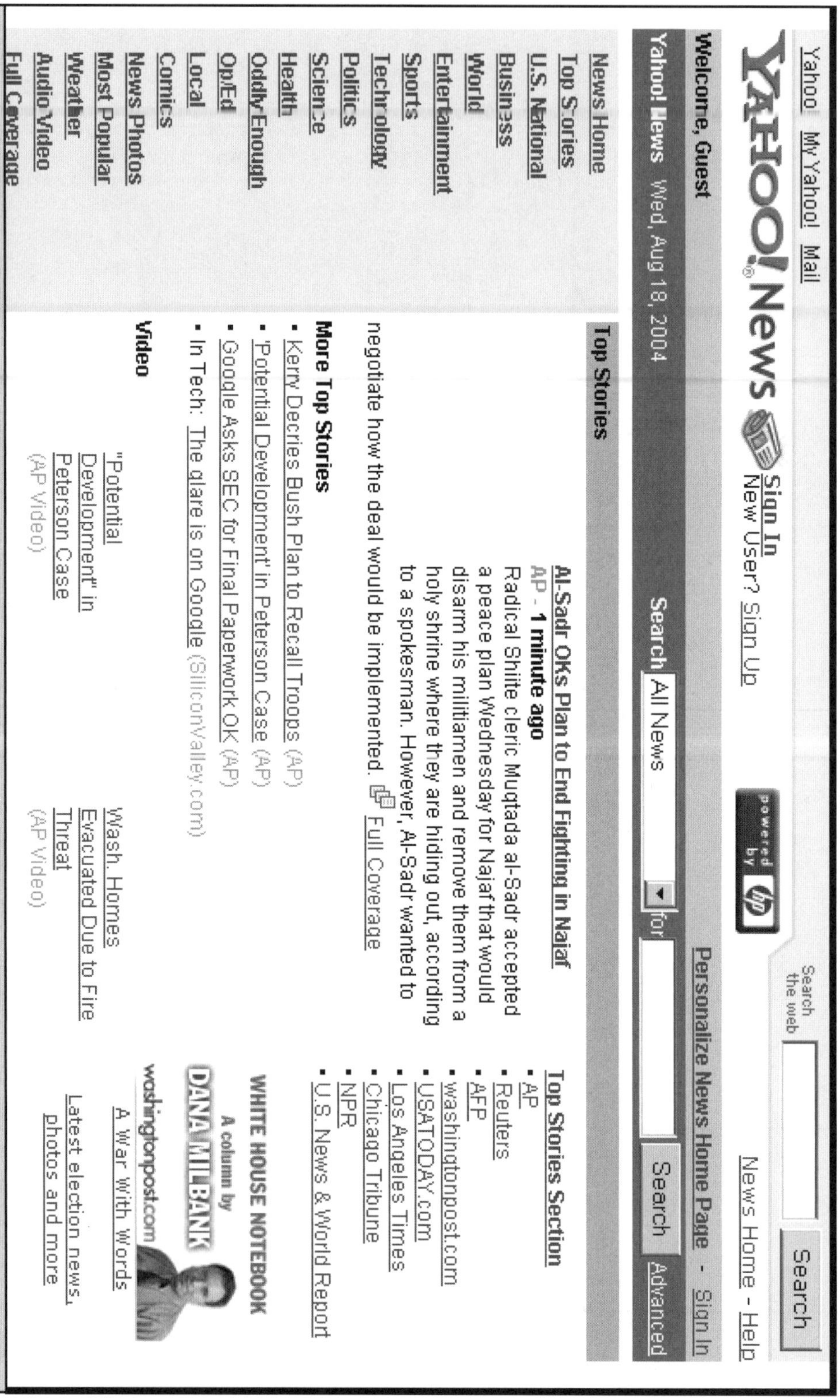

Yahoo! MyYahoo! Mail

YAHOO! News

Sign In
New User? Sign Up

powered by hp

Search
the web

News Home - Help

Personalize News Home Page - Sign In

Search | All News ▼ | for | Search | Advanced

Welcome, Guest

Yahoo! News   Wed, Aug 18, 2004

News Home
Top Stories
U.S. National
Business
World
Entertainment
Sports
Technology
Politics
Science
Health
Oddly Enough
Op/Ed
Local
Comics
News Photos
Most Popular
Weather
Audio/Video
Full Coverage

Top Stories

negotiate how the deal would be implemented. 🖶 Full Coverage

Al-Sadr OKs Plan to End Fighting in Najaf
AP - **1 minute ago**
Radical Shiite cleric Muqtada al-Sadr accepted
a peace plan Wednesday for Najaf that would
disarm his militiamen and remove them from a
holy shrine where they are hiding out, according
to a spokesman. However, Al-Sadr wanted to

More Top Stories

· Kerry Decries Bush Plan to Recall Troops (AP)
· "Potential Development" in Peterson Case (AP)
· Google Asks SEC for Final Paperwork OK (AP)
· In Tech: The glare is on Google (SiliconValley.com)

Video

"Potential
Development" in
Peterson Case
(AP Video)

Wash. Homes
Evacuated Due to Fire
Threat
(AP Video)

Top Stories Section
· AP
· Reuters
· AFP
· washingtonpost.com
· USATODAY.com
· Los Angeles Times
· Chicago Tribune
· NPR
· U.S. News & World Report

WHITE HOUSE NOTEBOOK
A column by
DANA MILBANK
washingtonpost.com
A War with Words

Latest election news,
photos and more

Figure 6-4. Yahoo!® News, Home Page (http://news.yahoo.com)

Type Code		Bibliographic Level*	MARC 21 Workform
a	Language material	a, c, d, m	Books
t	Manuscript language material	a, c, d, m	
a	Language material	b, s	Serials
g	Projected medium	a, b, c, d, m, s	Visual Materials
k	Two-dimensional nonprojected graphic	a, b, c, d, m, s	
r	Three-dimensional artifact or naturally occurring object	a, b, c, d, m, s	
o	Kits	a, b, c, d, m, s	
p	Mixed material	c, d	Mixed Materials
e	Cartographic material	a, b, c, d, m, s	Maps
f	Manuscript map	a, c, d, m	
c	Printed music	a, b, c, d, m, s	Scores
d	Manuscript music	a, c, d, m	
i	Nonmusical sound recording	a, b, c, d, m, s	Sound Recordings
j	Musical sound recording	a, b, c, d, m, s	
m	Computer file	a, b, c, d, m, s	Computer Files

Table 6-1. *MARC 21* Workforms

*Bibliographic-Level Codes

a = monographic-component part (i.e., a monograph that is part of a larger bibliographic unit)

b = serial-component part (i.e., a serial that is part of a larger bibliographic unit)

c = collection (i.e., a group of items described by a comprehensive record)

d = subunit (i.e., a portion of an archival unit)

m = monograph

s = serial

digital unless it is clear that the resource was originally a physical item and the digital version retains the look and feel of the original.

In the following chapters, most items are considered born digital. When cataloging for reproductions is discussed, *LCRI* 1.11A is applied. This rule states that for reproductions, the bibliographic information for the original item may be used for description, with a note that provides information about the reproduction and additional *MARC 21* codes for the electronic format.

TYPE OF RECORD CODE

The **Type of Record (leader/06)** code distinguishes different types of content and materials. There are 14 allowable values for this code. For electronic resources, the **Type of Record** code is determined based on the significant aspect of the content rather than on the physical form. For example, an electronic resource that is predominantly textual in nature would receive the **Type of Record** code for language material, which is code "a." This guideline applies to graphic materials, carto-graphic materials, sound, and moving-image resources, etc. There is a

Type of Record code for computer files, but this code is limited to certain kinds of electronic resources, specifically computer software, numeric data, computer-oriented multimedia, and online systems or services. Even for these classes, if a resource contains a significant aspect that causes it to fall into another type of record category, the cataloger should code for that significant aspect. Each of the next three chapters provide detailed explanations of how to determine the **Type of Record** code. For a listing of all codes, refer to the *MARC 21* manual. Further information on determining the **Type of Record** code for electronic resources is available from *LC Update No. 3 to USMARC for Bibliographic Data, 1997.*

BIBLIOGRAPHIC-LEVEL CODE

The **Bibliographic Level (leader/07)** is defined in *OCLC Bibliographic Formats and Standards* as "the relationship between the item being cataloged and its constituent parts" (OCLC, 2002, FF12). It is based on the mode of issuance of the resource. There are six allowable codes for the **Bibliographic Level** field, but the most important codes for electronic resources are the three standard modes of issuance: "m" for monograph, "s" for serial, and the forthcoming "i" for integrating resources.

MARC 21 WORKFORM

> **Workform:** The template for a particular kind of catalog record. Workforms are based on a combination of the type of record and the bibliographic level; only the correct workform will supply the necessary array of fixed fields.

There are currently eight different *MARC 21* bibliographic workforms. The workform is based on the combination of the **Type of Record** and **Bibliographic Level** codes. The most common workforms are the books workform, the serials workform, and the computer files workform. Additional workforms are available for visual materials, mixed materials, maps, scores, and sound recordings. At the time of this writing the workform for integrating resources is not yet available. Table 6-1 demonstrates the combinations that produce the various workforms. The table should be read from left to right following the cataloger's work flow as he or she examines the resource.

After the workform has been selected, the cataloger can perform original cataloging. Alternately, if the cataloger is performing copy cataloging, understanding how to evaluate an online resource can help the cataloger select high-quality records.

INFORMATION ABOUT OUR EXAMPLES

The examples in the following chapters serve as an introduction to descriptive cataloging for online resources. Each chapter begins with a basic description of the relevant type of issuance, followed by an in-depth look at a real online resource. This is followed by shorter examples that discuss how to catalog resources with characteristics that are common in online resources. The focus of the short examples is on how the electronic and online aspects of each resource are addressed in catalog records. For the examples, we selected established Web sites that we expect to exist in a familiar and stable format for some time to come. With only a few exceptions, the Web sites used as examples are freely available and no authentication or registration is required for access. Thus, anyone reading this book can go to the Web site in a given example to evaluate it while reading along. It is in the nature of online resources to change over time, so it is impossible to ensure that important bibliographic characteristics will not change, but we tried to choose examples that would minimize this problem.

The examples are based on records from OCLC that have been updated to meet the most recent cataloging rules and further edited for clarity. The OCLC *MARC 21* fixed-field display is the format familiar to the greatest number of librarians, so it has been retained. The underlying coding of *MARC 21* fields does not vary from system to system, so the information on how to code the records is valid regardless of the system or display used.

SUMMARY

Bibliographic analysis is the first step in cataloging. This universal process is also relevant when cataloging online resources. Understanding the significant bibliographic characteristics of a resource is essential for conducting original cataloging and assists in the identification of high-quality bibliographic records for copy cataloging. Even if your library does not use traditional cataloging, understanding the nature and characteristics of online resources can assist in organizing them under any conditions.

REFERENCES

Hiatt, Robert M. 1989. *Library of Congress Rule Interpretations.* Washington, DC: Library of Congress Cataloging Distribution Service.

Hirons, Jean L., ed. 2002. *CONSER Cataloging Manual.* Washington, DC: Library of Congress Cataloging Distribution Service.

Joint Steering Committee for the Revision of AACR2. 2002. *Anglo-American Cataloguing Rules, 2nd ed., 2002 rev.* Chicago: American Library Association.

Library of Congress Network Development and MARC Standards Office. 1999. *MARC 21 Format for Bibliographic Data.* Washington, DC: Library of Congress Cataloging Distribution Service.

Library of Congress Serial Record Division. 1994. *CONSER Editing Guide.* Washington, DC: Library of Congress Cataloging Distribution Service.

OCLC. 2002. *OCLC Bibliographic Formats and Standards*, 3rd ed. Dublin, OH: OCLC Online Computer Library Center.

7 ONLINE MONOGRAPHS: E-BOOKS AND MANUSCRIPTS

INTRODUCTION

Monographs are resources that are complete in one part or intended to be complete in a finite number of parts. The category of monographs encompasses a wide range of electronic resources, including e-books, electronic theses and dissertations, and digitized archival resources.

The majority of online monographs could be described as e-books: self-contained language resources that are paginated much like books and do not change over time. Online monographs tend to be cataloged on the *MARC 21* book workform. It may be possible for an online resource to be cataloged on a computer-file workform, but such examples are rare. Resources that meet the criteria for the computer-file workform, such as online systems or services, tend to be Web sites or online databases, which are typically cataloged as integrating resources. Almost any Web site is updated over time, and thus meets the definition of an integrating resource. Therefore, the examples in this chapter are self-contained, static, language resources cataloged in the *MARC 21* book workform.

In order to provide an overview of cataloging monographs, we are going to use a born-digital e-book as the first example. After describing how to catalog an e-book in depth, we will provide examples of other kinds of electronic monographs and show how to catalog them. Figures 7-2, 7-4, and 7-6 show the full *MARC 21* records.

LONG EXAMPLE: BORN-DIGITAL MONOGRAPH

BIBLIOGRAPHIC CHARACTERISTICS

Electronic book or e-book is a term that has taken on a variety of different meanings depending on the context. E-book can refer to a certain

E-book: This term can refer to many different things, including a certain kind of content, a method of delivery, even specific hardware or software. This book uses the term e-book to refer to monographic electronic resources that are predominantly textual in nature.

```
Project Gutenberg's The Wisdom of Father Brown, by G. K. Chesterton
#3 in our series by G. K. Chesterton

Copyright laws are changing all over the world. Be sure to check the
copyright laws for your country before downloading or redistributing
this or any other Project Gutenberg eBook.

This header should be the first thing seen when viewing this Project
Gutenberg file.  Please do not remove it.  Do not change or edit the
header without written permission.

Please read the "legal small print," and other information about the
eBook and Project Gutenberg at the bottom of this file.  Included is
important information about your specific rights and restrictions in
how the file may be used.  You can also find out about how to make a
donation to Project Gutenberg, and how to get involved.


**Welcome To The World of Free Plain Vanilla Electronic Texts**

**eBooks Readable By Both Humans and By Computers, Since 1971**

*****These eBooks Were Prepared By Thousands of Volunteers!*****


Title: The Wisdom of Father Brown

Author: G. K. Chesterton

Release Date: February, 1995 [EBook #223]
[This file was last updated on July 7, 2004]

Edition: 11

Language: English

Character set encoding: ASCII

*** START OF THE PROJECT GUTENBERG EBOOK THE WISDOM OF FATHER BROWN ***
```

Figure 7-1. *The Wisdom of Father Brown,* ASCII Text Version (www.gutenberg.org/dirs/etext95/wifrb11.txt)

kind of content, a method of delivery, even specific hardware or software. For the purposes of this chapter, an e-book is defined as a monographic electronic resource that is predominantly textual in nature. We will use a free e-book version of *The Wisdom of Father Brown,* available from Project Gutenberg, as our primary example (see Figure 7-1). To begin cataloging, the cataloger must examine the resource for cataloging purposes. This means the cataloger must open or otherwise process the resource to view it and gather bibliographic information from the chief source. In this example, the cataloger views the e-book by opening a browser to the URL www.gutenberg.org/dirs/ etext95/wifrbll.txt. Doing so displays the e-book as a single, large text file such that the entire book is displayed at once. The scroll bar on the right side of the browser window is used to move forward through the book. There are no page numbers, illustrations, menus, or other navigation tools within the e-book itself. The beginning of this e-book contains the basic bibliographic information about the book, including the title, author, copyright information, and information about the production of the e-book.

Significant bibliographic aspect: The entire work of *The Wisdom of Father Brown* resides in a single ASCII text file.

Type of issuance: This resource is self-contained and complete in one part. It is a monograph.

Sources of information: The chief source of information is the resource itself, preferring any part of the resource that provides the most complete information. In this case, information may be taken from any part of the text file. Most of the relevant bibliographic information is at the beginning of the file. Some relevant bibliographic information can be taken from the publisher's Web site.

Reproduction or born digital: This is a born-digital resource. Although this work was originally published in print, this electronic version is not a reproduction of a print work. It is a new publication in an electronic medium.

Type of Record code: Because this is a predominantly textual resource, the type code is a for language material.

Bibliographic Level code: Because this is a monographic resource, the bibliographic level is m.

MARC 21 workform: Books.

CODING THE *MARC 21* RECORD FOR A BORN-DIGITAL MONOGRAPH

Leaders

Textual e-books have the **Type of Record (leader/06)** coded a for language material and **Bibliographic Level (leader/07)** coded m for monograph.

The **Type of Control (leader/08)** is left blank, because this field is used only for archival resources.

The **Encoding Level (leader/17)** is I to indicate full-level cataloging. This is an OCLC code rather than a *MARC 21* code, and indicates that the record meets the requirement for second-level description according to *AACR2* 1.0D2.

The **Descriptive Cataloging Form (leader/18)** is coded a, indicating that description is based on the rules of *AACR2*.

008

The **Type of Date (008/06)** is s, indicating that a single date is used. Consequently, only the **Beginning Date (008/07-10)** field is used for the publication date, in this case 2002.

The **Country of Publication (008/15-17)** is ilu, which is the *MARC 21* country code for Illinois.

Both the **Beginning Date** and **Country of Publication** are based on the information from the **Publication, Distribution, Etc. (260)** field.

Illustrations (008/18-21) is left blank because this resource does not have any illustrations.

Target Audience (008/22) is left blank. This is an optional field that tends to be used primarily for juvenile materials.

Form of Item (008/23) is s, indicating that this is an electronic resource.

Nature of Contents (008/24-27) is left blank. This field is used for specific types of resources (e.g., bibliographies or dictionaries) and is not used for a narrative work of fiction.

Government Publication (008/28) is blank because this is not a government publication.

Conference Publication (008/29) is 0, indicating this is not a conference publication.

Festschrift (008/30) is 0, indicating this is not a festschrift.

Index (008/31) is 0, indicating the resource does not contain an index to its own contents.

Literary Form (008/33) is 1, indicating this is a work of fiction.

Biography (008/34) is blank, indicating that the resource does not contain biographical materials

006

Because the **Type of Record** code a in the leader reflects the *textual* nature of e-books, additional fixed fields must be added to reflect their electronic nature, specifically an **Additional Material Characteristics (006)** field and a **Physical Description (007)** field.

In the **Additional Material Characteristics (006)** field, the character in the first position determines the content in the rest of the positions. Therefore, the first character, known as the **Form of Material (006/00)**, is m, indicating that this resource is a computer file.

The **006** for computer files has three data elements: **Target Audience**, **Type of Computer File**, and **Government Publication**.

Target Audience (006/05) is left blank because this is not a juvenile resource.

Type of Computer File (006/09) is d, indicating that this resource is a document.

Government Publication (006/11) is blank because the resource is not a government publication.

007

The **Physical Description (007)** field is also designed so that the character in the first position determines the content in the rest of the positions. The first character, known as the **Category of Material (007/00)**, is c for computer file.

Specific Material Designation (007/01) is r, indicating that this is a remote-access resource.

Color (007/03) is b, indicating that this is a black-and-white resource.

Dimensions (007/04) is n, which indicates that this code is not applicable. This is the appropriate code for all remote-access resources.

The remaining fields are optional: **Sound (007/05)**, **Image bit depth (007/06–08)**, **File Formats (007/09)**, **Quality Assurance Targets (007/20)**, **Antecedent/Source (007/11)**, **Level of Compression (007/12)**, and **Reformatting Quality (007/13)**.

General material designation (GMD). *AACR2* defines GMD as the term indicating a broad class of material to which an item belongs, such as a sound recording or electronic resource. The list of prescribed GMD terms is in rule 1.1C.

Variable Fields

MARC 21 records for e-books include the descriptive fields that are created for print monographs plus additional fields and subfields to reflect their electronic nature. Some differences stand out in particular. For remote electronic resources, the general material designation [electronic resource] is placed in the **Title Proper (245)**, subfield **h** (*AACR2* 1.1C). Remote electronic resources do not have a **Physical Description (300)** field (*AACR2* 9.5). Certain note fields are required for electronic resources (*AACR2* 9.7). These are nature and scope note, systems-requirements note, mode-of-access note, source-of-title proper note, and item-described note.

The source of title proper note can be combined with the item described note. The **Electronic Location and Access (856)** field contains the URL or other type of location identifier. Furthermore, the nature of remote electronic resources in general provides challenges for coding some of the common variable fields. These will be discussed in turn.

Number and Code Fields (01X-04X)

The **Cataloging Source (040)** is not coded manually; it is added automatically by the cataloging utility.

The **Geographic Area Code (043)** is used for enhanced subject access to names of geographical areas. This field is used when a geographic name is used in a subject-access field (**6XX**). The code comes from the "MARC Code List for Geographic Areas" (LC Network Development and MARC Standards Office, 2003).

```
040   MNJ ‡c MNJ ‡d OCLCQ
043   e-uk-en
```

Classification and Call Number Fields (05X-08X)

This example has two classification fields, a **Dewey Decimal Call Number (082)** and a **Locally Assigned LC-type Call Number (090)**. For remote electronic resources, these fields serve more as subject classifications than call numbers. It is essentially impossible for them to serve as a physical item–location device, that is, a call number, because remote electronic resources do not materially exist. Still, subject classification is a useful tool in retrieval: classification numbers help co-locate similar items in online catalogs and may also be used for deriving other user tools, such as browsable subject lists.

```
082   04    823/.912 ‡2 20
090         PR4453.C4 ‡b W57 2002
```

Main Entry Fields (1XX)

The author, G. K. Chesterton, is the main entry of this work. His name, in the authorized form according to his record in the National Authority File, is placed in the **Main Entry-Personal Name (100)** field.

```
100  1_ Chesterton, G. K. ‡q (Gilbert
         Keith),  ‡d 1874-1936.
```

Title and Title-Related Fields (20X-24X)

The title of the book is placed in the **Title Statement (245)** subfield **a**.

The first indicator 1 specifies that the title is an added entry.

The second indicator 4 specifies that there are four nonfiling characters in subfield **a**.

The general material designation [electronic resource] is placed in the subfield **h** according to *AACR2* 1.1C.

The author's name, in this case transcribed from the work itself, is placed in the subfield **c**.

```
245  14 The wisdom of Father Brown ‡h
         [electronic resource] / ‡c G.K.
         Chesterton.
```

Edition, Imprint, Etc. Fields (250-270)

Edition information from the chief source is placed in the **Edition Statement (250)**.

The file characteristics of the resource are placed in the **Computer File Characteristics (256)** field *(AACR2 9.3B1)*. The Library of Congress omits this field, *(LCRI 9.3B1)*. Chapter 9 of *AACR2* states that all remote electronic resources are considered to be published.

Publication information is placed in the **Publication, Distribution, Etc. (260)** field. The place of publication is in subfield **a**. This information is placed in brackets because it does not come from the chief source, but instead from the publisher's Web site.

The publisher's name is placed in subfield **b**, and the date of publication in subfield **c**.

```
250     Ed. 11.
256     Electronic data.
260     [Urbana, Ill.] : ‡b Project
        Gutenberg, ‡c [2002]
```

Physical Description, Etc. Fields (3XX)

According to *AACR2* 9.5, electronic resources that are only available by remote access do not receive a physical description.

Series Statement Fields (4XX)

Series statements for electronic resources may be taken from information issued by the publisher (*AACR2* 9.0B2). Therefore, such information may be taken from a source other than the resource itself, such as a publisher Web site.

In this example, the series statement has been taken from the resource itself, the second line of the text file. It has been transcribed to the **Series Statement (490)**. The 0 in the first indicator signifies that the series is not traced and is not an added entry.

The volume number has been placed in the volume/sequential designation, subfield **v**.

A check of the National Authority File indicates that the series has not been established. In this case, the treatment of the series statement is an individual cataloging decision that is not specifically related to the electronic nature of this resource.

```
490  0_  Series by G.K. Chesterton ; ‡v
             no. 3
```

Note Fields: Part 1 (50X-53X)

The order of notes according to *AACR2* does not match perfectly the order of the appropriate *MARC 21* fields. Various guidelines, utilities, and ILS's provide conflicting information. For the sake of clarity, the notes fields are listed in the numerical order of *MARC 21* tags.

Chapter 9 of *AACR2* prescribes many notes for electronic resources. The source of the title proper is provided in a **General Note (500)** (*AACR2* 9.1B2 and 9.7B3).

```
500      Title from head of table of con-
             tents.
```

An edition statement is provided in a **General Note (500)** (*AACR2* 9.2B1).

```
500      This corrected edition was made
             available in November, 2002.
```

A note relating to the resource's edition and history, in this case, the release date, is provided in a **General Note (500)** (*AACR2* 9.7B7).

```
500        "Release date: February, 1995,
           Etext #223."
```

Another note relating to the resource's edition and history, describing the work's original publication date, is provided in a **General Note (500)**.

```
500        Originally published in 1914.
```

The table of contents are provided in a **Contents Note (505)** (*AACR2* 9.7B18). This note is optional.

```
505  00 ‡t The absence of Mr Glass -- ‡t
        The paradise of thieves -- ‡t
        The duel of Dr Hirsch -- ‡t The
        man in the passage -- ‡t The
        mistake of the machine -- ‡t
        The head of Caesar -- ‡t The
        purple wig -- ‡t The perishing
        of the Pendragons -- ‡t The god
        of the gongs -- ‡t The salad of
        Colonel Cray -- ‡t The strange
        crime of John Boulnois -- ‡t
        The fairy tale of Father Brown.
```

The type and extent of resource is provided in a **Type of Computer File or Data Note (516)** (*AACR2* 9.7B8). Although this note is not mandatory, the rule states that this information should be included if it is considered important and is not contained elsewhere in the description.

```
516        Text (electronic book).
```

A summary of the content is provided in a **Summary (520)** note (*AACR2* 9.7B17). This is an optional note.

```
520        The second collection of Father
           Brown stories. A dozen detec-
           tive stories featuring the
           seemingly naive Essex priest.
```

The date on which the resource was viewed for cataloging is placed in a **General Note (500)** (*AACR2* 9.7B22). Known as the "Item described" note, this note is mandatory.

```
500        Description based on contents
           viewed April 22, 2004.
```

Note Fields: Part 2 (53X-58X)

The mode of access is provided in a **System Details (538)** note (*AACR2 9.7B1c*). The system requirements are provided in a **System Details (538)** note (*AACR2 9.7B1b*).

The cataloger includes an additional **System Details (538)** note to describe system requirements for the version of the resource in the ZIP format.

```
538       Mode of access: World Wide Web
          or anonymous FTP.
538       System requirements: Internet
          access; web browser or FTP
          client.
538       Additional system requirements
          for zip file: computer; decom-
          pression utility.
```

Subject Access Fields (6XX)

Subject analysis is a complex practice that requires training, skill, and judgment. With regards to electronic monographs, the *BIBCO Core Record Standard for Monographic Electronic Resources* states that the cataloger should "assign a complement of headings that provides access to the primary/essential subject and/or form of the work" (BIBCO, 2003).

As in works in any other format, subject headings should be based on the subject content of the resource. This resource is given the following **Subject Added Entries**: one **Corporate Name (610)**, two **Topical Terms (650)**, and **Geographic Name (651)**.

```
650  _0   Brown, Father (Fictitious char-
          acter) ‡v Fiction.
610  20   Catholic Church. ‡z England ‡x
          Clergy ‡v Fiction.
650  _0   Priests ‡z England ‡v Fiction.
651  _0   England ‡v Fiction.
```

BIBCO also encourages the addition of entries for the form or genre of the resource. This record has two entries for **Index Term-Genre/Form (655)**. For this field, the appropriate genre term is coded in subfield **a** and the source for that term is coded in subfield **2**. The first term, Mystery fiction, is a genre term from the *Guidelines on Subject Access to Individual Works of Fiction, Drama, Etc.* (Subcommittee on the Revision of the Guidelines., et al., 2000). The second term, `Electronic books`, designates the form and is a local term.

```
655  _7   Mystery fiction. ǂ2 gsafd
655  _7   Electronic books. ǂ2 local
```

Added Entry Fields (70X-75X)

A **Corporate Name Added Entry (710)** is created for the publisher and distributor, `Project Gutenberg` (*AACR2* 21.30E1).
   The first indicator of 2 indicates that the name is in direct order.

```
710  2_  Project Gutenberg.
```

Series Added Entry Fields (80X-830)

In this case, the series does not require an added entry. The series is transcribed into the **Series Statement (490)**.

Holdings, Location, Alternate Graphs, etc. Fields (841-88X)

This e-book is available from a Web site and from a file transfer protocol (FTP) site. As a result, the *MARC 21* record for this resource has two fields for **Electronic Location and Access (856)**.
   The first **856** is for the text file available from a Web site. The first indicator is 4, indicating that the access method is the hypertext transfer protocol (HTTP), and the second indicator is 0, indicating that the address in the field is for the resource itself.
   The uniform resource identifier is placed in subfield **u**.

```
856  40  ǂu http://www.gutenberg.org/dirs/
             etext95/wifrb11.txt
```

The second **856** is for the text file available using the file transfer protocol (FTP).
   The first indicator is 1, indicating that the access method is FTP. The second indicator is 0, indicating that the address in the field is for the resource itself.
   The FTP host name is placed in the subfield **a**.
   The file path to the resource is placed in subfield **d**.
   The file name (called the electronic name in the *MARC 21* manual) is placed in the subfield **f**.
   The FTP logon name is placed in the subfield **l**.
   The uniform resource identifier is placed in the subfield **u**.

The password information is placed in subfield **z**.

```
856  10 ‡z Password, if requested, is
        your e-mail address. ‡u
        ftp://sailor.gutenberg.org/pub/g
        utenberg/etext95/wifrb11.txt ‡a
        sailor.gutenberg.org ‡d
        /pub/gutenberg/etext95 ‡f
        wifrb11.txt ‡l anonymous
```

Figure 7-2 shows the complete record for this example.

Type: a	ELvl: I	Srce: d	Audn:	Ctrl:	Lang:	eng
BLvl: m	Form: s	Conf: 0	Biog:	MRec:	Ctry:	ilu
	Cont:	GPub:	LitF: 1	Indx: 0		
Desc: a	Ills:	Fest: 0	DtSt: s	Dates:	2002,	

```
006          m     d
007          c ‡b r ‡d b ‡e n
040          MNJ ‡c MNJ ‡d OCLCQ
043          e-uk-en
082    04    823/.912 ‡2 20
090          PR4453.C4 ‡b W57 2002
100    1_    Chesterton, G. K. ‡q (Gilbert Keith),
             ‡d 1874-1936.
245    14    The wisdom of Father Brown ‡h [elec-
             tronic resource] / ‡c G.K.
             Chesterton.
250          Ed. 11.
256          Electronic data.
260          [Urbana, Ill.] : ‡b Project
             Gutenberg, ‡c [2002]
490    0_    Series by G.K. Chesterton ; ‡v no. 3
500          Title from head of table of contents.
500          "Release date: February, 1995, Etext
             #223."
500          This corrected edition was made
             available in November, 2002.
500          Originally published in 1914.
500          Description based on contents viewed
             April 22, 2004.
505    00    ‡t The absence of Mr Glass -- ‡t The
             paradise of thieves -- ‡t The duel
             of Dr Hirsch -- ‡t The man in the
             passage -- ‡t The mistake of the
             machine -- ‡t The head of Caesar --
```

Figure 7-2. Full _MARC 21_ Record for a Born-Digital Monograph

		‡t The purple wig -- ‡t The perishing of the Pendragons -- ‡t The god of the gongs -- ‡t The salad of Colonel Cray -- ‡t The strange crime of John Boulnois -- ‡t The fairy tale of Father Brown.
516		Text (electronic book).
520		The second collection of Father Brown stories. A dozen detective stories featuring the seemingly naive Essex priest.
538		Mode of access: World Wide Web or anonymous FTP.
538		System requirements: Internet access; web browser or FTP client.
538		Additional system requirements for zip file: computer; decompression utility.
650	_0	Brown, Father (Fictitious character) ‡v Fiction.
610	20	Catholic Church. ‡z England ‡x Clergy ‡v Fiction.
650	_0	Priests ‡z England ‡v Fiction.
651	_0	England ‡v Fiction.
655	_7	Mystery fiction. ‡2 gsafd
655	_7	Electronic books. ‡2 local
710	2_	Project Gutenberg.
856	40	‡u http://www.gutenberg.org/etext95/ wifrb11.txt
856	10	‡z Password, if requested, is your e-mail address. ‡u ftp://sailor .gutenberg.org/pub/gutenberg/etext95/w ifrb11.txt ‡a sailor.gutenberg.org ‡d /pub/gutenberg/etext95 ‡f wifrb11.txt ‡l anonymous

Figure 7-2. (continued)

Science and Human Rights

NATIONAL ACADEMY OF SCIENCES
Committee on Human Rights

Science and Human Rights

Carol Corillon, Editor

NATIONAL ACADEMY PRESS
Washington, D.C.   1988

**Figure 7-3. *Science and Human Rights*, Title Page
(http://print.nap.edu/pdf/NI000207/pdf_image/R1.pdf)**

SHORT EXAMPLE: ONLINE REPRODUCTION

A true online reproduction will maintain the visual qualities of the original resource. Often, reproductions are image files that have been created using a scanning process. Such reproductions will often contain the identical bibliographic information of the original print resource, such as the publication information. In such a case, *LCRI* 1.11A can be applied. This allows the bibliographic information for the original resource to be used with the addition of a **Reproduction Note (533)**.

BIBLIOGRAPHIC CHARACTERISTICS

Reproduction Note (533): This note may be used for online resources that are visual reproductions of physical materials. Such reproductions are usually image files created from scans that maintain the appearance of the original material.

In this example, we have a digitized version of the book *Science and Human Rights*. This e-book is available for free from the National Academies Press Web site at www.nap.edu/books/NI000207/html/. The introductory page has a hyperlinked table of contents. Clicking on one of the links, such as "Front Matter," opens an application within the Web browser that displays one page at a time and provides tools for navigating the book. The user can select a page number, go back to the table of contents, print the page, skip ahead one page or one chapter, or search the full text of the book. The title page of the book indicates that the book was published in 1988, prior to the development of the World Wide Web. The book appears to be scanned images of a printed text. At the bottom of the Web page is a link to more information about the OpenBook format. The first page of this e-book is a scanned image of the title page from the printed book.

Significant bibliographic aspect: The e-book *Science and Human Rights* (see Figure 7-3). The work is contained on a Web site at the URL www.nap.edu/books/NI000207/html/.

Type of issuance: This resource is self-contained and complete in one part. It is a monograph.

Source of information: The chief source of information is the resource itself, especially the title page. Other relevant information is available on the publisher's Web site.

Reproduction or born digital: This resource maintains the look and feel of the print resource. For example, the title page is a direct reproduction of the print and the pagination is maintained. It is a reproduction.

Type of Record code: The code is a for language material.

Bibliographic Level code: The code is m for monograph.

MARC 21 work form: Books.

CODING THE *MARC 21* RECORD FOR AN ONLINE REPRODUCTION

Because this electronic resource is a reproduction, it can be cataloged according to *LCRI* 1.11A. This rule allows the cataloger to use the bibliographic information for the original printed book, plus a general material designation for the electronic version, a note relating the details of the electronic version of the resource, a physical-description fixed field applicable to the reproduction, and an electronic location and access field. The bibliographic information for the original work is provided for the following areas:

- title and statement of responsibility
- edition
- material (or type of publication) specific details
- publication, distribution, etc.
- physical description
- series

The general material designation of [electronic resource] is added to the **Title Proper (245)**.

```
245  00 Science and human rights ‡h
        [electronic resource] / ‡c
        Carol Corillon, editor.
```

A **Reproduction Note (533)** is created to provide details relating to the reproduction.

The type of reproduction, in this case Electronic reproduction, is placed in a subfield **a**.

The place of reproduction is placed in a subfield **b**.

The agency responsible for reproduction is placed in subfield **c**.

Two notes about reproduction, subfield **n**, are provided to describe the mode of access and system requirements.

A fixed-length data elements of reproduction field, subfield **7**, provides information about the reproduction.

These data elements correspond to the **Fixed-length Data Elements (008)** field. The first element, at position 0, is equivalent to the **Type of Date/Publication Status (008/06)** and is coded s for single date.

Positions 1 to 4 represent **Date 1 (008/07-10)**, and are coded uuuu to indicate that the reproduction date is unknown.

Positions 5 to 8 represent **Date 2 (008/11-14)**, and are coded #### because only the first date is relevant for a monographic resource.

Positions 9 to 11 represent **Place of Publication, Production, or Execution (008/15-17)**, and are coded dcu, the *MARC 21* code for Washington, D.C.

Position 11 represents **Frequency** (continuing resources **008/18**). It is coded n indicating that the **Frequency** field is not applicable in this case.

Position 12 represents **Regularity** (continuing resources **008/19**). It is coded #, indicating that the **Regularity** field is not applicable in this case.

Position 13 represents **Form of item (008/23)**, and is coded s, indicating that the reproduction is an electronic resource.

```
533       Electronic reproduction. ‡b
          Washington, D.C. : ‡c National
          Academies Press. ‡n Mode of
          access: World Wide Web. ‡n
          System requirements: Adobe
          Acrobat reader. ‡7
          suuuu####dcun#s
```

A **Physical Description (007)** field is added for the reproduction.

The **Category of Material (007/00)** is c for computer file.

The **Specific Material Designation** is r for remote-access resource.

Color (007/03) is b, indicating that this is a black-and-white resource.

Dimensions (007/04) is n because dimensions are not applicable to remote-access resources.

Image bit depth (007/06-08) is relevant in this case because the resource consists of image files. However, this value is unknown, so three fill characters, | | |, are used.

```
007       c ‡b r ‡d b ‡e n ‡g | | |
```

The URL is placed in an **Electronic Location and Access (856)** field. The first indicator is 4, indicating that the access method is HTTP, and the second indicator is 0, indicating that the URL is to the resource itself.

```
856  40 ‡u http://www.nap.edu/books
        /NI000207/html/
```

Figure 7-4 is the full *MARC 21* record for an online reproduction.

```
Type: a   ELvl: I   Srce: d   Audn:      Ctrl:       Lang: eng
BLvl: m   Form: s   Conf: 1   Biog:      MRec:       Ctry: dcu
          Cont:     GPub: f   LitF: 0    Indx: 0
Desc: a   Ills:     Fest: 0   DtSt: s    Dates:   1988,

      006             m    d
      007             c ‡b r ‡d b ‡e n ‡g |||
      040             NSF ‡c NSF ‡d PAM ‡d OCL
      019             23354268
      043             n-us---
      090             JC571 ‡b .S4 1988
      245    00       Science and human rights ‡h [elec-
                      tronic resource] / ‡c Carol Corillon,
                      editor.
      260             Washington, D.C. : ‡b National Academy
                      Press : ‡b [Available from [the]
                      Committee on Human Rights], ‡c 1988.
      265             Committee on Human Rights, National
                      Academy of Sciences, 2101
                      Constitution Ave., N.W., Washington,
                      D.C. 20418
      300             Xiii, 92 p. ; ‡c 23 cm.
                      At head of title page: National
                      Academy of Sciences, Committee on
                      Human Rights.
      500             Based on a symposium held at the
                      National Academy of Sciences,
                      Washington, D.C., April 27, 1987.
      500             Committee chairman: Eliot Stellar.
      533             Electronic reproduction. ‡b
                      Washington, D.C. : ‡c National
                      Academies Press. ‡n Mode of access:
                      World Wide Web. ‡n System require-
                      ments: Adobe Acrobat reader. ‡7
                      suuuu####dcun#s
      650    _0       Civil rights ‡v Congresses.
      650    _0       Scientists ‡x Civil rights ‡v
                      Congresses.
      650    _2       Ethics, Medical ‡z United States ‡x
                      Congresses.
      650    _2       Human Rights ‡z United States ‡x
                      Congresses.
```

Figure 7-4. Full *MARC 21* Record for an Online Reproduction

```
700   1_   Corillon, Carol.
700   1_   Stellar, Eliot, ‡d 1919-
710   2_   National Academy of Sciences (U.S.).
           ‡b Committee on Human Rights.
856   40   ‡u http://www.nap.edu/books/NI000207/
           html/
```

Figure 7-4. (continued)

SHORT EXAMPLE: RESOURCES THAT ARE TRADITIONALLY UNPUBLISHED

> **Manuscripts**: *AACR2* defines manuscripts as writings made by hand, typescripts, inscriptions, etc. Print manuscripts are generally not published, but all remote-access resources are considered to be published according to *AACR2* 9.4B2.

Print manuscript resources are traditionally assigned the **Type of Record (leader/06)** code t for manuscript language materials. These are resources, such as personal letters or dissertations, that are not considered to be published. However, *AACR2* 9.4B2 states that all remote-access resources are considered to be published. Besides affecting the **Type of Record** code, this rule means that the publication information is included in *MARC 21* records for online manuscript materials. This information is included in the **Publication, Distribution, Etc. (260)** field.

BIBLIOGRAPHIC CHARACTERISTICS

In this example, we have a dissertation titled *Operators at the Borders: The Hero as Change Agent in Border Literature* (Figure 7-5). This electronic dissertation is available for free from the Texas A&M Web site at http://txspace.tamu.edu/handle/1969/550. The introductory page has bibliographic information about the dissertation and links to the file that contains the actual dissertation. Cataloging an electronic dissertation has only minor differences from cataloging a general e-book. The differences stem from special cataloging rules for theses and dissertations. The dissertation is predominantly textual and is in the PDF format; it was born digital.

Significant bibliographic aspect: The ETD *Operators at the Borders: The Hero as Change Agent in Border Literature*, which is located at the URL http://txspace.tamu.edu/handle/1969/550.

Type of issuance: This resource is self-contained and complete in one part. It is a monograph.

Source of information: The ETD itself and the Texas A&M Web site.

Reproduction or born digital: This is a born-digital resource. It does not exist in any other format.

OPERATORS AT THE BORDERS: THE HERO AS CHANGE AGENT
IN BORDER LITERATURE

A Dissertation

by

JONATHAN HANDELMAN

Submitted to the Office of Graduate Studies of
Texas A&M University
in partial fulfillment of the requirements for the degree of

DOCTOR OF PHILOSOPHY

May 2003

Major Subject: English

Figure 7-5. *Operators at the Borders: The Hero as Change Agent in Border Literature* Title Page (http://txspace.tamu.edu/handle/1969/550)

Type of Record code: The code is a for language material.
Bibliographic Level code: The code is m for monograph.
MARC 21 work form: Books.

CODING THE *MARC 21* RECORD FOR RESOURCES THAT ARE TRADITIONALLY UNPUBLISHED

The **Type of Record (leader/06)** for an electronic thesis or dissertation (ETD) is a for language material. This is a departure from the rules for coding print theses and dissertations. Print theses and dissertations are coded t for manuscript language material, which is the appropriate code for unpublished resources. However, *AACR2* 9.4B2 states that all remote-access electronic resources are considered to be published. For this reason, a is the appropriate code for ETDs.

  Type: a

  The **Country of Publication (008/15)** is txu, the *MARC 21* country code for Texas. Again, this is a departure from the practice for print theses and dissertations. Because they are considered unpublished manuscripts, they typically do not have a country code in this field.

  Ctry: txu

  Because the **Type of Record** code a in the leader reflects the *textual* nature of e-books, additional fixed fields must be added to reflect their electronic nature, specifically an **Additional Material Characteristics (006)** field and a **Physical Description (007)** field.

  In the **Additional Material Characteristics (006)** field, the **Form of Material (006/00)**, is m, indicating that this resource is a computer file.

  Type of Computer File (006/09) is d, indicating that this resource is a document.

  The other fields, **Target Audience (006/05)** and **Government Publication (006/11)**, are left blank.

  006 m d

  In the **Physical Description (007)** field, the **Category of Material (007/00)**, is c for computer file.

  Specific Material Designation (007/01) is r, indicating that this is a remote-access resource.

  Color (007/03) is b, indicating that this is a black-and-white resource.

  Dimensions (007/04) is n, the appropriate code for all remote-access resources.

The remaining fields are optional.

```
007     c ‡b r ‡d b ‡e n
```

The general material designation [electronic resource] is placed in the **Title Proper (245)** subfield **h**.

```
245  10 Operators at the borders ‡h
        [electronic resource] : ‡b the
        hero as change agent in border
        literature / ‡c by Jonathan
        Steven Handelman.
```

Publication information is placed in the **Publication, Distribution, Etc. (260)** field. Normally, print theses and dissertations are considered to be unpublished manuscripts and thus do not have the place of publication and name of publisher recorded in subfields **a** and **b**. Since remote electronic resources are considered to be published, this information is included for ETDs. In this case, the information is enclosed in brackets per *AACR2* 9.0B2, because it is taken outside of the prescribed sources of information. This information is not explicitly stated on the ETD itself or the Texas A&M Web site. The cataloger provided this information based on outside knowledge.

```
260     [College Station, Tex. : ‡b Texas
        A&M University, ‡c 2003.]
```

The source of the title proper is provided in a **General Note (500)** (*AACR2* 9.1B2 and 9.7B3).

```
500     Title from author supplied meta-
        data.
```

The type and extent of resource is provided in a **Type of Computer File or Data Note (516)** (*AACR2* 9.7B8). Although this note is not mandatory, the rule states that this information should be included if it is considered important and is not contained elsewhere in the description.

```
516     Text (Dissertation).
```

The date on which the resource was viewed for cataloging is placed in a **General Note (500)** note (*AACR2* 9.7B22). Known as the "Item described" note, this note is mandatory.

```
500     Description based on contents
        viewed May 25, 2004.
```

The mode of access is provided in a **System Details (538)** note (*AACR2* 9.7B1c).

The system requirements are provided in a **System Details (538)** note (*AACR2* 9.7B1b).

```
538          Mode of access: World Wide Web.
538          System requirements: Web
             browser, Adobe Acrobat Reader
```

The URL is placed in an **Electronic Location and Access (856)**
field.

```
856  40   ‡u http://txspace.tamu.edu/han-
          dle /1969/550
```

Figure 7-6 shows a full *MARC 21* record for electronic theses and
dissertations.

```
Type: a   ELvl: K  Srce: c  Audn:     Ctrl:   Lang: eng
BLvl: m   Form: s  Conf: 0  Biog:     MRec:   Ctry: txu
          Cont: bm GPub:     LitF: 0  Indx: 0
Desc: a   Ills:    Fest: 0  DtSt: s  Date: 2003,

    006   m      d
    007          c ‡b r ‡d b ‡e n
    040          TXA ‡c TXA ‡d OCLCQ
    100   1_     Handelman, Jonathan Steven, ‡d 1967-
    245   10     Operators at the borders ‡h [elec-
                 tronic resource] : ‡b the hero as
                 change agent in border literature /
                 ‡c by Jonathan Steven Handelman.
    260          [College Station, Tex. : ‡ Texas A&M
                 University, ‡c 2003.]
    500          "Major Subject: English."
    500          Title from author supplied metadata.
    502          Thesis (Ph. D.)--Texas A & M
                 University, 2003.
    504          Includes bibliographical references.
    516          Text (Dissertation).
    520   3_     This study of borders in literature
                 investigates the ways the frontier and
                 then the border entered the national
                 consciousness and developed into the
                 entities they are presently. The focus
                 here on the border in literature is
                 organized around the role of border
                 heroes as they bring instability and
                 change to the geographic border region
```

**Figure 7-6. Full *MARC 21* Record for an Electronic
Thesis/Dissertation**

```
                  and to more metaphoric border
                  regions. This study not only
                  addresses the individual border
                  hero's role and attributes, but also
                  focuses more generally on the border
                  hero's role as an emblem of the
                  struggle for change. Toward this end,
                  I support the importance to border
                  criticism of border agents by showing
                  their presence and essential partici-
                  pation in the work of Américo
                  Paredes, some of the earliest writing
                  on borders and border agents.
     500          Description based on contents viewed
                  May 25, 2004.
     538          Mode of access: World Wide Web.
     538          System requirements: Web browser,
                  Adobe Acrobat Reader
     650   _4     Major English.
     653          Border
     653          Border literature
     653          Paredes
     653          Hero
     856   40     ‡u http://txspace.tamu.edu/
                  handle/1969/550
```

Figure 7-6. (continued)

SUMMARY

A cataloging record for online monographs includes the familiar descriptive bibliographic elements in the *MARC 21* record along with additional information required to describe the electronic characteristics of the resources. Many of the additional elements, such as the general material designation in the **245**, are found in almost all records for electronic resources. However, the nuances of electronic resources also create cataloging challenges, such as the problems addressed in the examples in this chapter. The most challenging aspect of cataloging online monographs is determining that a resource is, indeed, a monograph. Content on the World Wide Web tends to be dynamic, and the cataloger must ensure that an individual resource meets the definition of a monograph. Another challenge is distinguishing between born-digital resources and reproductions. Sometimes this is easy to determine, sometimes it is not. Judgment is must be applied when making cataloging decisions. The last example in this chapter demonstrates that online resources are always considered published, a characteristic that influences cataloging in the fixed fields and publication area of description. After learning the basics of cataloging online monographs, most are easy to catalog. When faced with the occasional challenge, it is always advisable to consult authoritative cataloging manuals.

REFERENCES

BIBCO. *BIBCO Core Record Standard for Monographic Electronic Resources*. 2003. Washington, DC: Program for Cooperative Cataloging. Available: www.loc.gov/catdir/pcc/bibco/coreelectro.html. Accessed January 27, 2005.

Hiatt, Robert M. 1989. *Library of Congress Rule Interpretations*. Washington, DC: Library of Congress Cataloging Distribution Service.

Joint Steering Committee for the Revision of AACR2. 2002. *Anglo-American Cataloguing Rules, 2nd ed, 2002 rev*. Chicago: American Library Association.

Library of Congress Network Development and MARC Standards Office. 1999. *MARC 21 Format for Bibliographic Data*. Washington, DC: Library of Congress Cataloging Distribution Service.

Library of Congress Network Development and MARC Standards Office. 2003. "MARC Code List for Geographic Areas." Washington, DC: Library of Congress Cataloging Distribution Service. Available: www.loc.gov/marc/geoareas/gacshome.html. Accessed January 27, 2005.

Subcommittee on the Revision of the Guidelines on Subject Access to Individual Works of Fiction, Subject Analysis Committee, Cataloging and Classification Section, Association of Library Collections and Technical Services. Hiroko Aikawa, Jan DeSirey, Linda Gabel, Susan Hayes, Kathy Nystrom, Mary Dabney Wilson, and Pat Thomas, Chair. 2000. *Guidelines on Subject Access to Individual Works of Fiction, Drama, etc.*, 2nd ed. Chicago: American Library Association.

8

ONLINE SERIALS: E-JOURNALS AND PERIODICALS IN AGGREGATOR DATABASES

INTRODUCTION

Serials are continuing resources, issued in a succession of discrete parts, which have no predetermined conclusion. The individual parts often bear some kind of organizational labeling, such as volume, issue, with associated numbering. Common types of serials include popular magazines, academic journals, newspapers, and annual reports. While serials cataloging is addressed in the *Anglo-American Cataloging Rules, 2nd edition* ([*AACR2*] Joint Steering Committee for the Revision of AACR2, 2002) in Chapter 12, the most authoritative resource for serials cataloging is the *CONSER Cataloging Manual* ([*CCM*] Hirons, 2002). Module 31 of *CCM* specifically addresses cataloging remote-access electronic serials. The *CONSER Editing Guide* ([*CEG*] LC Serials Record Division, 1994) provides guidelines for *MARC 21* tagging in serials records. Both *CCM* and *CEG* are produced by CONSER, the cooperative serials cataloging program. In this chapter, *CCM* and *CEG* are the primary references.

Many long-established serials naturally migrated to the Web, but in the online environment, they may be expressed as either a serial or integrating resource. The cataloger must carefully determine if an online resource is indeed a serial. The key is that the resource must issue new content in discrete parts rather than integrating new content into the whole of the resource. This is typically indicated by a clear numerical designation on the resource. Another strong indication is a browseable list of the discrete parts of the serial, often indicated as a list of back issues. Sometimes this list is available from the resource home page; sometimes it is at a level below the home page.

Bibliographic records for online serials are quite similar to records for print serials. The differences tend to reflect coding that describes the electronic format of the online serial. Thus, *MARC 21* records for online serials almost always have the following features:

- **Form of Original Item (008/22)** and **Form of Item (008/23)** fields set to s for electronic.
- **Additional Material Characteristics (006)** field and a **Physical Description (007)** field.

- The general material designation [electronic resource] will be placed in the subfield h of the **Title Statement (245)** field.
- "Title from" note in a **General Note (500)** field.
- A "Latest issue consulted" note in a **General Note (500)** field.
- A "Mode of access" note in a **System Details Note (538)** field.
- An **Electronic Location and Access (856)** field.

If the serial is available in another physical format (typically a print version of the resource), the record will have a linking entry, either an **Additional Physical Form (776)** field or a **Preceding Entry (780)**. The record will have a note indicating the other physical format in an **Additional Physical Form Available (530)** field or a subfield **i** of the **776**.

Our first example of an online serial is a freely available serial that has published issues online since its inception. Following this example, we will look at online serials that present cataloging challenges and discuss how to address those challenges. Figures 8-3, 8-5, 8-6, 8-10, 8-12, and 8-14 are examples of full records.

LONG EXAMPLE: BORN-DIGITAL, ONLINE-ONLY SERIAL

As the Web continues to be used as a stable medium for publishing popular and academic serials, there are more and more born-digital, online-only serials. This type of online serial is the simplest type of online serial to catalog. The lack of a concurrently published alternate physical format simplifies description. Such a resource does not require linking fields, nor is there any problem with conflicts in bibliographic information, such as coverage. Cataloging serials that were born online is fairly straightforward.

BIBLIOGRAPHIC CHARACTERISTICS

D-Lib Magazine has been published online since its inception. Every issue was born digital, and it has never been published in print. It is a purely electronic online serial. To begin cataloging, the cataloger must examine the resource for cataloging purposes; this means open or otherwise process the resource to view it and gather bibliographic

D-Lib® Magazine

Search

[ ] Go

About D-Lib Magazine

Current Issue
  Table of Contents
  Featured Collection
  In Brief
  Clips & Pointers

Indexes
  Back Issues
  Author Index
  Title Index

Subscriptions

Search Guidelines

Mirror Sites

Author Guidelines

Contact D-Lib

•••

DOI
10.1045/dlib.magazine

ISSN
1082-9873

In the Current Issue
Full-length Features

July/August 2004
Vol. 10 No. 7/8
Table of Contents

•••

EDITORIAL
The Changing Landscape of Scholarly Publishing
by Bonita Wilson, *CNRI*

•••

LETTERS
To the Editor

•••

COMMENTARY
Thirteen Ways of Looking at ...Digital Preservation
by Brian Lavoie and Lorcan Dempsey, *OCLC Research*

•••

ARTICLES
The Role of ERPANET in Supporting Digital Curation and Preservation in Europe
by Seamus Ross, *HATII and ERPANET*

The Continuing Access and Digital Preservation Strategy for the UK Joint Information Systems Committee (JISC)

by Neil Beagrie, *The British Library*

The Integration of Non-OAI Resources for Federated Searching in DLIST, an Eprints Repository
by Anita Coleman, Paul Bracke, and S. Karthnik, *University of Arizona*

•••

CONFERENCE REPORTS
Report on the Fourth ACM, IEEE Joint Conference on Digital Libraries (JCDL): 7 - 11 June 2004, Tucson, Arizona
by Schubert Foo, *Nanyang Technological University, Singapore*

If you Build It, Will They Come? Participant Involvement in Digital Libraries
by Sarah Giersch, *iLumina Digital Library*; Eugene A. Klotz, *The Math Forum @ Drexel*; Flora McMartin, *MERLOT*; Brandon Muramatsu, *University of California, Berkeley*; K. Ann Renninger, *Swarthmore College*; Wesley Shumar, *Drexel University* and Stephen A. Weimar, *The Math Forum @ Drexel*

Also This Month
Digital Collections

FEATURED COLLECTION

Earth as Art
A gallery of beautiful images of our planet taken by the Landsat-7 satellite.

[Image courtesy of NASA Landsat Project Science Office and USGS EROS Data Center.]

Digital Library Community Activities

In Brief
Short items of current awareness.

In the News
Recent press releases and announcements.

Clips & Pointers
Documents, deadlines, calls for participation.

Archives
Back Issues and Indexes

Back Issues
Complete archive of D-Lib Magazine.

Author Index
Alphabetical list of authors and contributors.

Title Index
Alphabetical list of content by title.

Additional Links
Other Resources

Ready Reference
Links to other digital library sites.

Meetings, Conferences, Workshops
Calendar of activities associated with digital libraries research and technologies.

D-Lib Forum
Supporting the community developing the technology of the global digital library.

D-Lib Magazine is produced by the **Corporation For National Research Initiatives (CNRI)**, has been sponsored by the **Defense Advanced Research Project Agency (DARPA)** on behalf of the Digital Libraries Initiative under Grant No. N66001-98-1-8908, and is currently being funded by the **National Science Foundation** (NSF) under Grant No.IIS-0243042.

Figure 8-1. *D-Lib Magazine* Home Page (www.dlib.org)

information from the prescribed sources of information. In this example, the cataloger views the serial by opening a browser to the URL www.dlib.org. This displays the homepage of the resource. *D-Lib Magazine* clearly displays the numbering and chronology of the current issue on the home page. In addition to this, there is a link to back issues in the menu on the left side of the home page. Clicking this link opens a page that clearly shows the individual issues of the serial. This indicates that content is issued in successive, discrete parts, confirming the serial nature of the resource.

>Significant bibliographic aspect: The serial *D-Lib Magazine*. The work is contained on a Web site under the domain name www.dlib.org.

>Type of issuance: This is a continuing resource issued in a succession of discrete parts. It is a serial.

>Sources of information: The chief source of information is the resource itself, preferably whatever part of the resource provides the most complete information. In this case, most of the relevant bibliographic information is available on the serial home page. Additional relevant information is available on various pages of the Web site, accessible by clicking hyperlinks from the home page.

>Reproduction or born digital: This is a born-digital resource. New issues are published online.

>**Type of Record** code: Because this is a predominantly textual resource, the type code is a.

>**Bibliographic Level** code: Because this is a serial, the bibliographic level is s.

>*MARC 21* workform: Serial.

CODING THE *MARC 21* RECORD FOR A BORN-DIGITAL, ONLINE-ONLY SERIAL

Leaders

Textual serials have the **Type of Record (leader/06)** coded a for language material and **Bibliographic Level (leader/07)** coded s for serial.

The **Type of Control (leader/08)** is left blank because this field is used only for archival resources.

The **Encoding Level (leader/17)** is blank, indicating that this is a full-level catalog record input by a member of the Program for Cooperative Cataloging.

The **Descriptive Cataloging Form (leader/18)** is coded a, indicating that description is based on the rules of *AACR2*.

Title Index | Author Index | Search | Contents

BACK ISSUES

D-Lib Magazine
July/August 2004

Volume 10 Number 7/8

ISSN 1082-9873

Back Issues

To browse the contents pages of back issues of **D-Lib Magazine**, select the appropriate item from the list below. You may also browse alphabetized lists of stories, editorials, and briefings by author or title or you may search the contents of the monthly magazine and reference pages.

2004	2003	2002	2001	2000
January	January	January	January	January
February	February	February	February	February
March	March	March	March	March
April	April	April	April	April
May	May	May	May	May
June	June	June	June	June
	July/August	July/August	July/August	July/August
	September	September	September	September
	October	October	October	October
	November	November	November	November
	December	December	December	December

Figure 8-2. *D-Lib Magazine* back issues (www.dlib.org/back.html)

008

The **Type of Date (008/06)** is c for continuing resource that is currently published.

Date 1 **(008/07-10)** is 1995, indicating the year in which this serial was first published.

Date 2 (008/11-14) defaults to 9999, indicating that the resource is still being published.

The **Place of Publication (008/15)** is vau, the *MARC 21* code for Virginia.

Frequency (008/18) is m for monthly.

Regularity (008/19) is r for regularly published.

Type of Continuing Resource (008/21) is p for periodical because this version is the original version of the resource.

Form of Original Item (008/22) and **Form of Item (008/23)** are both s for electronic (*CEG*).

Nature of Entire Work (008/24), which signifies that the serial is entirely composed of a certain kind of work, is blank.

Nature of Contents (008/25-27), which indicates that a serial is partly composed of certain kinds of works, is blank.

Government Publication (008/28) is blank, indicating that this resource is not published by the government.

Conference Publication (008/29) is 0, indicating that this is not a conference publication.

Original Alphabet or Script of Title (008/33) is blank. This field is only completed by the members of the National Serials Data Program or ISSN Canada.

Entry Convention (008/34) is 0, indicating the successive entry convention is used. This means that a new record is created each time the title changes for this serial.

Language (008/35-37) is eng, indicating that this resource is in English.

Cataloging Source (008/39) is d, indicating that the record was created by an institution that is not a national bibliographic agency or participant in a cooperative cataloging program.

006

Because the **Type of Record** code a in the leader reflects the textual nature of serials, additional fixed fields must be added to reflect their electronic nature, specifically an **Additional Material Characteristics (006)** field and a **Physical Description (007)** field.

In the **Additional Material Characteristics (006)** field, the character in the first position determines the content in the rest of the positions. Therefore, the first character, known as the **Form of Material (006/00)**, is m, indicating that this resource is a computer file.

The **006** for computer files has three data elements: **Target Audience**, **Type of Computer File**, and **Government Publication**.

Target Audience (006/05) is left blank because this is not a juvenile resource.

Type of Computer File (006/09) is d, indicating that this resource is a document.

Government Publication (006/11) is blank because the resource is not a government publication.

007

The **Physical Description (007)** field is also designed so that the character in the first position determines the content in the rest of the positions. The first character, known as the **Category of Material (007/00)**, is c for computer file.

Specific Material Designation (007/01) is r, indicating that this is a remote-access resource.

Color (007/03) is c, indicating that this is a multicolored resource.

Dimensions (007/04) is n, which indicates that this code is not applicable. This is the appropriate code for all remote-access resources.

The remaining fields are optional and are not included in this example: **Sound (007/05)**, **Image bit depth (007/06–08)**, **File Formats (007/09)**, **Quality Assurance Targets (007/20)**, **Antecedent/Source (007/11)**, **Level of Compression (007/12)**, and **Reformatting Quality (007/13)**.

Variable Fields

MARC 21 records for electronic serials include the descriptive fields that are created for print serials, plus additional fields and subfields to reflect their electronic nature. Some differences stand out in particular. For remote electronic resources, the general material designation [electronic resource] is placed in the **Title Proper** (245), subfield **h**. Remote electronic resources do not have a **Physical Description (300)** field. Some note fields are required for electronic resources and others are commonly seen. According to *CCM* 13.14, the most relevant notes for online serials are the source of title proper, variations in title, description based on note, latest issue consulted, beginning and/or ending dates of publication, numbering peculiarities, mode of access, and other physical formats. Less common notes are restrictions on access, type of electronic resource or data, system requirements, and information about documentation. Notes are input in numeric *MARC 21* tag order. The **Electronic Location and Access (856)** field contains the U.R.L or other type of location identifier. Furthermore, the nature of remote electronic resources in general provides challenges for coding some of the common variable fields. These will be discussed in turn.

Number and Code Fields (01X-04X)

Although the **Cataloging Source (040)** is one of the first variable fields in most *MARC 21* records, this field is not coded manually. It is automatically added by the cataloging utility.

This record for *D-Lib Magazine* contains control numbers assigned by various cataloging agencies.

The **Library of Congress Control Number (010)** is a unique number assigned to specific *MARC 21* records by the Library of Congress or a cooperative cataloging agency.

The **National Bibliographic Agency Control Number (016)** is a field for control numbers assigned by an agency other than the Library of Congress. When the first indicator is 7, the source of the number is specified by placing the *MARC 21* organization code in subfield **2**. This record has two **016**s, each with a subfield **2** of DNLM, the National Library of Medicine.

This record also has an **OCLC Control Number Cross-Reference (019)**. This field is part of OCLC's *Bibliographic Formats and Standards* and is not in the official *MARC 21* standard. This field is used to identify the OCLC number of duplicate records that have been deleted from WorldCat. Such duplicate-record numbers are common for electronic resources because of previous cataloging rules. Current cataloging rules stipulate the creation of one *MARC 21* record for various manifestations of an electronic serial.

Subfield **a** of the **International Standard Serial Number (022)** field is where the International Standard Serial Number (ISSN) is placed. The first indicator of this field is coded 0 indicating that this is a serial of international interest.

The **CODEN Designation (030)** field is for a unique number assigned to the title by the International CODEN Section of Chemical Abstracts Service (CODEN designation).

The **Source of Acquisition (037)** field contains information needed to order a resource. This field is frequently included in serial records, even for titles that are freely available on the Web.

The **Authentication Code (042)** field contains codes that verify that an authentication agency has reviewed the record. The codes identify specific agencies. In this case, `nsdp` refers to the National Serials Data Program, and `lcd` refers to CONSER.

```
010          sn 95004209
016    7_    9709374 ‡2 DNLM
016    7_    SR0084642 ‡2 DNLM
019          44317768
022    0_    1082-9873
030          DLMAF7
037          ‡b CNRI, 1895 Preston White
             Drive, Ste. 100, Reston, VA
             22091
042          nsdp ‡a lcd
```

Classification and Call Number Fields (05X-08X)

This example has three classification fields, a **Library of Congress Call Number (050)**, a **National Library of Medicine Call Number (060)**, and a **Dewey Decimal Call Number (082)**. For remote electronic resources, these fields serve more as subject classifications than as call numbers. It is essentially impossible for them to serve as a physical-item location device, that is, a call number, because remote electronic resources have no material existence. Still, subject classification is a useful tool in retrieval: classification numbers help co-locate similar items in online catalogs and may also be used for deriving other user tools, such as browseable subject lists.

```
050    14    ZA4080
060    10    Z 669
082    10    025 ‡2 12
```

Main Entry Fields (1XX)

The title is the main entry heading of this work (*CCM* 4.7). Like many serials, the personal authorship for this title is diffuse, and the resource does not qualify for entry under a corporate body as defined by *CCM* 4.4. The record does not require a **Uniform Title (130)** because it does not conflict with any other title. In this case, the **Title Proper (245)** serves as the main entry and no **1XX** field is required.

> **Uniform Title (130)**: A uniform title is used for online serials to differentiate between two or more manifestations of a work published under identical titles proper.

Title and Title-Related Fields (20X-24X)

The **Abbreviated Title (210)** and **Key Title (222)** fields are only input by ISSN centers. The **Abbreviated Title** is used for indexing and identification purposes and in this case is based on the key title. The first identifier of 0 specifies that this title is not an added entry. The blank second indicator specifies that the abbreviated title is based on the key title.

The **Key Title** is a unique title used for ISSN purposes. The first indicator is undefined in the *MARC 21* standard. The second indicator of 0 means that there are no nonfiling characters.

Title Statement (245) subfield **a** is where the title of the serial is placed. The first indicator 0 is used when the title is the main entry. The second indicator 0 specifies that there are no nonfiling characters in subfield **a**.

The general material designation [electronic resource] is placed in the subfield **h**.

This record has two **Varying Form of Title (246)** fields. This field is used to code forms of the title appearing on the resource that differ from the title proper. The first indicator 3 specifies that a note will not be printed on the record and that the title will be made an added entry. The blank second indicator specifies that the varying titles are not of any particular type (such as a portion of a title or parallel title.)

```
210   0_    D-Lib mag.
222   _0    D-Lib magazine
245   00    D-Lib magazine ‡h [electronic
            resource].
246   3_    Digital library magazine
246   3_    D lib magazine
```

Edition, Imprint, Etc. Fields (250-270)

CCM 31.11 says to treat all electronic serials as published. Publication information is placed in the **Publication, Distribution, Etc. (260)** field. The place of publication is in subfield **a**, the publishers name in subfield **b**, and the date of publication in subfield **c**.

```
260         Reston, Va. : ‡b Corp. for National
            Research Initiatives, ‡c c1995-
```

Physical Description, Etc. Fields (3XX)

Current Publication Frequency (310) field is where the publication frequency of the resource is placed. The **Dates of Publication and/or Sequential Designation (362)** field contains the chronological or sequential designation for the resource. The first indicator 0 specifies that the field is in the formatted style, rather than an unformatted note. The formatted note is used in this case because the first issue of this resource is available online and the title is still being published.

```
310        Monthly
362  0_    July 1995-
```

Note Fields: Part 1 (50X-53X)

CCM Module 31 provides instructions for notes specific to cataloging online serials. The source of the title proper is provided in a **General Note (500)** according to *CCM* 31.3.3. The note should include the date on which the title was viewed in parentheses.

```
500        Title from journal home page
           (viewed Sept. 7, 1999).
```

The latest issue consulted is provided in a **General Note (500)** when more than one issue is used for description. This note is typically provided for online resources according to *LCRI* 12.7B23 and *CCM* 8.1.2.

```
500        Latest issue consulted: Vol. 8,
           no. 2 (Feb. 2002).
```

Inconsistencies with numbering are recorded in a **Numbering Peculiarities Note (515)**. This is typically a unique field for each resource, as different resources have different problems. Many cataloging references provide examples of how to format this field, including the *MARC 21* manual and the *CEG*.

```
515        Issues for Jan. 1999- numbered
           v. 5, no. 1- ; July/Aug. issues
           combined, 1996-
```

A summary of the contents can be provided in a **Summary Note (520)**. The first indicator of 8 means that no display constant will be generated. This field is not mandatory for serials.

```
520  8_    Presents "D-Lib Magazine," a
           monthly electronic publication
           related to digital libraries.
           Includes commentaries and news
```

```
                           articles. Offers an archive of
                           back issues and a site search
                           engine. Provides access to
                           working groups, digital library
                           research projects, events cal-
                           endars, and related technical
                           reports. Notes access terms and
                           conditions and links to mirror
                           sites. Links to the Corporation
                           for National Research
                           Initiatives, the coordinator of
                           the magazine.
```

Note Fields: Part 2 (53X-58X)

The mode of access is provided in a **System Details Note (538)** according to *CCM* 31.14.5.

The system requirements are provided in a **System Details Note (538)** according to *CCM* 31.14.4.

```
    538                    Mode of access: World Wide Web.
    538                    System requirements: Web
                           browser.
```

This record has two **Issuing Body Notes (550)**. This note is required when the cataloger wishes to create an added entry for a corporate body, but the name of the corporate body is not mentioned in the other areas of the catalog record. These notes are provided according to *CCM* 13.5.

```
    550                    Produced by the Corporation for
                           National Research Initiatives
                           for the Information
                           Infrastructure Technology and
                           Applications Task Group of the
                           High Performance Computing and
                           Communications Program.
    550                    Early issues have subtitle: the
                           magazine of the Digital Library
                           Forum.
```

Subject Access Fields (6XX)

Subject analysis is a complex practice that requires training, skill, and judgment. With regards to serials, *CCM* states that the cataloger should

"Generally, select headings that correspond with the subject matter of the serial as a whole, as opposed to the topics of certain sections of the serial, special theme issues of periodicals, etc." (Hirons, 2002, Module 15, p. 5). Subject headings are discussed in *CCM* Module 15.

This resource is assigned six **Topical Terms (650)**. The first four are Library of Congress subject headings, indicated by the second indicator of 0. The last two are Medical Subject Headings, indicated by the second indicator of 2.

```
650   _0    Digital libraries ‡v
             Periodicals.
650   _0    Electronic publishing ‡v
             Periodicals.
650   _0    Libraries and electronic pub-
             lishing ‡v Periodicals.
650   _0    Library information networks ‡v
             Periodicals.
650   02    Information Storage and
             Retrieval.
650   02    Information Systems.
```

Added Entry Fields (70X-75X)

Three **Corporate Name Added Entries (710)** are created for the corporate bodies that issue the resource (*CCM* 18.3).

```
710   2_    Corporation for National
             Research Initiatives.
710   2_    D-Lib Forum.
710   2_    Federal High Performance
             Computing Program (U.S.). ‡b
             Information Infrastructure
             Technology and Applications
             Task Group.
```

Linking Entry Fields (76X-78X)

Linking fields: Linking fields are commonly used in serial records to show bibliographic relationships between works. Records for online serials frequently contain linking fields for title changes, format changes, and other physical formats published simultaneously.

Linking fields are commonly used in serials to show relationships between works. For online serials, linking fields are often used to show title changes over time and to link a record for an electronic resource to the record for its print version. *D-Lib Magazine* does not fit any circumstances that require linking fields: it has not experienced a title change and is not published in print. We will look at the use of linking fields for online serials in other examples.

Holdings, Location, Alternate Graphs, etc. Fields (841-88X)

This serial is available from a Web site and has one **Electronic Location and Access (856)** field. For resources with persistent uniform resource locators (PURLs), place two u subfields in the field, with the PURL in the first and the standard URL in the second according to *CCM* 31.15.5.

```
856  40    ‡u
           http://bibpurl.oclc.org/web/1110
           ‡u http://www.dlib.org/
```

Figure 8-3 shows a full *MARC 21* record for a born-digital, online-only serial.

Type: a	ELvl:	Srce: d	GPub:	Ctrl:		Lang: eng
BLvl: s	Form: s	Conf: 0	Freq: m	MRec:		Ctry: vau
S/L: 0	Orig: s	EntW:	Regl: n	ISSN: 1	Alph:	
Desc: a	SrTp: p	Cont:	DtSt: c	Dates: 1995, 1999		

```
006          m    d
007          c ‡b r ‡d c ‡e n
010          sn 95004209
016    7_    9709374 ‡2 DNLM
016    7_    SR0084642 ‡2 DNLM
019          44317768
022    0_    1082-9873
030          DLMAF7
             ‡b CNRI, 1895 Preston White Drive,
             Ste. 100, Reston, VA 22091
042          nsdp ‡a lcd
050    14    ZA4080
060    10    Z 669
082    10    025 ‡2 12
210    0_    D-Lib mag.
222    _0    D-Lib magazine
245    00    D-Lib magazine ‡h [electronic
             resource].
246    3_    Digital library magazine
246    3_    D lib magazine
260          Reston, Va. : ‡b Corp. for National
             Research Initiatives, ‡c c1995-
310          Monthly
362    0_    July 1995-
```

Figure 8-3. Full *MARC 21* Record for a Born-Digital, Online-Only Serial

500		Title from journal home page (viewed Sept. 7, 1999).
500		Latest issue consulted: Vol. 8, no. 2 (Feb. 2002).
515		Issues for Jan. 1999- numbered v. 5, no.1- ; July/Aug. issues combined, 1996-
520	8_	Presents "D-Lib Magazine," a monthly electronic publication related to digital libraries. Includes commentaries and news articles. Offers an archive of back issues and a site search engine. Provides access to working groups, digital library research projects, events calendars, and related technical reports. Notes access terms and conditions and links to mirror sites. Links to the Corporation for National Research Initiatives, the coordinator of the magazine.
538		Mode of access: World Wide Web.
538		System requirement: Web browser.
550		Produced by the Corporation for National Research Initiatives for the Information Infrastructure Technology and Applications Task Group of the High Performance Computing and Communications Program.
550		Early issues have subtitle: the magazine of the Digital Library Forum.
650	_0	Digital libraries ‡v Periodicals.
650	_0	Electronic publishing ‡v Periodicals.
650	_0	Libraries and electronic publishing ‡v Periodicals.
650	_0	Library information networks ‡v Periodicals.
650	02	Information Storage and Retrieval.
650	02	Information Systems.
710	2_	Corporation for National Research Initiatives.
710	2_	D-Lib Forum.
710	2_	Federal High Performance Computing Program (U.S.). ‡b Information Infrastructure Technology and Applications Task Group.
856	40	‡u http://bibpurl.oclc.org/web/1110 ‡u http://www.dlib.org/

Figure 8-3. (continued)

SHORT EXAMPLE: ONLINE JOURNAL ALSO ISSUED IN PRINT (SINGLE-RECORD APPROACH)

Serials available online often exist in another format, either in print or on a direct-access medium such as CD-ROM. The print or direct-access format often precedes the existence of the online version, and, thus, has catalog copy available prior to the creation of the electronic record. In such a case, CONSER practice allows two methods of cataloging. CONSER allows creating a separate record for the electronic version, but also permits adding information about the online version to the print record, thus creating a single record for both formats.

The guidelines for deciding whether to create a single or separate record are in *CCM* 31.2.3. The rule of thumb is that the single-record approach is permissible when the bibliographic record for the print version provides adequate access to the online. It is best used when the resources are essentially identical in content. If the online version has significant differences, such as additional content or a difference in title, then the separate-record approach is preferable. In any case, creating separate records for electronic versions is permissible. We use a free online journal to demonstrate both approaches to catalog online serials, with an example of the single-record approach first. See Figure 8-5 for a full *MARC 21* record for a journal that is available online and in print.

> **Single-record approach**: Cataloging the print and online manifestations of a serial title on the same MARC record. This is one of two CONSER-approved methods for cataloging online serials that are published simultaneously with a print version.

BIBLIOGRAPHIC CHARACTERISTICS

The *Journal of Technology Education* (*JTE*) is an open-access journal published by Virginia Tech. It is available online at http://scholar.lib.vt.edu/ejournals/JTE. The home page has a list of all issues available online, beginning with volume 1, number 1, published in fall 1989. A search of WorldCat indicates that this journal is also published in print. The simultaneous existence of the print and online versions affects cataloging and coding.

   Significant bibliographic aspect: The serial *Journal of Technology Education*. The work is contained on a Web site under the domain http://scholar.lib.vt.edu/ejournals/JTE.

   Type of issuance: This is a continuing resource issued in a succession of discrete parts. It is a serial.

   Source of information: The chief source of information is the resource itself, which is contained on its Web site. Other relevant

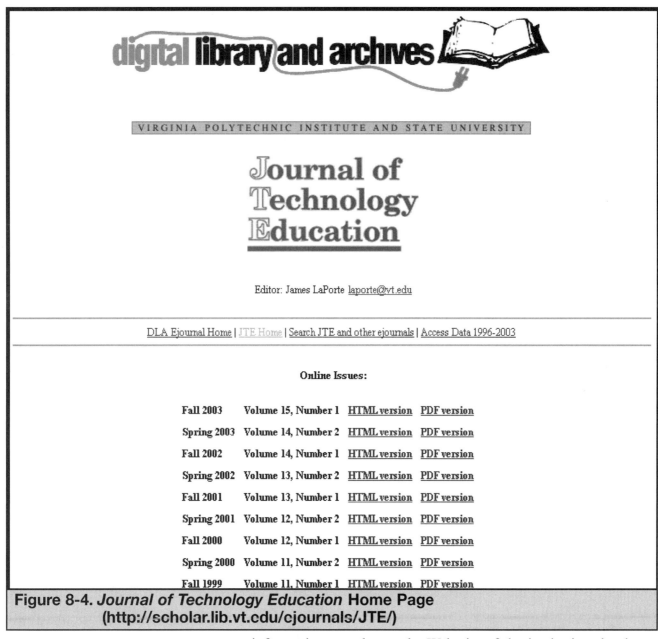

Figure 8-4. *Journal of Technology Education* **Home Page (http://scholar.lib.vt.cdu/cjournals/JTE/)**

information may be on the Web site of the institution that hosts and publishes the journal.

Reproduction or born digital: This resource is simultaneously published in print and online. The electronic version is considered born digital.

Type of Record code: The code is a for language material.

Bibliographic Level code: The code is s for serial.

MARC 21 work form: Serial.

CODING THE *MARC 21* RECORD USING THE SINGLE-RECORD APPROACH

When cataloging an online serial using the single-record approach, add the following tags to the record for the original item (*CCM* 31.2.3).

- Code **Form of Original Item (008/22)** and **Form of Item (008/23)** for the original version rather than the online version.
- Note the availability of the online version in an **Additional Physical Form Available Note (530)**.
- Add an **Added Entry—Uncontrolled or Related Added Entry (740)** or a name/title **Added Entry (7XX)** when the title of the online version differs.
- Provide the location of the online version in an **Electronic Location and Access Field (856)**.
- If the electronic version has a separate ISSN, but another record has not been created, add an **Additional Physical Form Entry (776)** placing the title in a subfield **t** and the ISSN in a subfield **x**.
- Optionally, add a **Physical Description Fixed Field (007)** for an electronic resource.

In the single-record approach, the leader is coded for the print version of the resource. In the **008**, the **Form of Original Item (008/22)** and **Form of Item (008/23)** are coded for the print version rather than the online version. Therefore, they are both blank, the appropriate code for print resources.

```
Form:
Orig:
```

The **Physical Description (007)** field for the online version is optional, but typically added.

The **Category of Material (007/00)**, is c for computer file.

Specific Material Designation (007/01) is r, indicating that this is a remote-access resource.

Color (007/03) is c, indicating that this is a multicolored resource.

Dimensions (007/04) is n, which indicates that this code is not applicable. This is the appropriate code for all remote-access resources.

The remaining fields are optional and are not included in this example: **Sound (007/05)**, **Image bit depth (007/06–08)** , **File Formats (007/09)**, **Quality Assurance Targets (007/20)**, **Antecedent/Source (007/11)**, **Level of Compression (007/12)**, and **Reformatting Quality (007/13)**.

The **Additional Material Characteristics (006)** field is not added.

The variable fields are generally coded for the print version of the resource, with a few additions: a note stating the availability of the online version, a title added entry (if necessary), a linking field, and an electronic-location note. In this case, the titles of the print and online versions are the same, so a title added entry is not needed.

An **Additional Physical Form Entry (776)** is added to provide a linking entry and a note on the additional physical form available.

```
776  08   ‡i Also issued online: ‡t
          Journal of technology education
          (Online) ‡w (DLC) 2003238319 ‡w
          (OCoLC)35922665
```

Since the serial is available online, the URLs are place in **Electronic Location and Access (856)** fields. For resources with PURLs, CONSER recommends placing two **u** subfields in the field, the PURL in the first being and the standard URL for the resource in the second. Since the record is for the print resource, the second indicator in these 856 fields is 1, indicating that the URLs are to versions of the resource described by the record.

```
856  41   ‡z Also available online: ‡u
          http://bibpurl.oclc.org/web/4731
          ‡u http://scholar.lib.vt.edu/
          ejournals/JTE/
856  41   ‡u http://borg.lib.vt.edu/
          ejournals /JTE/jte.html
```

SHORT EXAMPLE: ONLINE JOURNAL ALSO ISSUED IN PRINT (SEPARATE-RECORD APPROACH)

CODING THE *MARC 21* RECORD USING THE SEPARATE-RECORD APPROACH

Separate-record approach:
Cataloging the print and online manifestations of a serial title on separate MARC records. This is one of two CONSER-approved methods for cataloging online serials that are published simultaneously with a print version.

When cataloging using the separate-record approach, the digital version itself is described using all relevant *MARC 21* tags. CONSER considers electronic versions of print publications to be simultaneous versions (except in special cases, such as when it is clear that an online serial is a reproduction.) For this reason, *JTE* is an independent resource with a record coded on a serials workform.

Form of Original Item (008/22) and **Form of Item (008/23)** are both s for electronic.

```
Type: a   ELvl:    Srce: d   GPub: s  Ctrl:     Lang: eng
BLvl: s   Form:    Conf: 0   Freq: f  MRec:     Ctry: vau
S/L: 0    Orig:    EntW:     Reql: r  ISSN: 1   Alph: a
Desc: a   SrTp: p  Cont:     DtSt: c  Dates: 1989,1999
```

007		c ‡b r ‡d c ‡e n
010		90649316 ‡z sn 89006813
040		NSD ‡c NSD ‡d DLC ‡d NSD ‡d DLC ‡d NST ‡d GUA ‡d OCLCQ ‡d DLC ‡d CGU
022	0_	1045-1064
037		‡b Mark Sanders, 144 Smyth Hall, Virginia Tech, Blacksburg, VA 24061-0432
042		nsdp ‡a lc
050	00	T61 ‡b .J69
082	00	607.1 ‡2 20
210	0_	J. technol. educ.
222	_0	Journal of technology education
245	00	Journal of technology education.
246	13	JTE
260		Blacksburg, Va. : ‡b Technology Education Program, Virginia Polytechnic Institute and State University, ‡c c1989-
300		v. ; ‡c 23 cm.
310		Semiannual
362	0_	Vol. 1, no. 1 (fall 1989)-
500		Description based on surrogate; title from cover.
550		Cosponsored by the International Technology Education Association and the Council on Technology Teacher Education.
650	_0	Technology ‡x Study and teaching ‡v Periodicals.
650	_0	Technical education ‡v Periodicals.
710	2_	Virginia Polytechnic Institute and State University. ‡b Technology Education Program.
710	2_	International Technology Education Association.

Figure 8-5. Full *MARC 21* Record for Online Journal Also Issued in Print (Single-Record Approach)

```
710   2_    Council on Technology Teacher
             Education (U.S.)
776   08    ‡i Also issued online: ‡t Journal of
             technology education (Online) ‡w
             (DLC) 2003238319 ‡w (OCoLC)35922665
850         DLC ‡a GU ‡a InLP ‡a MnU ‡a ViBlbV
856   41    ‡z Also available online: ‡u
             http://bibpurl.oclc.org/web/4731 ‡u
             http://scholar.lib.vt.edu/ejournals/
             JTE/
856   41    ‡u
             http://borg.lib.vt.edu/ejournals/JTE/
             jte.html
```

Figure 8-5. (continued)

```
Form:     s
Orig:     s
```

Because the **Type of Record** code a in the leader reflects the textual nature of serials, additional fixed fields must be added to reflect their electronic nature, specifically an **Additional Material Characteristics (006)** field and a **Physical Description (007)** field.

In the **Additional Material Characteristics (006)** field, the **Form of Material (006/00)**, is m, indicating that this resource is a computer file.

Type of Computer File (006/09) is d, indicating that this resource is a document.

The other fields, **Target Audience (006/05)** and **Government Publication (006/11)**, are left blank.

```
006       m    d
```

In the **Physical Description (007)** field, the **Category of Material (007/00)** is c for computer file.

Specific Material Designation (007/01) is r, indicating that this is a remote-access resource.

Color (007/03) is c, indicating that this resource is multicolored.

Dimensions (007/04) is n, which indicates that this code is not applicable. This is the appropriate code for all remote-access resources. The remaining fields are optional.

```
007       c ‡b r ‡d c ‡e n
```

An ISSN is listed on the journal's homepage, but the Web site does not explicitly state whether this ISSN is for the electronic or print version of the resource. The ISSN Center assigns separate ISSNs to print and online resources, but not all simultaneous resources have two

ISSNs. It is common to find that the print version of a resource has been assigned an ISSN, but the online version has not. The cataloger must determine to which version this ISSN applies. In the record for the electronic version, the print ISSN is placed in the **International Standard Serial Number (022)** subfield **y**. Although subfield **y** is defined as being the incorrect ISSN, the ISSN for the print version is placed in this field (*CCM* 31.19).

```
022          ‡y 1045-1064
```

Uniform titles are used for serials to differentiate between two or more manifestations of a work published under identical titles proper. In this case, the title `Journal of technology education` was established as the title proper for the print version of this resource. Therefore, the record for the electronic version receives a **Uniform Title (130)**. The first indicator is 0 for the number of nonfiling characters. The second indicator is undefined. The uniform title is placed in subfield **a** and consists of the title proper with the addition of the qualifier `(Online)`. *CCM* provides further information about uniform titles for serials in Module 5 and uniform titles for electronic serials in Module 31.

```
130   0_    Journal of technology education
            (Online)
```

The general material designation [electronic / resource] is placed in the **Title Statement (245)** subfield **h**.

```
245   10    Journal of technology education
            ‡h [electronic resource].
```

The source of the title proper is provided in a **General Note (500)** (*CCM* 31.3.3). The note should include the date the title was viewed in parentheses.

```
500          Title from journal homepage
             (publisher's website, viewed
             May 19, 2003).
```

The latest issue consulted is provided in a **General Note (500)** when more than one issue is used for description. This note is typically provided for online resources according to *LCRI* 12.7B23 and *CCM* 8.1.2.

```
500          Latest issue consulted: Vol.
             14, no. 2 (spring 2003); title
             from journal homepage (pub-
             lisher's website, viewed Dec.
             18, 2003).
```

The mode of access is provided in a **System Details Note (538)** (*CCM* 31.14.5).

The system requirements are also provided in a **System Details Note (538)** (*CCM* 31.14.4).

```
538        Mode of access: World Wide Web.
538        System requirements: Web
           browser.
```

The **7XX** fields, or linking entry fields, provide information about related bibliographic items. In this case, an **Additional Physical Form Entry (776)** is created for the print version of the serial (*CCM* 31.16). The first indicator is 0, which causes the entry to be displayed as a note in library systems. The second indicator is 8, which causes the information in the subfield **i** to be used as the display label.

Subfield **t** is the title of the target item, in this case the title proper of the print journal.

Subfield **x** is the ISSN of the target item.

Subfield **w** is for record control numbers, in this case a Library of Congress Card Number and an OCLC Bibliographic Record Number.

```
776   08   ‡i Also issued in print: ‡t
           Journal of technology education
           ‡x 1045-1064 ‡w (DLC) 90649316
           ‡w (OCoLC)20001913
```

This serial is available from a Web site and has one **Electronic Location and Access (856)** field. For resources with PURLs, CONSER recommends placing two **u** subfields in the field, with the PURL in the first and the standard URL for the resource in the second.

```
856   40   ‡u http://bibpurl.oclc.org/web/
           4731
           ‡u http://scholar.lib.vt.edu/
           ejournals /JTE
```

SHORT EXAMPLE: AGGREGATOR-NEUTRAL RECORD

Aggregator-neutral record: A MARC record that is used to represent all online versions of a serial. Aggregator-neutral records do not contain any version-specific information other than the URLs where each version is available. Only URLs for issue-level aggregators, rather than article-level aggregators, are included.

Some serials are available from multiple online providers. Initially, the accepted practice was to create a new record for each version of the serial. Thus, an electronic serial that was available from three Web sites would have three separate records. It eventually became clear that this practice was confusing and difficult for catalogers to maintain. Among other problems, serials sometimes moved to new providers or whole

```
Type: a ELvl:     Srce: d  GPub:    Ctrl:     Lang: eng
BLvl: s  Form: s  Conf: 0  Freq: f  MRec:     Ctry: vau
S/L:  0  Orig: s  EntW:    Regl: r  ISSN:     Alph:
Desc: a  SrTp: p  Cont:    DtSt: c  Dates: 1989,1999
```

006		m d
007		c ‡b r ‡d c ‡e n
010		2003238319
040		GZI ‡c GZI ‡d OCL ‡d N@F ‡d OCL ‡d OCLCQ ‡d IUL ‡d OCLCQ ‡d DLC
019		44327244
022		‡y 1045-1064
042		lcd
050	_4	T61 ‡b .J68
082	04	070.572
082	04	600.05
082	04	370.05
049		TXAM
130	0_	Journal of technology education (Online)
245	10	Journal of technology education ‡h [electronic resource].
246	13	JTE
260		[Blacksburg, VA] : ‡b Council of Technology Teacher Education and the International Technology Education Association, ‡c 1989-
310		Semiannual
362	0_	Vol. 1, no. 1 (fall 1989)-
500		Title from journal homepage (publisher's website, viewed May 19, 2003).
500		Latest issue consulted: Vol. 14, no. 2 (spring 2003); title from journal homepage (publisher's website, viewed Dec. 18, 2003).
520	8_	Presents the online journal, "Journal of Technology Education (JTE)," as part of the Scholarly Communications Project of Virginia Polytechnic Institute and State University in Blacksburg. "JTE"

Figure 8-6. Full *MARC 21* Record for Online Journal Also Issued in Print (Separate-Record Approach)

		provides a forum for scholarly discussion on topics relating to technology education. Allows users to search "JTE." Links to the home page of the Project.
538		Mode of access: World Wide Web.
538		System requirements: Web browser.
550		Cosponsored by: the International Technology Education Association; and: the Council on Technology Teacher Education.
650	_0	Technology ‡x Study and teaching ‡v Periodicals.
650	_0	Technical education ‡v Periodicals.
650	_4	Electronic journals.
650	_4	Technology ‡v Periodicals.
650	_4	Education ‡v Periodicals.
710	2_	International Technology Education Association.
710	2_	Council on Technology Teacher Education (U.S.)
776	08	‡i Also issued in print: ‡t Journal of technology education ‡x 1045-1064 ‡w (DLC) 90649316 ‡w (OCoLC)20001913
856	40	‡u http://bibpurl.oclc.org/web/4731 ‡u http://scholar.lib.vt.edu/ejournals/ JTE

Figure 8-6. (continued)

providers were acquired and re-branded, thus rendering the descriptive data incorrect in existing records.

In July 2003, CONSER adopted a new policy of creating one record for an online serial, even if it was available from multiple providers. This kind of record is known as an aggregator-neutral record. Aggregator-neutral records do not differ appreciably from other online serial records. Generally, the difference is that the names of vendors are absent from the record as uniform title qualifiers, added entries, or in notes. The name of the vendor is provided only for the "Description based on" or "Title from" note. The description must apply to all versions of the serial, so some descriptive information, such as special access information relevant to only one provider, is excluded. All relevant URLs are provided in **Electronic Location and Access (856)** fields. Only URLs for issue-level aggregators, rather than article-level aggregators, are included. Further information about aggregator-neutral records is available from the CONSER Web site at www.loc.gov/acq/conser/agg-neutral-recs.html. The guidelines for creating aggregator-neutral records are in *CCM* 31.2.3.B.

Figure 8-7. *American Journal of Bioethics* at bioethics.net (www.bioethics.net)

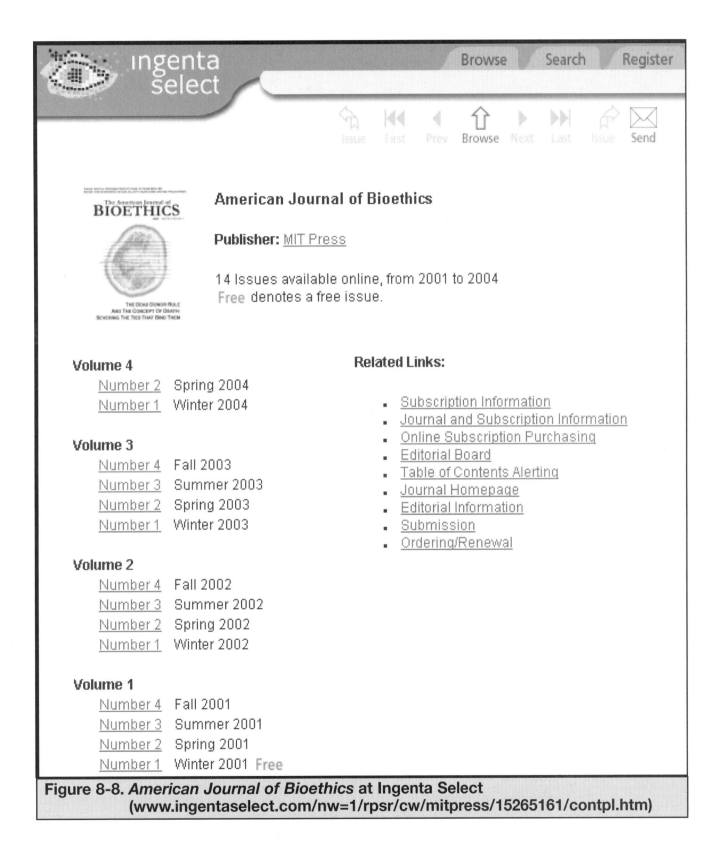

Figure 8-8. *American Journal of Bioethics* **at Ingenta Select (www.ingentaselect.com/nw=1/rpsr/cw/mitpress/15265161/contpl.htm)**

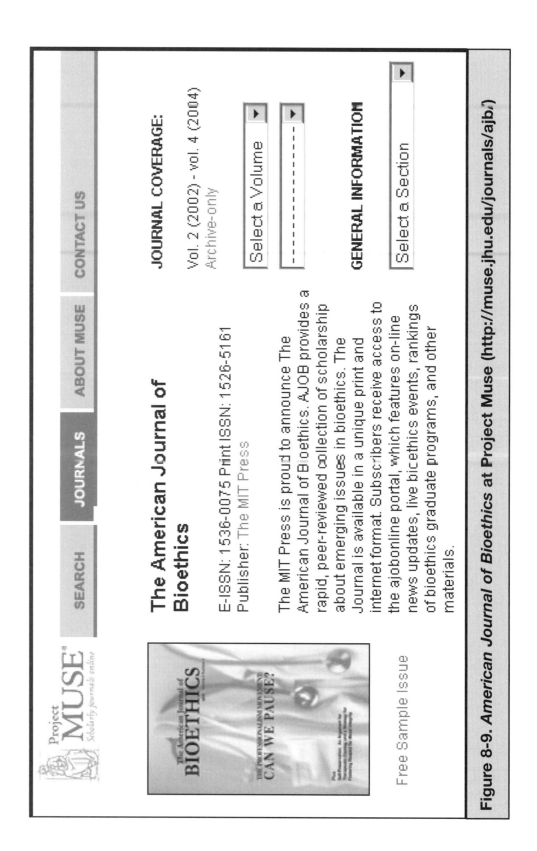

Figure 8-9. *American Journal of Bioethics* **at Project Muse (http://muse.jhu.edu/journals/ajb/)**

The problem with multiple providers is common among serials that require a subscription for access. We will use such a serial, available from three separate Web sites, to demonstrate the aggregator-neutral record.

BIBLIOGRAPHIC CHARACTERISTICS

The *American Journal of Bioethics* (*AJOB*) is provided through three separate Web sites. It has a dedicated Web site at www.bioethics.net and is also provided through the vendors Project Muse and Ingenta Select. A cataloger may have access to only one, or to multiple versions, of this serial. In general, the cataloger should use the publisher's Web site as the basis of description. If a separate host or archiving site has the first issue, then it should be used as the basis for description. In this case, volume 1, issue 1, published in winter 2001 is available from www.bioethics.net.

Significant bibliographic aspect: The serial *American Journal of Bioethics*. It is available from three Web sites. The publisher's Web site or the site with the first issue should be preferred as the basis for description.

Type of issuance: This is a continuing resource issued in a succession of discrete parts. It is a serial.

Source of information: The chief source of information is the resource itself, which is contained on its Web site. Other relevant information may be on any of the Web sites that host the serial.

Reproduction or born digital: This resource is simultaneously published in print and online. The electronic version is considered born digital.

Type of Record code: The code is a for predominantly textual.

Bibliographic Level code: The code is s for serial.

MARC 21 work form: Serial.

CODING THE *MARC 21* RECORD USING THE AGGREGATOR-NEUTRAL RECORD

Form of Original Item (008/22) and **Form of Item (008/23)** are both s for electronic.

```
Form:      s
Orig:      s
```

Because the **Type of Record** code a in the leader reflects the textual nature of serials, additional fixed fields must be added to reflect their electronic nature, specifically an **Additional Material Characteristics (006)** field and a **Physical Description (007)** field.

In the **Additional Material Characteristics (006)** field, the character in the first position determines the content in the rest of the positions. Therefore, the first character, known as the **Form of Material (006/00)**, is m indicating that this resource is a computer file.

The **006** for computer files has three data elements: **Target Audience, Type of Computer File**, and **Government Publication**.

Target Audience (006/05) is left blank because this is not a juvenile resource.

Type of Computer File (006/09) is d indicating that this resource is a document.

Government Publication (006/11) is blank because the resource is not a government publication.

```
006          m    d
```

The **Physical Description (007)** field is also designed so that the character in the first position determines the content in the rest of the positions. The first character, known as the **Category of Material (007/00)**, is c for computer file.

Specific Material Designation (007/01) is r, indicating that this is a remote-access resource.

Color (007/03) is c, indicating that this is a multicolored resource.

Dimensions (007/04) is n, which indicates that this code is not applicable. This is the appropriate code for all remote-access resources.

The remaining fields are optional and are not included in this example: **Sound (007/05), Image bit depth (007/06–08), File Formats (007/09), Quality Assurance Targets (007/20), Antecedent/Source (007/11), Level of Compression (007/12)**, and **Reformatting Quality (007/13)**.

```
007          c ‡b r ‡d c ‡e n ‡f u
```

The International Standard Serial Number (ISSN) is placed in the subfield **a** of the **International Standard Serial Number (022)** field. The first indicator of this field is coded 0 indicating that this is a serial of international interest. The print ISSN is placed in the subfield **y**. Although subfield **y** is defined as being the incorrect ISSN, the ISSN for the print version is placed in this field (*CCM* 31.19).

```
022  0_    1536-0075 ‡y 1526-5161
```

In this case, the title American journal of bioethics was established as the title proper for the print version of this resource. To differentiate the title for the electronic version, the record for the electronic version receives a **Uniform Title (130)**. The first indicator is 0 for the number of nonfiling characters. The second indicator is undefined. The uniform title is placed in subfield **a** and consists of the title proper with the addition of the qualifier (Online).

```
130  0_    American journal of bioethics
           (Online)
```

The title of the serial is placed in the **Title Statement (245)** subfield **a**. The first indicator, 1, indicates that the title is an added entry rather than the main entry. The second indicator, 0, specifies that there are no nonfiling characters in subfield **a**.

The general material designation [electronic resource] is placed in the **Title Statement (245)** subfield **h**.

The abbreviation *AJOB* is placed in the subfield **b** (*CCM* 6.3.3).

```
245  10    American journal of bioethics
           ‡h [electronic resource] : ‡b
           AJOB.
```

The source of the title proper and the date on which the resource was viewed for cataloging is placed in a **General Note (500)** (*CCM* 31.3.4). For aggregator-neutral records, the version used for description should be included.

```
500        Title from title screen
           (Ingenta Select website, viewed
           July 11, 2001).
```

When more than one issue is used for description, the latest issue consulted is provided in a **General Note (500)** (*CCM* 8.1.2 and 31.9).

```
500        Latest issue consulted: Vol. 3,
           no. 4 (fall 2003) (Project
           Muse, viewed Mar. 10, 2004).
```

The mode of access is provided in a **System Details Note (538)**, according to *CCM* 31.14.5. For aggregator-neutral records, a system-requirements note is not provided unless the note applies to all versions of the resource.

```
538        Mode of access: World Wide Web.
```

The **7XX** fields, or linking entry fields, provide information about related bibliographic items. In this case, an **Additional Physical Form Entry (776)** is created for the print version of the serial (*CCM* 31.16). The first indicator is 0, which causes the entry to be displayed as a note in library systems. The second indicator is 8, which causes the information in the subfield **i** to be used as the display label.

Subfield **t** is the title of the target item, in this case the title proper of the print journal.

Subfield **x** is the ISSN of the target item.

Subfield **w** is for record control numbers, in this case a Library of Congress Card Number and an OCLC Bibliographic Record Number.

```
776  08    ‡i Also issued in print: ‡t
```

<pre>
            American journal of bioethics
            ‡x 1526-5161 ‡w (DLC)sn
            99009204 ‡w (OCoLC)42279301
</pre>

For serials available from multiple providers, URLs to each provider may be added when creating an aggregator-neutral record. The three relevant URLs are placed in **Electronic Location and Access (856)** fields.

<pre>
    856   40   ‡u http://muse.jhu.edu/journals/
                 ajb/
    856   40   ‡u http://www.ingentaselect.com/
                 rpsv/cw/mitpress/15265161/contp1
                 .htm
    856   40   ‡u http://www.bioethics.net/
</pre>

Figure 8-10 shows a full *MARC 21* record for an aggregator-neutral record.

<pre>
Type: a   ELvl: Srce: c   GPub: Ctrl: Lang: eng
BLvl: s   Form: s   Conf: 0   Freq: q   MRec: Ctry: mau
S/L: 0   Orig: s   EntW: Regl: r   ISSN: 1   Alph: a
Desc: a   SrTp: p   Cont: DtSt: c   Dates: 2001,1999

      006   m   d
      007   c ‡b r ‡d c ‡e n ‡f u
      010   2001213395 ‡z 2002252795
      040   NSD ‡c NSD ‡d OCLCQ ‡d EYM ‡d WAU ‡d
                    OCLCQ ‡d WAU ‡d OCLCQ
      012   ‡l 1
      019   49735042
      022   0_   1536-0075 ‡y 1526-5161
      037   ‡b MIT Press Journals, 5 Cambridge
                    Center, Suite 4, Cambridge, MA 02142
      042   nsdp ‡a lcd
      050   14   QH332
      082   10   174 ‡2 13
      130   0_   American journal of bioethics
                    (Online)
      210   0_   Am. j. bioeth. ‡b (Online)
      210   10   Am J Bioeth ‡2 dnlm
      222   _0   American journal of bioethics ‡b
                    (Online)
</pre>

Figure 8-10. Full *MARC 21* Record for an Aggregator-Neutral Record

```
245   10    American journal of bioethics ‡h
            [electronic resource] : ‡b AJOB.
246   30    AJOB
260         Cambridge, Mass. : ‡b MIT Press, ‡c
            c2001-
310         Quarterly
362   0_    Vol. 1, no. 1 (winter 2001)-
500         Title from title screen (Ingenta
            Select website, viewed July 11,
            2001).
500         Latest issue consulted: Vol. 3, no. 4
            (fall 2003) (Project Muse, viewed
            Mar. 10, 2004).
538         Mode of access: World Wide Web.
650   _0    Bioethics ‡v Periodicals.
650   _0    Medical ethics ‡v Periodicals.
650   12    Bioethics ‡v Periodicals.
776   08    ‡i Also issued in print: ‡t American
            journal of bioethics ‡x 1526-5161 ‡w
            (DLC)sn 99009204 ‡w (OCoLC)42279301
856   40    ‡u http://muse.jhu.edu/journals/ajb/
856   40    ‡u
            http://www.ingentaselect.com/rpsv/cw/m
            itpress/15265161/contp1.htm
856   40    ‡u http://www.bioethics.net/
```

Figure 8-10. (continued)

SHORT EXAMPLE: ONLINE SERIAL WITH A TITLE CHANGE

Online serials frequently possess multiple relationships with other resources. A common example is a serial that is published in print and online and has experienced a title change. In such a case, the *MARC 21* record will have two linking entries: an **Additional Physical Form Entry (776)** to link to the record of the print version of the resource and a **Preceding Entry (780)** to link to the record of the former title of the resource. Note that the **Preceding Entry (780)** will link to the former *online* version of the resource, not the former print version, because the online version is the version that is being cataloged.

BIBLIOGRAPHIC CHARACTERISTICS

The journal *Library Collections, Acquisitions, and Technical Services* (*LCATS*) is published by Elsevier. It is available to subscribers online at www.sciencedirect.com/science/journal/14649055. The home page has a list of all issues available online, beginning with volume 23, issue 1, published in spring 1999. The Web page indicates that the journal was formerly published under a different title and provides a link to the Web site of the former title. A search of union catalogs indicates that this journal is also published in print. For this journal, the record will have linking fields to records for the former title and the print version of the title.

Significant bibliographic aspect: The serial *Library Collections, Acquisitions, and Technical Services*. The work is provided through the ScienceDirect Web site.

Type of issuance: This is a continuing resource issued in a succession of discrete parts. It is a serial.

Source of information: The chief source of information is the resource itself, which is contained on its Web site. Other relevant information is available on the publisher's Web site.

Reproduction or born digital: This resource is simultaneously published in print and online. The electronic version is considered born digital.

Type of Record code: The code is a for predominantly textual.

Bibliographic Level code: The code is s for serial.

MARC 21 work form: Serial.

CODING THE *MARC 21* RECORD FOR AN ONLINE SERIAL WITH A TITLE CHANGE

CONSER considers electronic versions of print publications to be simultaneous versions. For this reason, *LCATS* is an independent resource with a record coded on a serials workform.

Form of Original Item (008/22) and **Form of Item (008/23)** are both s for electronic.

```
Form:    s
Orig:    s
```

Because the **Type of Record** code a in the leader reflects the textual nature of serials, additional fixed fields must be added to reflect their electronic nature, specifically the **Additional Material Characteristics (006)** and **Physical Description (007)** fixed fields.

In the **Additional Material Characteristics (006)** field, the **Form of Material (006/00)**, is m, indicating that this resource is a computer file.

Type of Computer File (006/09) is d, indicating that this resource is a document.

The other fields, **Target Audience (006/05)** and **Government Publication (006/11)**, are left blank.

```
006        m      d
```

In the **Physical Description (007)** field, the **Category of Material (007/00)**, is c for computer file.

Specific Material Designation (007/01) is r, indicating that this is a remote-access resource.

Color (007/03) is c indicating that this resource is multicolored.

Dimensions (007/04) is n, which indicates that this code is not applicable. This is the appropriate code for all remote-access resources. The remaining fields are optional.

```
007        c ‡b r ‡d c ‡e n
```

In the record for the electronic version, the print ISSN is placed in the **International Standard Serial Number (022)** subfield **y**. Although subfield **y** is defined as being the incorrect ISSN, the ISSN for the print version is placed in this field (*CCM* 31.19).

```
022        ‡y 1464-9055
```

Uniform titles are used for serials to differentiate between two or more manifestations of a work published under identical titles proper. In this case, the title Library collections, acquisitions, and technical services was established as the title proper for the print version of this resource. Therefore, the record for the electronic version receives a **Uniform Title (130)**. The first indicator is 0 for the number of nonfiling characters. The second indicator is undefined. The uniform title is placed in subfield **a** and consists of the title proper with the addition of the qualifier (Online). *CCM* provides further information about uniform titles for serials in Module 5 and uniform titles for electronic serials in Module 31.

```
130   0_   Library collections, acquisi-
           tions, & technical services
           (Online)
```

The general-material designation [electronic resource] is placed in the **Title Proper (245)** subfield **h**.

```
245   10   Library collections, acquisi-
           tions & technical services
           ‡h [electronic resource]/.
```

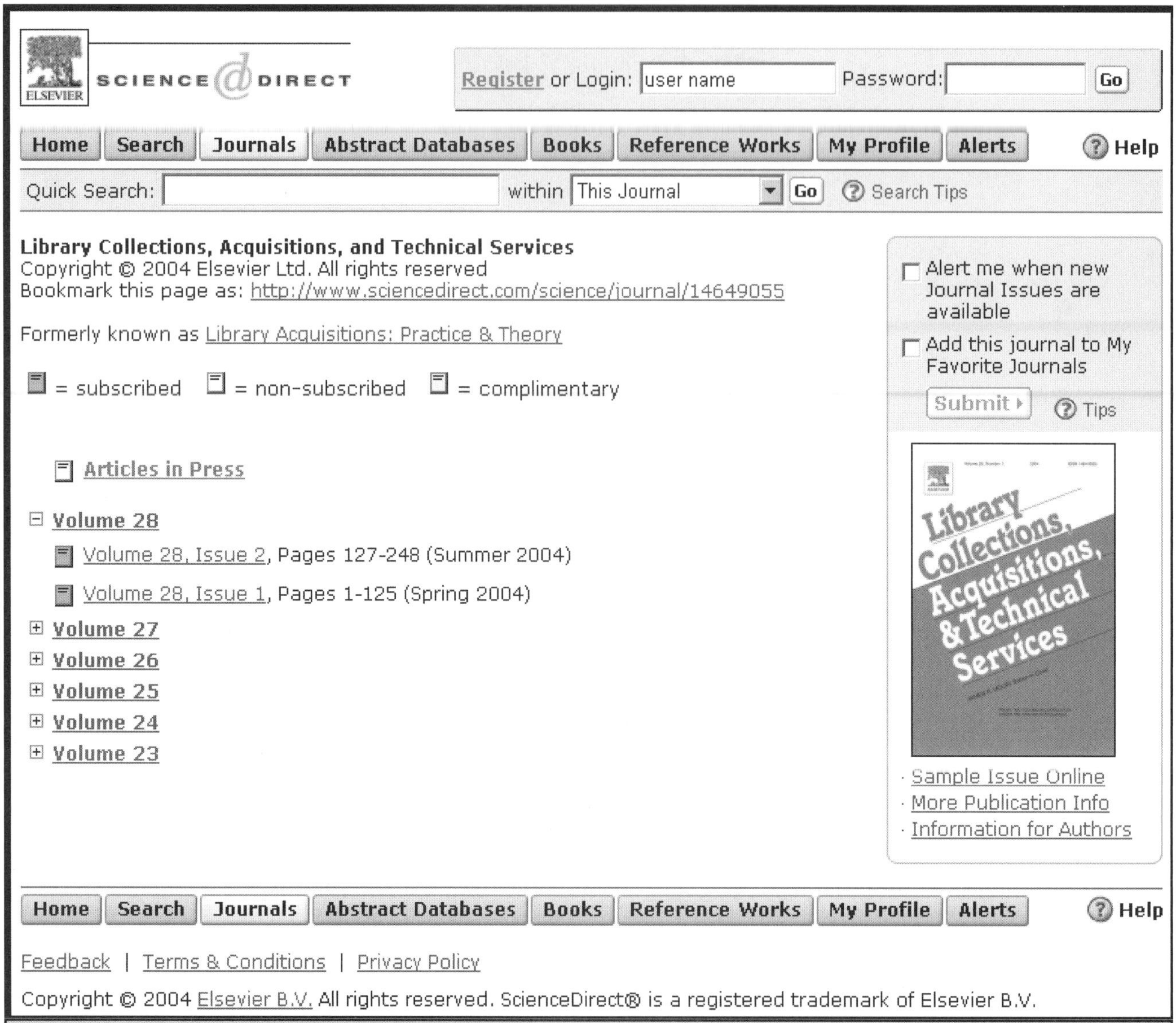

Figure 8-11. *Library Collections, Acquisitions, and Technical Services,* **Home Page**
(www.sciencedirect.com/science/journal/14649055)

CCM Module 31 provides instructions for notes specific to cataloging online serials. The source of the title proper is provided in a **General Note (500)**, according to *CCM* 31.3.3. The note should include the date the title was viewed in parentheses.

```
500           Title from introductory page
              (viewed Sept. 9, 2002).
```

The latest issue consulted is provided in a **General Note (500)** when more than one issue is used for description. This note is provided for online resources according to *LCRI* 12.7B23 and *CCM* 8.1.2.

```
500          Latest issue consulted: Vol.
             26, issue 2 (summer 2002).
```

The mode of access is provided in a **System Details Note (538)** according to *CCM* 31.14.5. The system requirements are provided in a **System Details Note (538)** according to *CCM* 31.14.4.

```
538          Mode of access: World Wide Web.
538          System requirements: Web
             browser.
```

An **Additional Physical Form Entry (776)** is created for the print version of the serial (*CCM* 31.16). The first indicator is 0, which causes the entry to be displayed as a note in library systems. The second indicator is set to 8, which prevents a predefined display constant from being generated.

The desired display text is placed in subfield **i** (*CCM* 31.16).

Subfield **t** is the title of the target item, in this case the title proper of the print journal.

Subfield **x** is the ISSN of the target item.

Subfield **w** is for record control numbers, in this case a Library of Congress Card Number and an OCLC Bibliographic Record Number.

```
776    18    ‡i Also available in print: ‡t
             Library collections, acquisi-
             tions & technical services ‡x
             1464-9055 ‡w (DLC)sn 99031280
             ‡w (OCoLC)40968090
```

A **Preceding Entry (780)** is created for the earlier title according to *CCM* 14.2.1. The first indicator is 0, which causes a note to display in online catalogs. The second indicator 0 represents that the title being cataloged continues the title in the linking field.

The title of the target work is placed in subfield **t**.

The Library of Congress Control Number and OCLC number are placed in **w** subfields.

```
780    00    ‡t Library acquisitions: prac-
             tice & theory (Online) ‡w (DLC)
             2002238867 ‡w (OCoLC)39061108
```

This serial is available from a Web site and has one **Electronic Location and Access (856)** field. Although it is not mandatory, serials requiring a subscription for access frequently have a note for access restrictions placed in the subfield **z**.

```
856    40    ‡z Subscription required for
             access. ‡u http://www.sciencedi-
             rect.com/science/jour-
             nal/14649055
```

Figure 8-12 is an example of a full record for an online serial that
is also available in print and has had a title change.

```
Type: a   ELvl:     Srce: d  GPub:  Ctrl:  Lang:eng
BLvl: s   Form:  s  Cont: U  Freq:q MRec:  Ctry:enk
S/L:  0   Orig:  s  EntW:    Regl:r ISSN:  Alph:
Desc: a   SrTp:  p  Cont:    DtSt:c Dates:1999,1999


006          m    d
007          c ‡b r ‡d c ‡e n
010          2002238866
040          IUA ‡c IUA ‡d OCL ‡d OCLCQ ‡d IUL ‡d
             OCLCQ
022          ‡y 1464-9055
042          Lcd
050    _4    Z689 ‡b .L515
049          TXAM
130    0_    Library collections, acquisitions, &
             technical services (Online)
245    10    Library collections, acquisitions &
             technical services ‡h [electronic
             resource].
246    1_    ‡i Popularly known as: ‡a LCATS
246    3_    Library collections, acquisitions, and
             technical services
260          [Oxford ; ‡a New York] : ‡b Pergamon
310          Quarterly
362    0_    Vol. 23, issue 1 (spring 1999)-
500          Title from introductory page (viewed
             Sept. 9, 2002).
500          Latest issue consulted: Vol. 26, issue 2
             (summer 2002).
538          Mode of access: World Wide Web.
650    _0    Acquisitions (Libraries) ‡v Periodicals.
650    _0    Collection management (Libraries) ‡v
             Periodicals.
650    _0    Technical services (Libraries) ‡v
             Periodicals.
776    18    ‡i Also available in print: ‡t Library
             collections, acquisitions & technical
             services ‡x 1464-9055 ‡w (DLC)sn
             99031280 ‡w (OCoLC)40968090
```

**Figure 8-12. *Full MARC 21* Record for Online Serial Also in
Print and with a Title Change**

```
780    00    ‡t Library acquisitions: practice &
              theory (Online) ‡w (DLC) 2002238867
              ‡w (OCoLC)39061108
856    40    ‡z Subscription required for access.
              ‡u http://www.sciencedirect.com/
              science/journal/14649055
```

Figure 8-12. (continued)

SHORT EXAMPLE: SERIAL DISCONTINUED IN PRINT, CONTINUED ONLINE

Serials sometimes cease in print and move exclusively online. This is considered a major change (*CCM* 16.4.1) and requires a new record. Because the print title precedes the online title, the resulting record for the online resource is linked to the print record using a **Preceding Entry (780)** field rather than an **Additional Physical Form Entry (776)** field. The record may also have a **Linking Entry Complexity Note (580)** if the print and electronic were published simultaneously for some time.

BIBLIOGRAPHIC CHARACTERISTICS

The *Journal of Extension* (*JOE*) is an open-access journal published by U.S. Cooperative Extension System. It is available online at www.joe.org. The home page has a link to back issues. Clicking the link reveals a list of issues, starting with volume 8 in 1970. Research indicates that the online version of the journal was published simultaneously with the print version from 1987 to 1993. In 1993, the journal moved exclusively online.

Significant bibliographic aspect: The serial *Journal of Extension*. The work is contained on a Web site under the domain www.joe.org.

Type of issuance: This is a continuing resource issued in a succession of discrete parts. It is a serial.

Source of information: The chief source of information is the resource itself, which is contained on its Web site.

Reproduction or born digital: This resource was published simultaneously in print and online from 1987 to 1993. Since 1993, it has been published exclusively online. It is considered born digital.

Type of Record code: The code a for predominantly textual.

Bibliographic Level code: The code s for serial.

MARC 21 work form: Serial.

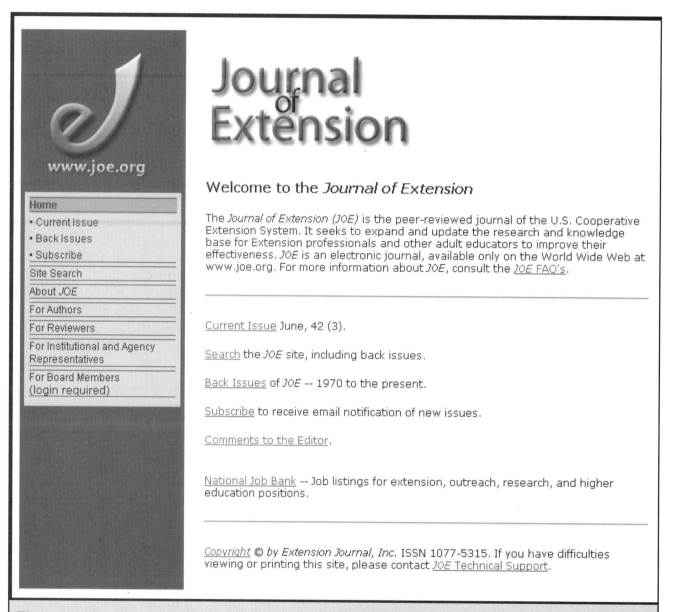

Figure 8-13. *Journal of Extension*, Home Page (www.joe.org)

CODING THE *MARC 21* RECORD FOR SERIALS DISCONTINUED IN PRINT, CONTINUED ONLINE

Form of Original Item (008/22) and Form of Item (008/23) are both s for electronic.

Form: s

```
Orig:      s
```

Because the **Type of Record** code a in the leader reflects the textual nature of serials, additional fixed fields must be added to reflect their electronic nature, specifically an **Additional Material Characteristics (006)** field and a **Physical Description (007)** field.

In the **Additional Material Characteristics (006)** field, the character in the first position determines the content in the rest of the positions. Therefore, the first character, known as the **Form of Material (006/00)**, is m, indicating that this resource is a computer file.

The **006** for computer files has three data elements: **Target Audience**, **Type of Computer File**, and **Government Publication**.

Target Audience (006/05) is left blank because this is not a juvenile resource.

Type of Computer File (006/09) is d, indicating that this resource is a document. **Government Publication (006/11)** is blank because the resource is not a government publication.

```
006        m     d
```

The **Physical Description (007)** field is also designed so that the character in the first position determines the content in the rest of the positions.

The first character, known as the **Category of Material (007/00)**, is c for computer file. **Specific Material Designation (007/01)** is r, indicating that this is a remote access resource.

Color (007/03) is c, indicating that this is a multicolored resource.

Dimensions (007/04) is n, which indicates that this code is not applicable. This is the appropriate code for all remote-access resources.

The remaining fields are optional and are not included in this example: **Sound (007/05)**, **Image bit depth (007/06–08)**, **File Formats (007/09)**, **Quality Assurance Targets (007/20)**, **Antecedent/Source (007/11)**, **Level of Compression (007/12)**, and **Reformatting Quality (007/13)**.

```
007        c ǂb r ǂd c ǂe n ǂf u
```

The ISSN is placed in the subfield **a** of the **International Standard Serial Number (022)** field. The first indicator of this field is coded 0, indicating that this is a serial of international interest.

The print ISSN is placed in the subfield **y**. Although subfield **y** is defined as being the incorrect ISSN, the ISSN for the print version is placed in this field (*CCM* Module 31). This journal was previously assigned an ISSN that was later cancelled. This is placed in subfield **z**.

```
022        1077-5315 ǂz 1077-5307 ǂy 0022-
           0140
```

In this case, the title `Journal of extension` was established as the title proper for the print version of this resource. To differentiate the title for the electronic version, the record for the electronic version receives a **Uniform Title (130)**. The first indicator is 0 for the number of non-filing characters. The second indicator is undefined.

The uniform title is placed in subfield **a** and consists of the title proper with the addition of the qualifier (`Online`).

```
130  0_   Journal of extension (Online)
```

The general material designation `[electronic resource]` is placed in the **Title Statement (245)** subfield **h**.

```
245  00   Journal of extension
          ‡h [electronic resource]/.
```

The chronological or sequential designation for the resource is placed in the **Dates of Publication and/or Sequential Designation (362)** field. The first indicator 0 specifies that the field is in the formatted style, rather than an unformatted note. The formatted note is used in this case because the first issue of this resource is available online and the title is still being published.

```
362  0_   Vol. 25, no. 3 (fall 1987)-
```

The source of the title proper and the date on which the resource was viewed for cataloging are placed in a **General Note (500)** (*CCM* 31.3.4).

```
500       Title from caption (viewed on
          Aug. 12, 2004).
```

The latest issue consulted is provided in a **General Note (500)** when more than one issue is used for description. This note is typically provided for online resources (*LCRI* 12.7B23 and *CCM* 8.1.2).

```
500       Latest issue consulted: Vol.
          36, no. 1 (Feb. 1998)/.
```

The existence of another physical medium is recorded in an **Additional Physical Form Available (530)** note (*CCM* 31.14.7). (An alternative is to put this note in the **776** subfield **i**.)

```
530       Also issued in print format,
          1987-1993.
```

The mode of access is provided in a **System Details Note (538)** (*CCM* 31.14.5).

```
538       Mode of access: World Wide Web
          browser, email, or gopher.
```

In this case, because the relationship of the online to the print version is a chronological relationship (the online replaced the print at a certain point in time) the linking relationship is provided in a **Preceding Entry (780)** field (*CCM* 14.2.1 and 31.16.1).

The title of the preceding entry is placed in subfield **t**.

The ISSN of the preceding entry is placed in the subfield **x**.

The Library of Congress Control Number and OCLC number are placed in **w** subfields.

```
780   00   ‡t Journal of extension ‡x
           0022-0140 ‡w (DLC)sn 85000080
           ‡w (OCoLC)1714173
```

This serial is available from a Web site and has one **Electronic Location and Access (856)** field. For resources with PURLs, CONSER recommends placing two **u** subfields in the field, with the PURL in the first and the standard URL for the resource in the second.

```
856   40   ‡u
           http://bibpurl.oclc.org/web/7319
           ‡u http://www.joe.org/
```

Figure 8-14 is a full record for a serial that has been discontinued in print and is only available online.

```
Type: a   ELvl:      Srce:    GPub:    Ctrl:   Lang: eng
BLvl: s   Form: S    Conf: 0  Freq: b  MRec:   Ctry: oru
S/L: 0 Orig:         EntW:    Regl: x  ISSN: 1 Alph: a
Desc: a   SrTp: P    Cont:    DtSt: c  Dates: 1987,1999


 006          m     d
 007          c ‡b r ‡d c ‡e n ‡f u
 010          sn 94002758 ‡z sn 94002757
 040          AGL ‡c AGL ‡d NSD ‡d GUA ‡d OCL ‡d
              AGL ‡d NSD ‡d MFM ‡d AGL ‡d OCL ‡d
              AGL ‡d GUA ‡d N@F ‡d OCLCQ ‡d CGU ‡d
              OCLCQ
 012          ‡l y
 019          34147958 ‡a 44366997
 022          1077-5315 ‡z 1077-5307 ‡y 0022-0140
 037          ‡b Extension Journal, Inc., Journal
              Editorial Office, joe-ed@joe.org ‡c
              Free
 042          nsdp ‡a lcd
 043          n-us---
 050     14   LC5201 ‡b .J66
```

Figure 8-14. Full *MARC 21* Record for Serial Discontinued in Print, Continued Online

070	0_	LC45.4.J682
072	_0	C210
072	_0	U000
082	10	374 ‡2 12
130	0_	Journal of extension (Online)
210	0_	J. ext. ‡b (Online)
222	_0	Journal of extension ‡b (Online)
245	00	Journal of extension ‡h [electronic resource].
246	1_	‡i Also known as: ‡a JOE
246	1_	‡i Also known as: ‡a Electronic journal of extension
246	1_	‡i Also known as: ‡a EJOE
260		Eugene, OR : ‡b Extension Journal, ‡c [1987-
310		6 no. a year, ‡b 1995-
321		Quarterly, ‡b fall 1993-1994
362	0_	Vol. 25, no. 3 (fall 1987)-
500		Title from caption (viewed on Aug. 12, 2004).
500		Latest issue consulted: Vol. 36, no. 1 (Feb. 1998).
530		Also issued in print format, 1987-1993.
538		Mode of access: World Wide Web browser, email, or gopher.
650	_0	Non-formal education ‡z United States ‡v Periodicals.
650	_0	Home economics extension work ‡z United States ‡v Periodicals.
650	_0	Agricultural extension work ‡z United States ‡v Periodicals.
780	00	‡t Journal of extension ‡x 0022-0140 ‡w (DLC)sn 85000080 ‡w (OCoLC)1714173
856	40	‡u http://bibpurl.oclc.org/web/7319 ‡u http://www.joe.org/

Figure 8-14. (continued)

SUMMARY

Serials have adapted quite successfully to the World Wide Web. When cataloging online serials, the familiar descriptive elements are included in the *MARC 21* record along with additional information required to describe the electronic characteristics of the resources. The characteristics of electronic resources present new challenges in the context of serials cataloging. As with monographs, one of the biggest challenges is determining the format. Is a resource indeed a serial? Some resources that are serials in print are presented as integrating resources online. Another major challenge is caused by the simultaneous publication of serials in print and online. CONSER has addressed this problem by allowing two options, the single-record approach and the separate-record approach. Libraries should carefully consider which option to use. When cataloging online serials using the separate-record approach, the guidelines of the aggregator-neutral record should be followed to guarantee consistency in cataloging. Because of their nature, serials will continue to undergo title changes, creating complex bibliographic relationships. Due to the electronic characteristics of online serials, it is not uncommon for *MARC 21* records to have multiple linking relationships. Fortunately, CONSER is continuing to update its guidelines for cataloging serials given these new challenges.

REFERENCES

Hiatt, Robert M. 1989. *Library of Congress Rule Interpretations*. Washington, DC: Library of Congress Cataloging Distribution Service.

Hirons, Jean L., ed. 2002. *CONSER Cataloging Manual*. Washington, DC: Library of Congress Cataloging Distribution Service.

Joint Steering Committee for the Revision of AACR2. 2002. *Anglo-American Cataloguing Rules,* 2nd ed., 2002 rev. Chicago: American Library Association.

Library of Congress Network Development and MARC Standards Office. 1999. *MARC 21 Format for Bibliographic Data*. Washington, DC: Library of Congress Cataloging Distribution Service.

Library of Congress Serial Record Division. 1994. *CONSER Editing Guide*. Washington, DC: Library of Congress Cataloging Distribution Service.

OCLC. 2002. *Bibliographic Formats and Standards,* 3rd ed. Dublin, OH: OCLC Online Computer Library Center.

9 ONLINE INTEGRATING RESOURCES: DATABASES AND WEB SITES

INTRODUCTION

Integrating resources change by means of successive updates that do not remain discrete; rather, the changes are integrated into the whole. An example of this is a frequently updating news Web site, which may add significant new content over a short period of time. The updates may be at regular intervals (such as once per week) or irregular. The frequency of the updates may be continuous (defined as more often than once a day), or at other intervals, such as daily, weekly, or monthly. The two types of online integrating resources are updating Web sites and updating databases.

Integrating resources have existed for some time in the form of loose-leaf publications, but they were only recognized as an independent type of issuance in the 2002 revision of *AACR2* (Joint Steering Committee for the Revision of AACR2, 2002). Subsequently, the *MARC 21* standard (LC Network Development and MARC Standards Office, 1999) was revised to accommodate these changes. The most significant change was the addition of a new **Bibliographic Level (leader/07)** of i for integrating resource.

Although *AACR2* and the *MARC 21* manual have been updated, the changes have been difficult to implement in cataloging utilities. At the time of this writing, OCLC still had not implemented the changes. For this reason, OCLC (2002b) outlined an interim policy for cataloging integrating resources in "Technical Bulletin 247: OCLC-MARC Format Update 2002." The policy requires integrating resources to be cataloged on the book workform (**Type of Record** a for language material and **Bibliographic Level** m for monograph) with an **Additional Material Characteristics (006)** field to code for integrating-resources characteristics. The examples in this chapter follow the interim policy, with additional notes describing future coding practices for important fields. The most thorough discussion of cataloging integrating resources is Appendix A of the *BIBCO Participants' Manual*. Titled *Integrating Resources: A Cataloging Manual ([IRCM] Boehr and Jacobs, 2003)*, it defines the current Program for Cooperative Cataloging's (PCC) policy for cataloging integrating resources.

The first example is a continuously updating Web site. Then there will be shorter examples of other integrating resources with distinct characteristics and a discussion on how to catalog them.

LONG EXAMPLE: CONTINUOUSLY UPDATING WEB SITE

BIBLIOGRAPHIC CHARACTERISTICS

The CNN Web site, located at www.cnn.com, contains complex, news-oriented content. Most of the hyperlinks on the site link to textual news articles, while others link to multimedia sound or video files. Some of the links go to content external to the CNN Web site. The Web site is updated with new articles throughout the day. New content is integrated into the whole of the Web site without maintaining discrete parts.

Significant bibliographic aspect: The CNN Web site, located at www.cnn.com.

Type of issuance: This is a continuing resource in which the updates are integrated into the whole. It is an integrating resource.

Sources of information: The chief source of information is the resource itself, preferring any part of the resource that provides the most complete information. In this case, most of the relevant bibliographic information is available on the home page. Additional relevant information is available on various pages of the Web site, accessible by clicking hyperlinks from the home page.

Reproduction or born digital? This is a born-digital resource.

Type of Record code: Because this is a predominantly textual resource, the type code is a for language material.

Bibliographic Level code: Because this is an integrating resource, the bibliographic level is m, under the interim practice defined in "Technical Bulletin 247: OCLC-MARC Format Update 2002." In the future, this resource will have a bibliographic level of i.

MARC 21 work form: Book.

Figure 9-1. CNN.com Home Page (www.cnn.com)

CODING THE *MARC 21* RECORD FOR A CONTINUOUSLY UPDATING WEB SITE

Leader

Textual Web sites have the **Type of Record (leader/06)** coded a for language material and **Bibliographic Level (leader/07)** coded m for monograph.

The **Type of Control (leader/08)** is left blank because this field is used only for archival resources.

The **Encoding Level (leader/17)** is I to indicate full-level cataloging.

The **Descriptive Cataloging Form (leader/18)** is coded a, indicating that description is based on the rules of *AACR2*.

Future practice: Once implemented, this resource will receive **Bibliographic Level (leader/07)** i for integrating resource.

008

The **Type of Date (008/06)** is m, indicating that multiple dates are used.

The **Beginning Date** field **(008/07-10)** is 199u, indicating that the initial date of publication is between 1990 and 1999.

The **Place of Publication (008/15)** is gau, which is the *MARC 21* country code for Georgia.

Illustrations (008/18-21) is coded a, indicating that the Web site has illustrations.

Target Audience (008/22) is left blank. This is an optional field that tends to be used primarily for juvenile materials.

Form of Item (008/23) is s, indicating that this is an electronic resource.

Nature of Contents (008/24-27) is left blank. This field is used for specific types of resources (e.g., bibliographies or dictionaries) and is not used for a news Web site.

Government Publication (008/28) is blank because this is not a government publication.

Conference Publication (008/29) is 0, indicating this is not a conference publication.

Festschrift (008/30) is 0, indicating this is not a festschrift.

Index (008/31) is 0, indicating the resource does not contain an index to its own contents.

Literary Form (008/33) is 0, indicating this is not a work of fiction.

Biography (008/34) is blank, indicating that the resource does not contain biographical materials.

After the implementation of **Bibliographic Level** i, the **Type of Date (008/06)** field will have three values: c for currently published, d for ceased, or u for unknown. In this case, the appropriate value would be c for continuing.

006

Because the **Type of Record** code a in the leader reflects the *textual* nature of this Web site, additional fixed fields must be added to reflect its electronic nature, specifically an **Additional Material Characteristics (006)** field and a **Physical Description (007)** field. Also, as a result of the interim coding policy, integrating resources receive an additional **006** for continuing resources to reflect integrating-resource characteristics.

In **Additional Material Characteristics (006)** fields, the character in the first position determines the content in the rest of the positions. The first **006** for this resource reflects the electronic nature of the resource. The first character, known as the **Form of Material (006/00)**, is m, indicating that this resource is a computer file.

The **006** for computer files has three data elements: **Target Audience**, **Type of Computer File**, and **Government Publication**.

Target Audience (006/05) is left blank because this is not a juvenile resource.

Type of Computer File (006/09) is d, indicating that this resource is a document.

Government Publication (006/11) is blank because the resource is not a government publication.

```
006        m        d
```

The second **006** for this resource reflects the continuing nature of this resource.

The **Form of Material (006/00)** is s, indicating that this resource is a continuing resource.

The **006** for continuing resources has five mandatory data elements: **Frequency**, **Regularity**, **Type of Resource**, **Form of Item**, and **Entry Convention**.

Frequency (006/01) is coded k, indicating this resource updates continuously.

Regularity (006/02) is left blank when **Frequency** is k.

Type of Resource (006/04) is coded w for updating Web site.

Form of Item (006/06) is coded s, indicating that this is an electronic resource.

> **Integrated-entry convention:**
> Under this convention, an item is cataloged under its latest title, responsible person, or corporate body. It is used for integrating resources and electronic serials that do not retain their earlier titles.

Entry Convention (006/17) is coded 2, indicating that the integrating-entry convention is used for changes in the main entry.

```
006       sk w s     2
```

After the implementation of **Bibliographic Level** i, the **006** for continuing resources will not be necessary. The appropriate codes will be added to the leader and **008** fields.

007

The **Physical Description (007)** field is also designed so that the character in the first position determines the content in the rest of the positions.

The first character, known as the **Category of Material (007/00)**, is c for computer file.

Specific Material Designation (007/01) is r, indicating that this is a remote access resource.

Color (007/03) is c, indicating that this is a multicolored resource.

Dimensions (007/04) is n, indicating that this code is not applicable. This is the appropriate code for all remote-access resources. The remaining fields are optional and are not included in this example: **Sound (007/05)**, **Image bit depth (007/06–08)**, **File Formats (007/09)**, **Quality Assurance Targets (007/20)**, **Antecedent/Source (007/11)**, **Level of Compression (007/12)**, and **Reformatting Quality (007/13)**.

```
007       c ‡b r ‡d c ‡e n
```

Variable Fields

MARC 21 records for integrating resources include the descriptive fields that are created for print integrating resources (loose-leaf publications) plus additional fields and subfields to reflect their electronic nature. Some differences stand out in particular. For remote electronic resources, the general material designation [electronic resource] is placed in the **Title Proper (245)** subfield **h**.

Remote electronic resources do not have a **Physical Description (300)** field. Certain note fields are required for electronic resources (*AACR2,* Chapter 9). These are nature and scope note, systems-requirements note, mode-of-access note, source-of-title-proper note, and item-described note. The source-of-title-proper note can be combined with the item-described note.

The **Electronic Location and Access (856)** field contains the URL or other type of location identifier. Furthermore, the nature of remote electronic resources in general provides challenges for coding some of the common variable fields. These will be discussed in turn.

Number and Code Fields (01X-04X)

This record has a **Library of Congress Control Number (010)** field, indicating that it was input by an agency that has authorization to do this. The Library of Congress and members of the Program for Cooperative Cataloging are the only agencies that are authorized to add this number to a record.

The **Cataloging Source (040)** field indicates that the original cataloging agency was the Library of Congress, which would explain the presence of the **Library of Congress Control Number** field. The **Cataloging Source** field is updated automatically by the cataloging utility.

This record also has an **OCLC Control Number Cross-Reference (019)** field. This field contains the OCLC control numbers of records that were duplicates and were deleted from WorldCat. It is added by OCLC.

```
010        00529724
040        DLC ‡c DLC ‡d WAU ‡d ZBL ‡d N@F
           ‡d GZN ‡d OCLCQ ‡d LML ‡d OCLCQ
           ‡d YQU ‡d LCP ‡d OCLCQ
019        34123060 ‡a 40171266 ‡a
           44312130 ‡a 44330684 ‡a
           50162764 ‡a 50165439 ‡a
           50398369 ‡a 50706526 ‡a
           51667459 ‡a 53190931 ‡a
           53870950
```

Classification and Call Number Fields (05X-08X)

This example has two classification fields, a **Dewey Decimal Call Number (082)** and a **Locally Assigned LC-type Call Number (090)**. For remote electronic resources, these fields serve more as subject classifications than call numbers. It is essentially impossible for them to serve as a physical item location device, that is, a call number, because remote electronic resources have no material existence. Still, subject classification is a useful tool in retrieval: classification numbers help co-locate similar items in online catalogs and may also be used for deriving other user tools, such as browseable subject lists.

```
050   _4   PN4888.T4 ‡b C66
```

```
082   04    070.195
```

Main Entry Fields (1XX)

According to *AACR2* 21.1C1, the title is the main entry heading of this work. The personal authorship for this title is diffuse, and the resource does not emanate from a corporate body as defined by rule 21.1B2. The record does not require a **Uniform Title (130)** because it does not conflict with any other title. In this case, the **Title Statement (245)** serves as the main entry and no **1XX** field is required.

Title and Title-Related Fields (20X-24X)

The title of the Web site is placed in the **Title Statement (245)** subfield **a**. The first indicator 0 is used when the title is the main entry. The second indicator 0 specifies that there are no nonfiling characters in subfield **a**.

The general material designation [electronic resource] is placed in the subfield **h**.

This Web site has experienced a title change, indicated in the **Former Title (247)** field. The range of dates for the former title is placed in subfield **f** (*LCRI* 12.7B4.1). Note that for integrating resources, ongoing maintenance of the record is often required. This includes maintenance for changes in the title proper and occasional changes to the dates in the fixed fields.

```
245   00    CNN.com ‡h [electronic
            resource].
247   10    CNN interactive ‡f <Oct. 1998-
            Jan. 2000>
```

Edition, Imprint, Etc. Fields (250-270)

Chapter 9 of *AACR2* states that all remote electronic resources are considered to be published. Publication information is placed in the **Publication, Distribution, Etc. (260)** field. The place of publication is in subfield **a**, and the publisher's name in subfield **b**. Normally, the date of publication is placed in subfield **c**, but determining the exact date of publication for an integrating resource is sometimes problematic. When this information is not known exactly, the estimated date should be placed in the **Dates of Publication and/or Sequential Designation (362)** field rather than in the **260** subfield **c** (*IRCM* I.6.1).

```
260           Atlanta, Ga.  :  ‡b Cable News
              Network
```

Physical Description, Etc. Fields (3XX)

The frequency of updates for the resource is placed in the **Current Publication Frequency** (**310**) field (*LCRI* 12.7B1). The word updated is added to indicate that this applies to the updates and not the issuance of the resource itself.

Since no explicit date is available for the **260** field, the estimated beginning date is provided in a **Dates of Publication and/or Sequential Designation** (**362**) field (*IRCM* I.9.9.2). The first indicator of 1 indicates that this is an unformatted note.

```
310           Continuously updated
362   1_      Began in 1990s?
```

Note Fields: Part 1 (50X-53X)

Most notes for online-continuing resources are prescribed in Chapter 9 of *AACR2*. *Integrating Resources: A Cataloging Manual* ([*IRCM*] Boehr and Jacobs, 2003) also provides instructions for notes specific to cataloging integrating resources.

The source of the title proper is provided in a **General Note** (**500**) (*AACR2* 9.1B2 and 9.7B3).

The date on which the resource was viewed for cataloging is placed in a **General Note** (**500**) (*AACR2* 9.7B22).

These two notes may be combined.

```
500           Title from home page (viewed
              Nov. 13, 2002).
```

A summary of the contents can be provided in a **Summary Note** (**520**). The first indicator of 0 means that the display constant "Summary" will be generated in the online catalog. This field is not mandatory for integrating resources.

```
520           Cable News Network Web site
              featuring United States and
              world news, weather reports,
              and current events in subject
              areas such as business, sports,
              technology, health, entertain-
              ment, politics, law, travel,
              food, arts, and style. Includes
              video and audio segments.
```

Note Fields: Part 2 (53X-58X)

The mode of access is provided in a **System Details (538)** note (*AACR2 9.7B1c*)

The system requirements are provided in a **System Details (538)** note (*AACR2* 9.7B1b).

```
538        Mode of access: World Wide Web.
538        System requirements: Web browser
```

Subject Access Fields (6XX)

Subject analysis is a complex practice that requires training, skill, and judgment. With regards to integrating resources, *IRCM* states "it is expected that records for integrating resource will contain subject headings" (Hixson, Banush, and Cristán, 2002, App. A, p. 74). Subject headings are discussed in Section 14 of *IRCM*.

This resource has been assigned one **Topical Term (650)**, a Library of Congress subject heading, as indicated by the second indicator of 0.

```
650   _0   Television broadcasting of news.
```

Added-Entry Fields (70X-75X)

A **Corporate Name Added Entry (710)** is created for the publisher and distributor, Cable News Network, (*AACR2* 21.30E1). The first indicator of 2 indicates that the name is in direct order.

```
710   2_   Cable News Network.
```

Linking Entry Fields (76X-78X)

Linking entries are permissible for integrating resources, but they are not as common as with serials. Title changes are recorded by adding a **Former Title (247)** field to the record. Some cases that may require the use of linking fields include the existence of an additional physical format, edition, or translation.

Holdings, Location, Alternate Graphs, Etc. Fields (841-88X)

The URL for this Web site is placed in an **Electronic Location and Access (856)** field.

```
856   40   ‡u http://www.cnn.com/
```

The full record for a continuously updating Web site is shown in Figure 9-2.

```
Type: a  ELvl: I  Srce:     Audn:     Ctrl:     Lang: eng
BLvl: m  Form: s  Conf: 0   Biog:     MRec:     Ctry: gau
         Cont:    GPub:     LitF: 0   Indx:  0
Desc: a  Ills: a  Fest: 0   DtSt: m   Dates: 199u,1999


   006             m    d
   006             sk w s        2
   007             c ‡b r ‡d c ‡e n ‡f u
   010             00529724
   040             DLC ‡c DLC ‡d WAU ‡d ZBL ‡d N@F ‡d
                   GZN ‡d OCLCQ ‡d LML ‡d OCLCQ ‡d YQU
                   ‡d LCP ‡d OCLCQ
   019             34123060 ‡a 40171266 ‡a 44312130 ‡a
                   44330684 ‡a 50162764 ‡a 50165439 ‡a
                   50398369 ‡a 50706526 ‡a 51667459 ‡a
                   53190931 ‡a 53870950
   050   _4        PN4888.T4 ‡b C66
   082   04        070.195
   245   00        CNN.com ‡h [electronic resource].
   247   10        CNN interactive ‡f <Oct. 1998-Jan.
                   2000>
   260             Atlanta, Ga. : ‡b Cable News Network
   310             Continuously updated
   362   1_        Began in 1990s?
   538             Mode of access: World Wide Web.
   538             System Requirements: Web browser
   500             Title from home page (viewed Nov. 13,
                   2002).
   500             Frequently updated.
   520             Cable News Network Web site featuring
                   United States and world news, weather
                   reports, and current events in sub-
                   ject areas such as business, sports,
                   technology, health, entertainment,
                   politics, law, travel, food, arts,
                   and style. Includes video and audio
                   segments.
   650   _0        Television broadcasting of news.
   710   2_        Cable News Network.
   856   40        ‡u http://www.cnn.com/
```

Figure 9-2. Full *MARC 21* Record for a Continuously Updating Web Site

SHORT EXAMPLE: FREQUENCY AND REGULARITY ARE UNKNOWN

Many online integrating resources fail to provide complete bibliographic information regarding publication: first date of publication, frequency, and regularity. The availability or lack of this information influences coding of the *MARC 21* records in both fixed and variable data fields. *IRCM* addresses the various combinations of this information that may be available. In the following example, we demonstrate cataloging a resource in which the frequency and regularity are unknown.

BIBLIOGRAPHIC CHARACTERISTICS

The United States Geological Survey (USGS) Web site, located at www.usgs.gov, contains a broad diversity of content related to geology, geography, and earth sciences. The Web site has textual documents, images, cartographic materials, data sets, and online services. When content is added, it is integrated into various locations on the site. This site is not a serial, and it does not provide discrete issues. It is clearly an integrating resource. The main Web site indicates the date of last update, but different sections of the site have different dates of update. There is no indication of the frequency or regularity of the updates.

Significant bibliographic aspect: The USGS Web site, located at www.usgs.gov.

Type of issuance: This is a continuing resource in which the updates are integrated into the whole. It is an integrating resource.

Source of information: Most of the relevant bibliographic information is available on the home page at www.usgs.gov. Additional relevant information is available on various pages of the Web site, which can be accessed by clicking hyperlinks from the home page.

Reproduction or born digital: This is a born-digital resource.

Type of Record code: Because this is a predominantly textual resource, the type code is a for language material.

Bibliographic Level code: Because this is an integrating resource, the bibliographic level is m under the interim practice defined in "Technical Bulletin 247: OCLC-MARC Format Update 2002." In the future, this resource will have a bibliographic level of i.

MARC 21 workform: Book.

Figure 9-3. United States Geological Survey, Home Page (www.usgs.gov)

CODING THE *MARC 21* RECORD WHEN THE FREQUENCY AND REGULARITY ARE UNKNOWN

Because the **Type of Record** code a in the leader reflects the textual nature of integrating resources, additional fixed fields must be added to reflect their electronic nature, specifically an **Additional Material Characteristics (006)** field and a **Physical Description (007)** field. Also, as a result of the interim coding policy, integrating resources receive an additional **006** for continuing resources to reflect integrating-resource characteristics.

The first **006** for this resource reflects the electronic nature of the resource.

The **Form of Material (006/00)** is m, indicating that this resource is a computer file.

The **006** for computer files has three data elements: **Target Audience**, **Type of Computer File**, and **Government Publication**.

Target Audience (006/05) is left blank because this is not a juvenile resource.

Type of Computer File (006/09) is d, indicating that this resource is a document.

Government Publication (006/11) is f because the resource is published by a federal agency.

```
006      m    d f
```

The second **006** for this resource reflects the continuing nature of this resource.

The **Form of Material (006/00)** is s indicating that this resource is a continuing resource.

The **006** for continuing resources has five mandatory data elements: **Frequency**, **Regularity**, **Type of Resource**, **Form of Item**, and **Entry Convention**.

Frequency (006/01) is coded u, indicating that the frequency is unknown.

Regularity (006/02) is u, indicating that the regularity is unknown.

Type of Resource (006/04) is coded w for updating Web site.

Form of Item (006/06) is coded s, indicating that this is an electronic resource.

Entry Convention (006/17) is coded 2, indicating that the integrating entry convention is used for changes in the main entry.

```
006      suu w s        2
```

In the **Physical Description (007)** field, the **Category of Material (007/00)**, is c for computer file.

Specific Material Designation (007/01) is r, indicating that this is a remote-access resource.

Color (007/03) is m, indicating that the image of the resource is produced in a combination of black-and-white and other color combinations.

Dimensions (007/04) is n, the appropriate code for all remote-access resources. The remaining fields are optional.

```
007        c ‡b r ‡d m ‡e n
```

The general material designation [electronic resource] is placed in the **Title Statement (245)** subfield **h**.

```
245 10    USGS ‡h [electronic resource] :
          ‡b science for a changing
          world.
```

In this case, the publication date is not explicitly stated on the Web site. Furthermore, the Web site is not the first iteration. Thus the publication date is not given in the **260** subfield **c**.

The estimated date of publication is placed in the **Dates of Publication and/or Sequential Designation (362)** field (*IRCM* I.6.1). The first indicator is 1, meaning that the note is unformatted.

Because the frequency and regularity are unknown, the **Current Publication Frequency (310)** field is omitted, (*IRCM* I.9.3.3).

This information is also reflected in the fixed fields, specifically in the **Additional Material Characteristics (006)** fields for **Frequency** and **Regularity**.

```
260        Reston, VA : ‡b United States
           Geological Survey
362        Began in 1996?
```

The source of the title proper is provided in a **General Note (500)** (*AACR2* 9.1B2 and 9.7B3).

The date on which the resource was viewed for cataloging is placed in a **General Note (500)** (*AACR2* 9.7B22). These two notes may be combined.

```
500        Title from title screen (viewed
           on Apr. 29, 2002).
```

A summary of the contents can be provided in a **Summary Note (520)**. The first indicator of 8 means that no display constant will be generated. This field is not mandatory for integrating resources.

```
520 8_     The U.S. Geological Survey pro-
           vides the Nation with reliable,
           impartial information to
           describe and understand the
           Earth. This information is used
```

to: minimize loss of life and
property from natural disas-
ters; manage water, biological,
energy, and mineral resources;
enhance and protect the quality
of life; and contribute to wise
economic and physical development.

The mode of access is provided in a **System Details (538)** note
(*AACR2* 9.7B1c). The system requirements are provided in a **System Details (538)**. ([*AACR2*] 9.7 B1b).

```
538   Mode of access: World Wide Web.
538   System requirements: Web Browser.
```

The URL for this Web site is placed in an **Electronic Location and Access (856)** field.

```
856   40    ‡u http://www.usgs.gov/
```

Figure 9-4 is the full record for a resource for which the frequency and regularity are not known.

```
Type: a  ELvl: I  Srce: D  Audn:     Ctrl:      Lang: eng
BLvl: m  Form: s  Conf: 0  Biog:     MRec:      Ctry: vau
         Cont:    GPub: F  LitF: 0   Indx:  0
Desc: a  Ills: a  Fest: 0  DtSt: m   Dates: 1996,1999


   006          m    d f
   006          suu w s         2
   007          c ‡b r ‡d m ‡e n
   040          WAU ‡c WAU ‡d OCL ‡d OCLCQ ‡d N@F
   019          34197936 ‡a 42256344 ‡a 44296137 ‡a 44296145 ‡a
                44311594 ‡a 44312228 ‡a 48920208 ‡a 48920255
   043          n-us---
   082   04     551.0223
   090          QE76 ‡b .G465
   049          TXAM
   110   2_     Geological Survey (U.S.)
   245   10     USGS ‡h [electronic resource] : ‡b science for
                a changing world.
   246   30     Science for a changing world
   246   1_     ‡i Title in HTML header: ‡a U.S. Geological
                Survey home page
   246   3_     U.S. Geological Survey
```

Figure 9-4 Full *MARC 21* Record for Resource When Frequency and Regularity Are Unknown

246	3_	US Geological Survey
246	3_	United States Geological Survey
260		Reston, VA : ‡b United States Geological Survey
362		Began in 1996?
500		Title from title screen (viewed on Apr. 29, 2002).
520	8_	The U.S. Geological Survey provides the Nation with reliable, impartial information to describe and understand the Earth. This information is used to: minimize loss of life and property from natural disasters; manage water, biological, energy, and mineral resources; enhance and protect the quality of life; and contribute to wise economic and physical development.
538		Mode of access: World Wide Web.
538		System requirements: Web browser
610	20	Geological Survey (U.S.)
650	_0	Geology ‡z United States.
650	_0	Earth sciences ‡z United States.
650	_0	Natural resources ‡z United States ‡x Management.
610	24	United States. Dept. of the Interior. Geological Survey.
650	_4	Geological mapping
650	_4	Geological surveys
651	_4	United States
856	40	‡u http://www.usgs.gov/

Figure 9-4 (continued)

SHORT EXAMPLE: COMPUTER FILE *MARC 21* FORMAT

All of the examples we have presented so far are predominantly textual resources, but some online resources, especially many integrating resources, are not predominantly textual. Such resources include computer programs, data files, multimedia resources, and online systems and services. When cataloging these resources, the **Type of Record (leader/06)** code is set to m for computer file, and the *MARC 21* computer file workform is used.

A **Physical Description (007)** field is added to the record but not an **Additional Material Characteristics (006)** for electronic

Figure 9-5. Weather.com Home Page (www.weather.com)

resources. Under the interim policy for integrating resources, an **Additional Material Characteristics (006)** for continuing resources is added. Additional information for coding the **Type of Record** for complex electronic resources is available in "Cataloging Electronic Resources: OCLC-MARC Coding Guidelines" (Weitz, 2003).

BIBLIOGRAPHIC CHARACTERISTICS

Weather.com provides a wide variety of weather-related services. The textual content includes brief weather forecasts and reports. The nontextual content consists of interactive maps, videos, and services that provide information related to weather, such as pollution reports. Although it contains textual content, it is not clear that the Web site is predominantly textual. "Cataloging Electronic Resources: OCLC-MARC Coding Guidelines" states "In case of doubt or if the most significant aspect cannot be determined, consider the item a computer file." (Weitz, 2003) When content is added, it is integrated into various locations on the site. It is clearly an integrating resource.

Significant bibliographic aspect: Weather.com, located at www.weather.com.

Type of issuance: This is a continuing resource in which the updates are integrated into the whole. It is an integrating resource.

Source of information: Most of the relevant bibliographic information is available on the home page at www.weather.com. Additional relevant information is available on various pages of the Web site, accessible by clicking hyperlinks from the home page.

Reproduction or born digital: This is a born-digital resource.

Type of Record code: This resource meets the definition of an online system or service. Consequently, the **Type of Record** code is m, indicating that it is a computer file.

Bibliographic Level code: Because this is an integrating resource, the bibliographic level is m under the interim practice defined in "Technical Bulletin 247: OCLC-MARC Format Update 2002." In the future, this resource will have a bibliographic level of i.

MARC 21 workform: Computer file.

CODING THE *MARC 21* RECORD USING THE COMPUTER-FILE *MARC 21* FORMAT

This resource meets the definition of an online system or service. Therefore, the **Type of Record** code is m. The combination of this code with the **Bibliographic Level** m results in a computer-file workform. The fixed fields in the computer-file workform are coded using the information from the chief source of information, which is the resource itself.

One fixed field in this workform is particularly influenced by the electronic nature of the resource, the **Type of Computer File (008/26)** field. In this case, it is coded m, indicating that the resource is a combination of different types of computer files, including computer models, numeric-data files, computer programs, and text files.

```
File:       m
```

An **Additional Material Characteristics (006)** for continuing resources must be added to reflect integrating-resource characteristics.

The **Form of Material (006/00)** is s, indicating that this resource is a continuing resource.

The **006** for continuing resources has five mandatory data elements: **Frequency, Regularity, Type of Resource, Form of Item**, and **Entry Convention**.

Frequency (006/01) is coded k, indicating that this resource updates continuously.

Regularity (006/02) is left blank when **Frequency** is k.

Type of Resource (006/04) is coded w for updating Web site.

Form of Item (006/06) is coded s, indicating that this is an electronic resource.

Entry Convention (006/17) is coded 2, indicating that the integrating entry convention is used for changes in the main entry.

```
006       sk w s      2
```

Furthermore, all online resources must have a **Physical Description (007)** fixed field for electronic resources.

The **Category of Material (007/00)**, is c for computer file.

Specific Material Designation (007/01) is r, indicating that this is a remote-access resource.

Color (007/03) is c, indicating that this is a multicolored resource.

Dimensions (007/04) is n, indicating that this code is not applicable. This is the appropriate code for all remote-access resources.

The remaining fields are optional and are not included in this example: **Sound (007/05), Image bit depth (007/06–08), File Formats (007/09), Quality Assurance Targets (007/20), Antecedent/Source (007/11), Level of Compression (007/12)**, and **Reformatting Quality (007/13)**.

```
007       c ǂb r ǂd c ǂe n
```

The general material designation [electronic resource] is placed in the subfield **h**. Other forms of the title may be placed in **246** fields.

```
245   04   The Weather Channel ǂh [elec-
           tronic resource] : ǂb
           weather.com.
246   30   weather.com
246   3_   Weather Channel on the Web
```

```
246  3_    Weather Channel online
246  3_    Weather Channel home page
```

When the date of publication is explicitly stated on the Web site, it is placed in subfield **c** of the **Publication, Distribution, Etc. (260)** field (*IRCM* I.6.1). Weather.com has a copyright statement at the bottom of the home page. This can be used in lieu of the publication date by placing a c before the date. When viewing other than the first iteration of the Web site, put this date in brackets (*IRCM* I.6.2). When the date is provided in the **260** subfield **c**, a **362** field is not required.

```
260        [Atlanta, Ga.] : ‡b The Weather
           Channel, ‡c [c1995]-
```

The frequency of updates for the resource is placed in the **Current Publication Frequency (310)** field (*LCRI* 12.7B1). The word updated is added to indicate that this applies to the updates and not the issuance of the resource itself.

```
310        Continuously updated.
```

The source of the title proper is provided in a **General Note (500)** (*AACR2* 9.1B2 and 9.7B3). The date on which the resource was viewed for cataloging is placed in a **General Note (500)** (*AACR2* 9.7B22).

```
500        Title from title screen.
500        Description based on contents
           viewed Nov. 20, 2001.
```

A **Formatted Contents Note (505)** can be supplied to describe the titles of parts of the resource.

The first indicator 0 signifies that the field contains the contents of the resource.

The second indicator is blank, signifying that this is a basic, rather than enhanced, contents note.

This field is not mandatory for integrating resources.

```
505  0_    Health : help for your seasonal
           sneezes, sniffles, wheezes, and
           aches -- Travel : stay on
           schedule with detailed weather
           for all types of travel --
           Events : forecasts for local
           events across the country --
           Recreation : take in the fore-
           cast before you take to nature
           -- Home & garden : tips for a
           beautiful garden and weather-
           wise house -- Ski : get fore-
           cast and detailed resort
```

```
                        information for local ski areas
                        -- Local -- World -- News --
                        Maps -- Weather tools.
```

A summary can be provided in a **Summary Note (520)**. The blank first indicator signifies that the display constant "Summary" will be generated. This field is not mandatory for integrating resources.

```
520                     "Delivers comprehensive weather
                        information for 80,000 loca-
                        tions worldwide and provides
                        relevant content to help users
                        plan for everyday life"--About
                        page.
```

The mode of access is provided in a **System Details** note **(538)** (*AACR2* 9.7B1c). The system requirements are provided in a **System Details** note **(538)** (*AACR2* 9.7B1b).

```
538                     Mode of access: World Wide Web.
538                     System requirements: Web
                        browser.
```

The URL for this Web site is placed in an **Electronic Location and Access (856)** field.

```
856   40     ‡u http://www.weather.com/
```

A Full record for a service that is continuously updated is shown in Figure 9-6.

```
Type: m ELvl:I Srce: d Audn:    Ctrl:     Lang: eng
BLvl: m File:m GPub:            MRec:     Ctry: gau
Desc: a                   DtSt: m Dates: 1995,1999

      006          suu w s          2
      007          c ‡b r ‡d c ‡e n
      040          SOU ‡c SOU ‡d OCLCQ ‡d N@F ‡d OCLCQ
                   ‡d LML
      019          44249428 ‡a 44254946 ‡a 44477810 ‡a
                   47696463
      082   04     551.63
      082   04     551.6
      090          QC995.4 ‡b .W4
      245   04     The Weather Channel ‡h [electronic
                   resource] : ‡b weather.com.
      246   30     weather.com
      246   3_     Weather Channel on the Web
```

Figure 9-6. Full *MARC 21* Record for a Continuously Updating Service

246	3_	Weather Channel online
246	3_	Weather Channel home page
260		[Atlanta, Ga.] : ‡b The Weather Channel, ‡c [c1995-
310		Continuously updated.
500		Title from title screen.
500		Description based on contents viewed Nov. 20, 2001.
505	0_	Health : help for your seasonal sneezes, sniffles, wheezes, and aches -- Travel : stay on schedule with detailed weather for all types of travel -- Events : forecasts for local events across the country -- Recreation : take in the forecast before you take to nature -- Home & garden : tips for a beautiful garden and weatherwise house -- Ski : get forecast and detailed resort information for local ski areas -- Local -- World -- News -- Maps -- Weather tools.
520		"Delivers comprehensive weather information for 80,000 locations worldwide and provides relevant content to help users plan for everyday life"--About page.
538		Mode of access: World Wide Web.
538		System requirements: Web browser.
650	_0	Weather ‡v Databases.
710	2_	Weather Channel.
856	40	‡u http://www.weather.com/

Figure 9-6. (Continued)

SUMMARY

Although integrating resources existed in the form of loose-leaf publication prior to the development of the World Wide Web, the popularity of the Web was a major factor in the development of integrating resources as a new type of issuance. *AACR2* and *MARC 21* have been updated to specifically address integrating resources, but some cataloging utilities and systems are still in the process of implementing the changes. Meanwhile, these resources still have to be cataloged. OCLC defined an interim practice for cataloging integrating resources in "Technical Bulletin 247: OCLC-MARC Format Update 2002" (Boehr and Jacobs, 2003). Online integrating resources are particularly challenging to catalog, not only because of the relative newness of the rules, but also because of their dynamic nature and the lack of uniformity. The examples in this chapter provide a basic overview of cataloging integrating resources. As catalogers gain experience with the new rules, record quality will improve. As with any cataloging, specific problems are best addressed by referring to official documentation.

REFERENCES

Boehr, Diane, and Alice E. Jacobs. 2003. *Integrating Resources: A Cataloging Manual* Washington, DC: Program for Cooperative Cataloging. Available: http://www.loc.gov/catdir/pcc/bibco/irman.pdf

Hiatt, Robert M. 1989. *Library of Congress Rule Interpretations*. Washington, DC: Library of Congress Cataloging Distribution Service.

Hixson, Carol, David Banush, and Ana Cristán, eds. 2002. *BIBCO Participants' Manual*. Washington, DC: Program for Cooperative Cataloging. Available: www.loc.gov/catdir/pcc/bibco/bpm.pdf. Accessed January 27, 2005.

Joint Steering Committee for the Revision of AACR2. 2002. *Anglo-American Cataloguing Rules,* 2nd ed., 2002 rev. Chicago: American Library Association.

Library of Congress Network Development and MARC Standards Office. 1999. *MARC 21 Format for Bibliographic Data*. Washington, DC: Library of Congress Cataloging Distribution Service.

OCLC. 2002a. *Bibliographic Formats and Standards,* 3rd ed. Dublin, OH: OCLC Online Computer Library Center.

OCLC. 2002b. "Technical Bulletin 247: OCLC-MARC Format Update 2002." Dublin, Ohio: OCLC Online Computer Library Center. Available: www.oclc.org/support/documentation/worldcat/tb/247/. Accessed January 27, 2005.

Weitz, Jay. 2003. "Cataloging Electronic Resources: OCLC-MARC Coding Guidelines." Dublin, OH: OCLC Online Computer Library Center. Available: www.oclc.org/support/documentation/worldcat/cataloging/electronicresources/. Accessed January 27, 2005.

10 ONLINE TRENDS TO WATCH

OPEN ACCESS

Open access is a scholarly publishing trend that promises to have a major impact on online-resource management in academic and specialized research libraries because it circumvents the need for licensing, activation of the resource by a vendor, or authentication of users. Open access refers to online scholarly resources that are made available to readers at no cost and with few or no usage restrictions. The philosophy behind this trend is that the cost of subscriptions and the burden of copyright restrictions are barriers to the free exchange of ideas, and, therefore, the removal of these barriers will promote scholarly discourse and maximize the availability of educational resources. The most common types of open-access resources are online journals, discipline-based repositories, and institutional repositories. Other types of online content that are often openly available but are presently less significant as scholarly resources include personal Web sites, Weblogs, discussion lists, and news feeds.

Open-access journals are becoming fairly common. These new publications function much like traditional scholarly journals, albeit with some notable differences. Like traditional scholarly journals, open-access journals are managed by editorial boards consisting of experts in their subject areas and often support peer review. Unlike most conventional journals, many open-access titles are published exclusively online because publishing in the print medium is so costly. Thus, they require alternative funding methods in lieu of subscription revenues. The most prominent open-access journal is *PLoS Biology* (www.plosbiology.org), published by the Public Library of Science. *PLoS Biology* was founded by scientists Patrick Brown and Michael Eisen and Nobel laureate Harold Varmus in response to dramatic increases in subscription costs for commercial journals. The *Directory of Open Access Journals* (www.doaj.org) currently provides the most comprehensive list of open-access journals.

Discipline-based repositories are databases of pre- and postprint scholarly articles deposited by the author. They are already common in the sciences and are beginning to gain ground in the social sciences and humanities. The oldest and most prominent of these repositories is *arXiv* (www.arxiv.org), which emphasizes disciplines that rely heavily on rapid communication, such as physics, computer science, astronomy, and mathematics. The articles in these databases, known as e-prints, are usually in the draft form that exists just prior to submission to a journal. The practice of making e-prints publicly available is perfectly legal, but nonetheless some commercial publishers refuse to publish previously circulated articles as a matter of policy.

Institutional repositories are established by and affiliated with academic institutions, such as universities, labs, and research centers, to preserve and make accessible the intellectual product of those institutions. In addition to e-prints, institutional repositories may house many other kinds of digital objects, including image collections, data sets, presentations, and multimedia. Institutional repositories are not yet as common as open-access journals or discipline-based repositories, but the concept is currently under development at many academic institutions (see Chapter 1).

> **Open-access repositories**:
> Discipline-based repositories are subject-oriented databases of pre- and postprint scholarly articles deposited by the author. Institutional repositories are established by and affiliated with academic institutions, such as universities, labs, and research centers, to preserve and make accessible the intellectual product of those institutions.

IMPACT ON LIBRARY WORK FLOWS

Open-access resources are simultaneously affecting publishing models, library collections, and resource management. The fundamental goal of open access, reducing barriers to information, is essentially in harmony with the purpose of libraries. However, just because open-access resources are freely accessible to library users does not mean they are free for libraries. Not only are libraries likely to be called upon to absorb some of the costs of open-access publishing, but they must also learn to manage selection, acquisition, and bibliographic control for open-access resources and possibly develop and maintain their own open-access collections.

The immediate impact of open-access resources on library work flow is in the area of selection. These resources do not entail fees or licenses, but they should nonetheless be subjected to the same evaluation criteria used for other information resources to ensure that they are appropriate to the library's collection aims. The fact that a given resource is available at no direct cost does not mean it is completely free. The library must expend time and effort to process and maintain access to freely available titles just as it does for titles that cost money.

If a resource is selected for the library's collection, the library must take the appropriate steps to acquire access. In some cases, this process can be as simple as having the selector submit a request to have the resource cataloged or added to a Web page. In other cases, interacting with open-access acquisition can be as problematic as traditional subscription-based resources or even more so. This is because open-access publications must derive funding from other sources.

Sustainable funding models are still subject to discussion and debate, but probable models include sponsorship by individual institutions or consortia and grant funding. Libraries may very well end up subsidizing these methods by providing financial support to authors who seek to publish in open-access journals or by contributing to consortia that support this type of publication. An even more direct method of subsidy is for the library to provide funding and infrastructure support for the local production of an open-access journal or repository and pay for operations out of general funds, endowments, or grants. Any of these avenues require the library to juggle budgets in new and unpredictable ways.

Like their traditional fee-based counterparts, open-access titles must be accounted for in the library's bibliographic tools, such as the library catalog, resource lists on the Web, federated-search systems, and context-sensitive linking tools. Because open-access is a conceptual model for the dissemination of information rather than a format, these titles are potentially compatible with any of these systems. (Interoperability varies depending on the metadata and technical characteristics of each resource). Open-access publications can be described using MARC records, and high-quality MARC records have already been created for many of them. Many of the common publication-access management services include open-access journal titles in their lists. Libraries that are directly managing open-access content through a locally hosted journal or repository face a somewhat different set of challenges, discussed in Chapter 1.

SUSTAINABILITY

Impact factor: A measure of the effectiveness of a journal, based on citation analysis. A high impact factor indicates that a journal is influential in its field.

Despite some notable successes and high-profile promoters, other experts doubt the sustainability of the open-access model. There are many stakeholders in the commercial publishing model, including publishers, libraries, and authors. The growth in open-access publishing affects these stakeholders differently, shifting responsibilities and roles. The reaction of scholarly authors is a major concern for the growth of open access. Specifically, they may be reluctant to change their behaviors to support open-access publishing when their academic advancement is at stake. Some of the burden of financing will shift to authors, who may have to account for publishing costs when planning research. Furthermore, many long-lived commercial publications have established impact factors: they are recognized as the authoritative publications in their field. The paramount concern for many authors pursuing tenure is the reputation of journal, not its funding model. Newly established open-access resources will face challenges in establishing reputations and attracting contributions from scholarly authors.

On the other hand, open-access shows great promise in promoting the fluid exchange of scholarship and is already having a significant impact on libraries that support scholarly research, but this publishing model has yet to prove its viability over the long term.

FUNCTIONAL REQUIREMENTS FOR BIBLIOGRAPHIC RECORDS (FRBR)

Functional Requirements for Bibliographic Records (FRBR): *FRBR* is an approach to bibliographic control that is gaining momentum in the online environment. The *FRBR* model articulates the complex relationship between intellectual content as an abstraction and the reality of information objects. *FRBR* also relates the specific needs of information-seeking users to each element of the bibliographic record and sets priorities for the data elements according to those goals. *FRBR* is a conceptual model rather than a metadata format or a set of cataloging rules; it is unclear when, or if, existing library catalogs will incorporate the *FRBR* model, but its principles are likely to guide the development of post-MARC bibliographic tools.

In 1998, the International Federation of Library Associations (IFLA) published a new conceptual model for bibliographic control that is receiving considerable attention in the cataloging community because of its potential implications for information organization and retrieval. *Functional Requirements for Bibliographic Records, Final Report* (known colloquially as *FRBR*) is a complex data model predicated on user tasks of finding, identifying, selecting, and obtaining information through the use of a bibliographic tool. The purpose of the model is to relate these generic tasks to the information presented in bibliographic records. Libraries are under increasing pressure to simplify bibliographic-control processes to accommodate the growing volume of published material in all formats as well as the unique aspects of information published online. Ultimately, *FRBR* provides conceptual support for determining which elements of bibliographic records are essential for information retrieval and which are merely desirable.

Much of the FRBR document is devoted to defining the attributes of various entities related to bibliographic records and establishing the lateral and hierarchical relationships that exist among these entities. At the core of the FRBR model are the bibliographic entities known as works, expressions, manifestations, and items. These entities, which range from intellectual abstractions to concrete physical objects, exist in hierarchical relationships to one another. For example, the primary intellectual content of Jan. L Harrington's Relational Database Design Clearly Explained comprises a work. Each successive edition of this title is a separate expression of the original work. The print run of this book, published by Morgan Kaufmann Publishers in 2002, represents a manifestation of one particular edition or expression; an online version of the same edition would be a separate manifestation. An individual copy of the book is an item-level entity. The FRBR model also defines entities with a responsibility relationship to the bibliographic entity (such as individuals or corporate bodies responsible for creating, editing, or publishing the resource) and entities with a subject relationship to the bibliographic entity (such as concepts, objects, events, and places).

SIGNIFICANCE OF THE *FRBR* MODEL

Although the *FRBR* model is based on existing cataloging formats and practices, there are three areas in which it departs significantly from current bibliographic-control principles. First, the *FRBR* model is explicit. Whereas earlier bibliographic theory relied on vague concepts such as finding objectives and choice objectives (Svenonius, 2000), *FRBR* explicitly defines the entities, attributes, and relationships that converge in a bibliographic record. In addition, a series of user objectives is correlated with each entity in the model at a highly granular level, with the priorities of the various attributes set according to how essential they are to the discovery of the bibliographic entity.

Second, *FRBR* is hierarchical. *FRBR* is the first bibliographic model to clearly articulate a framework for understanding the relationships between specific information objects and the intellectual abstractions they embody, a development that has major implications for managing online resources. In the present environment, one of the most difficult aspects of describing and organizing online resources is trying to understand the abstract relationships among resources, such as the relationships of online versions of a serial to one another and to a print counterpart. Traditional catalog records are generally used to describe information resources at the manifestation level, based on data extrapolated from an individual item or instance. Certain aspects of the bibliographic record extend outward to the more abstract entities; for example, a uniform title relates a specific manifestation to an intellectual work. However, the hierarchical relationship between the manifestation and the work is not apparent from the record itself, rather it is only revealed through the structure of entries and headings in the catalog as a whole. The *FRBR* model is concerned with making these relationships more transparent. Although *FRBR*-driven bibliographic systems do not yet exist, the information community already appears to be moving toward a similar model. For example, the existing ISSN system is currently being revised, and recent discussion suggests that the new ISSNs may incorporate a work-level identifier in addition to unique data for specific editions and formats.

Third, the *FRBR* model is user focused. Earlier bibliographic models were presented in terms of the library user. *FRBR* expands the concept of the user to refer not only to library users but also to libraries, publishers, and other content providers. In addition, *FRBR* recognizes that bibliographic data in the online environment supports not only information retrieval but also a variety of management functions. Discovery-related user tasks identified in the *FRBR* model include finding, identifying, selecting, and obtaining desired bibliographic entities. Perhaps the most significant aspect of this model is that the user tasks culminate in obtaining an information resource, an objective that is absent from earlier models. A subsequent study of the *FRBR* model in relation to the MARC format has led to further consideration of how bibliographic attributes relate to functions such as access con trol, management, and operation, which pertain primarily to resource use rather than discovery (Delsey, 2003). This approach is beginning to give shape to the relationship between resource discovery and resource management.

REFERENCES

Delsey, Tom. 2003. "Functional Requirements for Bibliographic Records User Tasks and Cataloguing Data: Part 1." *Catalogue & Index* no. 150 (Winter): 1–4.

IFLA Study Group on the Functional Requirements for Bibliographic Records. 1998. *Functional Requirements for Bibliographic Records, Final Report.* Munich: K. G. Saur.

Suber, Peter. 2004. "Open Access Overview." Available: www.earlham.edu/~peters/fos/overview.htm. Accessed January 27, 2005.

Svenonius, Elaine. 2000. *The Intellectual Foundation of Information Organization.* Cambridge, MA.: MIT Press.

INDEX

ABOUT THE AUTHORS

Anne Mitchell has been the metadata coordinator at the University of Houston Libraries since 2002. She was formerly the electronic resources cataloger for the University of Houston Libraries. She has published articles and given presentations on electronic-resource cataloging and work flow, and she has a particular interest in how libraries adapt metadata standards to localized needs. She received her MLIS from the University of Texas at Austin.

Brian Surratt joined the Texas A&M University Libraries in 2002 as the electronic resources cataloger and has published and presented on a variety of topics related to electronic-resource cataloging. He is now the metadata coordinator for Texas A&M's newly formed Digital Initiatives, Research, and Technology Department, where he focuses on metadata development and digital-collection management to facilitate scholarly communication. He is currently chairing the Standards Work Group for the Texas Heritage Digitization Initiative. He received his MLIS and Certificate of Graduate Studies in Information Technology from the University of South Carolina.